James J Menley

SON OF GOD TO SUPER STAR

Twentieth-Century Interpretations of Jesus

JOHN H. HAYES

Nashville, Tennessee   Abingdon Press

Son of God to Superstar

Library of Congress Cataloging in Publication Data

Son of God to Superstar.
  Bibliography: p.
  1. Jesus Christ—History of doctrines—20th century. I. Hayes, John
Haralson, 1934-
BT198.S645   232   75-30603

ISBN 0-687-39091-5
ISBN 0-687-39092-3 pbk.

MANUFACTURED BY THE PARTHENON PRESS AT
NASHVILLE, TENNESSEE, UNITED STATES OF AMERICA

ACKNOWLEDGMENT

Acknowledgment is made to the following for permission to use copyrighted material:

Abingdon Press for excerpts from "Primitive Christian Kerygma" by Rudolph Bultmann, which appeared in *Historical Jesus and Kerygmatic Christ*, copyright © 1964 by Abingdon Press.

Andover Newton Quarterly and the Reverend Joseph A. Johnson for excerpts from "Jesus: The Liberator."

Bantam Books for permission to quote excerpts reprinted from *The Passover Plot* by Dr. Hugh J. Schonfield; copyright © 1965 by Hugh Schonfield.

George Allen & Unwin, Ltd. for extracts from *Jesus of Nazareth* by Joseph Klausner.

Adam and Charles Black for extracts from Albert Schweitzer's *The Quest of the Historical Jesus*.

Bobbs-Merrill Publishing Company for permission to reprint excerpts from *The Man Nobody Knows* by Bruce Barton, copyright 1925 by The Bobbs-Merrill Company, Inc., 1952 by Bruce Barton.

James Brown Associates, Inc., Agents, and the author, for permission to reprint excerpts from "Sexuality and Jesus," by Tom Driver, copyright © 1965 by Union Theological Seminary in the City of New York.

Cambridge University Press for permission to quote materials from *The Background of the New Testament and its Eschatology* by T. W. Manson.

Collins Publishers for permission to use excerpts from *The Founder of Christianity* by C. H. Dodd.

Doubleday & Co. for permission to reprint excerpts from *The Sacred Mushroom and the Cross,* copyright © 1970 by John M. Allegro.

Fortress Press for permission to reprint excerpts from *Reimarus: Fragments*, ed. Charles H. Talbert, tr. Ralph S. Fraser, copyright 1970, Fortress Press, Philadelphia, Pa., in the Lives of Jesus Series, ed. Leander Keck.

Victor Gollancz, Ltd. for excerpts from *The Secret Gospel* by Morton Smith.

For my wife
SARAH
w'm kwl shpr' chkm' sgy' 'mh'
(Genesis Apocryphon XX 7)

PREFACE

The purpose of this volume is to introduce the interested reader to a spectrum of twentieth-century interpretations of the historical Jesus. The enormous number of published studies of Jesus during the past three quarters of a century makes any comprehensive and inclusive survey impossible. This volume attempts to present a representative selection of interpretations ranging from the most traditional to the most radical but with emphasis placed on those studies published during the last twenty-five years.

As far as possible, the interpreters of Jesus have been allowed to present their views in their own words. This explains the extensive use of quotations. Summaries of others' views tend to interpret more than does the use of direct quotes, and summations almost always lose the color and impact of the originals.

No assessment or critique of the individual presentations has been offered. The various studies of Jesus and the diversity of approaches do tend to offer indirect critiques of each other.

Internal footnoting has been used throughout the work. Full bibliographical information is given in the bibliography at the end of the book.

A special word of thanks is due Madeline Hawley, who has worked so diligently typing the manuscript for this volume.

J.H.H.
Candler School of Theology
Interdenominational Theological Center

CONTENTS

1. JESUS: THE HISTORICAL FIGURE

And Jesus went on with his disciples, to the villages of
Caesarea Philippi; and on the way he asked his disciples,
"Who do men say that I am?" And they told him, "John the
Baptist; and others say, Elijah; and others one of the
prophets." And he asked them, "But who do you say I am?"
Peter answered him, "You are the Christ."—Mark 8:27-29

The search for the outline and character of the historical
life of Jesus has, since the Age of Enlightenment, occupied
and fascinated many of the academic minds of the western
world as have few other historical problems. At times, this
so-called "quest of the historical Jesus" has moved outside
the confines of academic circles and engaged the attention of
the average man, sometimes enraging and occasionally
traumatizing him. As a historical endeavor, the quest has not
been limited to members or exponents of the Christian faith.
Many in the Christian church have, in fact, denounced the
quest as either irrelevant to the Christian faith or as
destructive of genuine belief. Others have proclaimed the
effort to be an indispensable requirement and an aid to
understanding the pristine character of the Christian religion
or as the means to recover a faith beyond the structures of
Christian orthodoxy which would be relevant to and
believable by modern man.

SOME ISSUES IN THE QUEST

In very general terms, it may be said that four primary aspects of the life of Jesus have been the focus of concern throughout the modern phase of the quest. In the first place, there has been a concern to understand Jesus within the context of his place in history, that is within the context of the Jewish community as part of the Roman Empire of the first century. Geographical, religious, cultural, and economic issues of first-century Judaism have been explored as avenues toward a comprehension of the historical Jesus. It is true that this concern for the historical context and sociocultural locale was not a dominant issue in the earliest discussions; however, with the passage of time it has assumed a greater role. This is due on the one hand to the greatly increased knowledge of the period through the influence of archaeological exploration and the discovery and study of ancient documents. On the other hand, this focus has been influenced by the stress on historical causation and sociological conditioning which has characterized historical, cultural, and psychological studies, especially in the area of biographical research. Every man is a child of his time and in some respects a mirror of his age.

It has been assumed therefore that a delineation of the contours of first-century Palestinian Judaism would allow the observer a glimpse if not a complete picture of the historical Jesus. What were the general conditions of life in Palestine at the time? What was the religious situation? What classes and divisions of society existed? What traits and characteristics of Palestinian life may have been dominant influences in his life? To what groups and classes of society may he have belonged, and how may these have influenced the course of his life? These are some of the types of questions which scholars have explored in their attempt to outline the features of the historical Jesus.

Out of this area of concern have come the assumptions that any portrayal of the Jesus of history must understand him in the context of first-century Palestinian Judaism and that the failure to do so renders any such portrayal suspect.

A second area of concern in the quest centers on the teachings of Jesus. What was the content of his message? What did he preach? What antecedents and frames of reference were available to his audience through which they could understand his message? What was the central concern of his teaching and preaching? Did he offer a new understanding of religion, a new approach to life, a new vision of social order, a new sense or understanding of God, and/or a new interpretation of the course of history? Or in his teaching and preaching did he offer merely a new synthesis of faith and ethics adapted from his contemporaries? Was the message of Jesus obscured, transformed, or merely transmitted by the early church? These are the types of questions explored in the concern to discover the content and message of the preaching and teaching of the historical Jesus.

Out of this area of concern has come the conclusion that any adequate understanding of the Jesus of history must present the content of his vision of life whether this vision was ethically, socially, religiously, and/or politically oriented.

A third concern of this area of research centers on the death of Jesus. A rather firm fact concerning the life of Jesus is that he was put to death during the rule of Pontius Pilate who was Roman procurator or *praefectus* over Judaea during the years A.D. 26–36. Why was Jesus put to death? What was there in his life and preaching that would have stirred the Jewish leaders and/or the Romans to seek his execution? Was his death the culmination of his life and career? Was it due to a misunderstanding or a miscarriage of justice? What role and influence did Jesus have in his own death? How did Jesus understand and face up to his death? These are the types of questions about his death explored in various interpretations of Jesus.

Out of this area of concern has come the conclusion that any portrait of the historical Jesus must take seriously the death of Jesus and seek to understand what actions and/or teachings in his life led to his crucifixion.

A final concern in research on Jesus centers on the origins of the church. Why did Jesus' ministry attract a following?

What was there in his life that could have given the impetus to the birth of the Christian community? What in his life and death could have become the ground of the primitive Christian faith? Why were his followers willing, if not compelled after his death, to carry on the movement which he had begun? Is it possible to understand the life and faith of Jesus? Is there any unbridgeable gap or continuity between the preaching and teaching of Jesus and that of the early church? These are the types of questions discussed by those concerned with the relationship of the life and faith of the early church to the life and faith of the historical Jesus.

Out of this area of concern has come the conviction that any historical depiction of the life and teachings of Jesus must explain what there was in his career which could account for the birth of the Christian community.

Before examining representative twentieth-century reconstructions of the Jesus of history, it will be helpful to review a spectrum of earlier interpretations of Jesus and then ask how it is possible to interpret the historical Jesus in such diverse ways.

SOME PRE-TWENTIETH-CENTURY LIVES OF JESUS

Prior to the eighteenth century, no one had examined the New Testament with the aim of reconstructing the historical outline of Jesus' life apart from faith in the Christ of Christian theology. This does not mean that the church had not been concerned with historical questions concerning Jesus' life and ministry. In some respects, the quest is as old as the church itself. The author of the Gospel of Luke, in his prologue (1:1-4), states that his purpose in writing was to present an "orderly account," implying that this had not been the case for the "many who have undertaken to compile a narrative of the things which have been accomplished among us." The selection of four Gospels as the canonical sources for the life of Jesus and the repudiation of the more than fifty so-called apocryphal Gospels by the church certainly reflect discrimination about which sources were to be accepted as primary for understanding Jesus.

Late in the second century, Tatian hoped to replace the four Gospels with a single version, a single portrait of Christ. His harmony of the life of Christ, called the *Diatessaron*, combined the materials in the Gospels generally following the outline of Matthew for the events prior to the trial and crucifixion of Jesus; for the latter Tatian followed the account found in John. His harmony eliminated the duplications in the Gospel traditions. His work manifests an element of critical analysis: where the Gospel accounts differed, he gave the account which to him appeared most probable. The *Diatessaron* was in use in the Syriac church until the fifth century and was translated into several other languages, although Tatian himself was declared a heretic.

The use of harmonies of the Gospels to present a unified picture of the life of Jesus was employed by Eusebius and St. Augustine in the fourth century. Part of the purpose behind such harmonies was to oppose the idea that the four Gospels were contradictory in many places—an idea which had been around and sometimes used against Christians since the second century. The belief in the divine inspiration of the Gospels stifled any serious critical appraisal of them, although Augustine was fully aware of the differences between them. Augustine sought to explain away these differences so that in the last analysis everything in all four Gospels was accurate and historical. Augustine was willing, unlike Tatian, to see the doublets in the Gospels as reflecting genuine historical events; Jesus performed similar acts and spoke identical or similar sayings on more than one occasion.

During the Middle Ages, poetic presentations of Jesus (beginning in the fourth century) and harmonies of the Gospels were used for teaching and devotion. Beginning in the sixteenth century, a proliferation of Gospel harmonies occurred among both Catholics and Protestants, including a new pattern which presented the Gospel traditions in parallel columns—what might be called the "synopsis" pattern. Behind these harmonies lay both the desire to present within one volume the total material on Jesus and the aim to combat skeptics who might criticize the Gospels because of their contradictions and differences. The number of harmonies during this period may reflect the renewed interest in the Bible, the influence of the moveable-type printing press, the budding "science" of historical research or all of these.

Probably the most influential harmony of the Gospels was that by Osiander (1498–1552) published in 1537. Its methodology is illustrated in its title which translates as: *Greek and Latin Gospel Harmony in four books, in which the gospel story is combined according to the four evangelists, in such a way that no word of any one of them is omitted, no foreign word added, the order of none of them disturbed, and nothing is displaced, in which, however, the whole is marked by letters and signs which permit one to see at a first glance the points peculiar to each evangelist, those which he has in common with the others, and with which of them.* Osiander adherred to the principle that if an action or saying of Jesus was reported two or three times in slightly differing form or in a different order then Jesus must have spoken the saying or accomplished the action two or three times over. Thus the daughter of Jairus was raised from the dead on three different occasions; Jesus cleansed the temple on three separate occasions; identical sayings found in different contexts were repeated by Jesus at different times in his career, and so on.

The Protestant Reformation produced no critical analysis of the Gospels, although both Luther and Calvin were aware of the differences between the Gospels and their sequence of events and the variations between events and sayings within the Gospels. Luther's verdict on this matter was not intended to encourage investigation into such matters: "The Gospels follow no order in recording the acts and miracles of Jesus, and the matter is not, after all, of much importance. If a difficulty arises in regard to the Holy Scriptures and we cannot solve it, we must just let it alone." Here his doctrine of the divine inspiration of scripture seems to have precluded any need for evaluative and critical judgment. This is not totally what one would have expected from Luther who elsewhere could criticize the book of James, which he described as a "right strawy epistle," and the book of Revelation for which he had little use.

Calvin, who differed with Osiander and refused to assume that the sequence of events and teachings in each gospel were historical, wrote a commentary on a harmony of the gospels. In this work, Calvin argued that "no fixed and distinct order of dates was observed by the evangelists in composing their narratives. The consequence is that they disregard the order of time and satisfy themselves with presenting in a summary manner, the leading transactions in the life of Christ."

The first thorough attempt to present a study of Jesus apart from the church's confessional and orthodox faith in Jesus as the divine son of God was made by Hermann Samuel Reimarus (1694–1768). His discussion of Jesus is contained in his *magnum opus,* a manuscript of over four thousand pages, which circulated during his lifetime in anonymous form. After his death, parts of his work were published— beginning in 1774—by the philosopher Lessing. In his "The Intention of Jesus and his Teaching," published in 1778, Reimarus argued that an absolute distinction must be drawn between the faith of the early church and what Jesus proclaimed and taught during his lifetime. He tried to outline the process by which the Gospels had come into existence, and he set the first three Gospels over against the fourth. For his reconstruction of Jesus' ministry, he tended to set aside the Fourth Gospel as more doctrinal than historical. Reimarus sought to understand Jesus within the context of first-century Judaism and claimed that Jesus had no desire to do away with Jewish religion and replace it with another. Jesus' preaching of the kingdom of heaven assumed the typical Jewish beliefs about the hope of a coming messianic kingdom which would free the Jews from foreign domination and political oppression. Jesus believed that under his leadership the kingdom of the messiah was about to dawn. In this coming kingdom, a new and deeper morality, which would fulfill and supercede the old law, would come into being. Jesus sent out his disciples to rally the Galileans to a popular uprising, and in Jerusalem he called for an open revolt against the Jewish leaders. No such uprising or revolt occurred, and Jesus' aim to establish an earthly kingdom and deliver the Jews from oppression failed, and he was put to death. Jesus performed cures but no miracles which would have rallied the people to his cause. After Jesus' death the disciples adopted a spiritualized interpretation of the messianic kingdom—an interpretation also borrowed from Judaism—and proclaimed that the messiah must appear twice, once in lowly human form and again in triumph. The disciples stole the body of Jesus, hid it, and after fifty days proclaimed his resurrection and the nearness of his second coming as the messiah triumphant.

Reimarus' portrayal of Jesus represented a radical break with Christian orthodoxy, and numerous refutations of it were published. How can one explain such a radical interpretation of Jesus within the context of eighteenth-century thought? In the first place, radical interpretations of Jesus had been earlier proclaimed however without the historical concerns of Reimarus. Socinus (1525–62) and Servetus, who was burned at the stake in Calvin's Geneva in 1553, had both denied the divinity of Jesus and regarded him as a human prophet and the founder of a religion. This is not to say that Reimarus was familiar with their thought but only to note that some aspects of his radical presentation were not without precedence. Secondly, interest in the origin of the Gospels and their relationship to each other was beginning to dawn. The recognition that the first three Gospels were not independent accounts of the career of Jesus but were interdependent was a significant development in New Testament studies. This understanding of the Gospels was just beginning to emerge at the time of Reimarus. For example, J. G. Herder (1744–1803), a younger contemporary of Reimarus, published investigations on the Gospels (1796–97) in which he argued that the first three Gospels were Palestinian and historical in origin while the Fourth Gospel was not historical but doctrinal in character. The common basis for the first three Gospels was an oral Aramaic gospel proclaimed by the earliest apostles (so also Lessing). Mark was, according to Herder, the oldest of the Gospels. Thirdly, rationalism, represented by the German Christian Wolff and English Deists such as Toland, Collins, Chubb, and Woolston and the Frenchman Voltaire, had begun to challenge the miraculous element in the Gospel traditions and to argue for religion within the bounds of reason. The miracles of Jesus were rationalized—for example, the dead were not raised but only awakened from a lethargic sleep—and Jesus' resurrection was understood as a phantom appearance seen by visionaries and dreamers if not an outright invention. The rationalists saw in Jesus a prophet and the founder of a more perfect form of "natural religion." Even Rousseau (in 1769) argued that Jesus' aims were to free the Jews from Roman rule and introduce them to true freedom. Fourthly, Reimarus was a creative, radical free-thinker, an advocate of rational religion, and was obviously intent upon an attack on the church's faith. Schweitzer describes Reimarus' work in the following statement: "Seldom has there been a hate so eloquent, so lofty a scorn; but then it is seldom that a work has been written in the just consciousness of so absolute a superiority to contemporary opinion" *(The Quest of the Historical Jesus,* 15).

Reimarus was the harbinger of things to come, although his work did not itself receive very widespread circulation nor exert an immediate or far reaching influence. To illustrate the developing interests in the Jesus of history, several representative interpretations will be noted.

During the nineteenth century, a number of authors produced studies of Jesus and his teachings based on the principles of philosophical rationalism. Rationalism argued that no more of religion can be accepted than is amenable to human intellect and logic and can justify itself at the bar of reason. Therefore full blown rationalism eliminated everything supernatural from the arena of belief. This meant that the life of Jesus must be exorcised of all things supernatural, either through outright denial or through reinterpretation. The rationalists believed that the desupernaturalization of the gospel traditions would provide the world with a Jesus whose life and teachings were acceptable to natural religion and reason and more relevant to contemporary man. The rationalists of course had no desire to do away with religion but merely to free it from supernaturalism so that it would more adequately mirror acceptable beliefs. In the United States, Thomas Jefferson reflected this concern, and his version of the New Testament eliminates all the miracles and concludes the Gospels with the death of Jesus.

A classic expression of this rationalistic interpretation of Jesus is the 1828 work by H. E. G. Paulus (1761–1851). For Paulus, Jesus was the supreme example of purity and serene holiness whose character was genuinely human and capable of imitation and emulation by all mankind. Much of his discussion is related to and an explanation of the Gospel miracles. Paulus does not doubt that the biblical writers intended to ascribe miracles to Jesus and that Jesus' disciples understood certain events in his life as miraculous. However, he argued that this was due to either their misunderstanding of certain events or their failure to recognize secondary causes which lay behind the so-called miracles. Paulus argued that the miracles of healing were performed by Jesus either through the exertion of his spiritual power over the nervous system of the sufferer or else through the use of curative medicines known only to him. The nature miracles are understood as reflections of the disciples' misunderstanding or are otherwise open to rational explanation. Jesus did not walk upon the water; he walked along the shore and in the mist surrounding the lake the disciples thought he walked upon the lake's surface. He did not still the storm; the ship at the moment of Jesus' awakening entered the shelter of a hill, and the disciples ascribed to him power over wind and sea. Jesus did not multiply the loaves and fishes; when Jesus began to distribute the food and share it, those present with provisions followed his good example and shared their supplies. The transfiguration was the result of an interview of Jesus with two dignified-looking men whom his disciples, only half awake in the early morning sunlight, thought were

Elijah and Moses. Raisings from the dead were deliverances from premature burial. Jesus' death on the cross was a death-like trance and the surface wound of the spear, the unguents, the cool grave, the storm, and the earthquake resuscitated him. Upon resuscitation, Jesus removed his burial clothes and dressed in a gardener's clothes. After this, he appeared to his disciples for forty days, and then accompanied by the same two men who appeared at the so-called transfiguration (actually secret followers), he bid farewell to his disciples on the Mt. of Olives and disappeared behind a cloud after which his two friends addressed the disciples. Afterward, Jesus died without this being known by his followers.

The rationalists gave extensive consideration to many of the teachings of Jesus stressing the moral and ethical elements. Often the sayings of Jesus were interpreted, restated, or paraphased. For example, the beatitude, "Blessed are the mourners for they shall be comforted," is restated by one rationalist (J. J. Hess, 1741–1828) as: "Happy are they who amid the adversities of the present make the best of things and submit themselves with patience; for such men, if they do not see better times here, shall certainly elsewhere receive comfort and consolation."

A number of nineteenth-century writers produced what may be called imaginary or fictionalized accounts of Jesus' life and ministry. A basic characteristic of practically all of these works is their attempt to discover the true plot of Jesus' life lying behind the disconnected episodes of the gospel accounts. As a rule, these lives of Jesus assume the existence of a secret society to which Jesus belonged or by whom he was controlled. Generally this secret society is identified with the Essenes who are described most fully in the writings of the first-century Jewish historian Josephus but who are not mentioned in the New Testament or the Jewish Talmud.

Examples of this type of approach are the works of K. F. Bahrdt (1741–1792); F. W. Ghillany (1807–76), who wrote under the pseudonym of Richard von der Alm; and Ludwig Noack (1819–85). Bahrdt's work, which was the earliest fully developed specimen, can serve to illustrate the approach. Bahrdt found the clue to his explanation of Jesus' life in the characters of Nicodemus and Joseph of Arimathea. Why, he asked, should these wealthy members of the Jewish upper class make their brief and enigmatic appearances in the New Testament? His answer was that they were Essenes, members of a secret society. This society, whose members had infiltrated practically all ranks and organizations in Judaism, had as its goals the desire to rescue the Jews from their nationalistic and sensuous messianic hopes and the aim of leading the Jews to a higher knowledge of spiritual truths. To do this, they set out to present to the nation a claimant of messiahship who would destroy these false and misleading messianic expectations. Jesus, shortly after his birth, fell under the control of this society which taught him about the falsity of the priesthood, the horror of Jewish sacrifices, and introduced him to the Greek philosophers Plato and Socrates. Upon hearing of the death of Socrates, Jesus as a lad resolved to emulate his heroic death. By the time he was twelve, Jesus' instruction by the society was far advanced.

Jesus' ministry was clearly planned from the beginning. He and John the Baptist, along with various Essene characters whom Bahrdt introduced into the story, in consultation, planned their public careers. Jesus had acquired medical skills from a Persian and Luke, the physician. In order to find some acceptance, Jesus, under the direction of the society, appeared as a messianic figure with many of the characteristics of the expected Jewish messiah—always, of course, with the purpose of freeing the Jews from their gross messianic beliefs. The miracles of Jesus were well orchestrated events which the gospel writers who were not members of the inner circle of the Essenes assumed to be miraculous. For example, the feeding of the five thousand was executed through the help of the society which had filled a cave with bread and passed it out to Jesus for distribution.

Contact with the Essene community was preserved throughout Jesus' career—his departure to secret places for prayer involved meetings in caves with the Essene leaders of which all his disciples were unaware. Jesus taught in two different ways—in simple terms for the general audience and in esoteric and mystic form for the initiates. The Gospel of John has preserved an expression of the latter.

Jesus' "death" was well planned by the community. He did not die but was only drugged. After three days his wounds were healed, and he could walk. Members of the Essene community played the role of angels in the resurrection stories. From his seclusion with the Essene community, he made later appearances, even to Paul on the way to Damascus. He continued to share in the life of the secret Essene community until his death.

Somewhat similar to these imaginary or fictionalized versions of the life of Jesus is Ernest Renan's *Life of Jesus* published in 1863. Renan (1823–92) was, however, a scholar of repute and was much more bound to the biblical text—although his imagination and literary artistry were given full expression. Renan was a Catholic, one of the first to offer a systematic treatment of the life of Jesus, and his work was addressed to a popular audience. The book was given an enthusiastic reception; it sold sixty thousand copies in the first six months and went through twenty-three editions during his lifetime. Renan's Jesus stands out as the embodiment of an idyllic humanity whose career centered on the common folk of Galilee, who are idealized almost beyond recognition by the sentimentalization of the author. In other words he produced a historical novel about Jesus. Schweitzer, speaking in sarcastic tones because Renan's vision of Jesus differed so radically from his own, wrote: "Renan's *Vie de Jesus* . . . is Christian art in the worst sense of the term—the art of the wax image. The gentle Jesus, the beautiful Mary, the fair Galilaeans who formed the retinue of the 'amiable carpenter,' might have been taken over in a body from the shop window of an ecclesiastical art emporium" (182). The ministry of Jesus is placed amid the blue skies, gentle breezes, seas of waving grain, the gleaming lilies, and the vibrant landscapes of Galilee. Even Renan's Jesus stoops to trickery in the raising of Lazarus, a miracle staged by Jesus to encourage the faltering faith of his disciples in him. In describing the scene in the Garden of Gethsemane, Renan wrote: "Did he recall the clear fountains of Galilee where He might have refreshed himself; the vineyard and the fig-tree under which he might have been seated; the young maidens who might perhaps have consented to love Him? Did He curse his bitter destiny, which had forbidden to him the joys conceded to all others? Did he regret his too lofty nature, and, the victim of his own grandeur, did he weep because he had not remained a simple artizan of Nazareth?" (*The Life of Jesus,* 318). In a final summation of the work of Jesus, Renan wrote:

This sublime person, who each day still presides over the destinies of the world, we may call divine, not in the sense that Jesus absorbed all divinity, or was equal to it (to employ the scholastic expression), but in this sense that Jesus is an individual who has caused his species to make the greatest advance towards the divine. Humanity as a whole presents an assemblage of beings, low, selfish, superior to the animal only in that their selfishness is more premeditated. But in the midst of this uniform vulgarity, pillars rise towards heaven and attest a more noble destiny. Jesus is the highest of these pillars which show to man whence he came and whither he should tend. In him is condensed all that is good and lofty in our nature. He was not sinless; he conquered the same passions which we combat; no angel of God comforted him, save his good conscience; no Satan tempted him, save that which each bears in his heart. And as many of the grand aspects of his character are lost to us by the fault of his disciples, it is probable also that many of his faults have been dissembled. But never has any man made the interests of humanity predominate in his life over the littlenesses of self-love as much as he. Devoted without reserve to his idea, he subordinated everything to it to such a degree that towards the end of his life, the universe no longer existed for him. It was by this flood of heroic will that he conquered heaven. . . . He lived only for his Father, and the divine mission which he believed it was his to fulfil.

As for us, eternal children, condemned to weakness, we who labor without harvesting, and shall never see the fruit of what we have sown, let us bow before these demi-gods. They knew what we do not know: to create, to affirm, to act. Shall

originality be born anew, or shall the world henceforth be
content to follow the paths opened by the bold creators of the
ancient ages? We know not. But whatever may be the
surprises of the future, Jesus will never be surpassed. His
worship will grow young without ceasing; his legend will call
forth tears without end; his sufferings will melt the noblest
hearts; all ages will proclaim that among the sons of men
there is none born greater than Jesus (375-76).

The first extensive interpretation of Jesus written by a Jew
was the work of Joseph Salvador published in Paris in 1838.
Salvador's work treats not only the historical Jesus but also
the history of the church to the end of the first century. A
number of Salvador's emphases are noteworthy. He argued
that Jesus never taught a single idea nor laid down any
precept that was not to be found in the Jewish scriptures or
the writings of the sages contemporary with Jesus. The
Sermon on the Mount for example was traced back to
influence from the book of Ben Sirach. The tone of Jesus'
teaching however differed from that of the Pharisaic Judaism
of his day. Pharisaic Judaism, he argued, placed its emphasis
on preparing men for earthly life and the transformation of
the life of society. Jesus, on the other hand, stressed the
religious and ethical life of the individual in terms of an
orientation to the future life, and he therefore adopted a
negative attitude toward civilized life and disregarded the
existing social order. The Pharisees were concerned to lay
down prescribed ceremonial laws and practices to preserve
and insure national persistence as a people. The laws were a
means of guarding Jewish nationalism. Jesus gave however
no thought to and was unconcerned about such matters.

Salvador claimed that much of what is written in the
Gospels was inserted or created in order to depict the life of
Jesus as the fulfillment of Old Testament scriptures. Much of
what was said about Jesus' birth, death, and resurrection
were derived from Oriental and Greek mythology. Salvador
defended the trial of Jesus against the charge of its illegality
often claimed by Christians. He compared the early church
with pagan religious corporations of Jesus' day.

Another view of Jesus which came to vogue in Germany near the end of the century denied the Jewish origin of Jesus. This view did not arise as a counter to the interpretation of Jesus by Jews but is merely mentioned at this point for the sake of convenience. It was an outgrowth of liberal interpretations of Jesus combined with a racist theory of the superiority of the Aryan peoples. Part of the concern of the studies reflecting this belief in the non-Semitic origin of Jesus was the desire to justify the Aryan nations' acceptance of Christianity. The view was espoused by Houston Stuart Chamberlain, Ernst Häckel, and others. Interestingly enough, some who advocated this view adopted the argument of the Jewish legend found in the Talmud which claimed that Jesus' father was a Roman soldier named Pandera. The theory of Jesus as an Aryan survived to become a dogmatic principle in Adolph Hitler's Nazism.

The work which perhaps had the greatest influence on the academic study of the historical Jesus was *The Life of Jesus Critically Examined* by David Friedrich Strauss (1808–74), published in two volumes (1835–36). Because of one of its special emphases, his presentation has been categorized as mythological. Strauss' work was thorough and scholarly and dealt with practically all the important issues which still haunt and fascinate New Testament research. Strauss gave detailed attention to the question of the New Testament sources for the life of Jesus and challenged the historical value of the Gospel of John. The first three Gospels he saw as composite structures created out of diverse narratives and discourses which made it impossible to use them to establish a fixed chronological order for the life of Jesus. The Gospels contain various strata of legend and narrative with John being the most dominated by apologetic and dogmatic purposes.

For Strauss, the messianic consciousness of Jesus was a historical fact in the sense that Jesus believed that after his earthly life was over he would be taken to heaven from which he would return to bring in his kingdom, a kingdom to be established by the supernatural intervention of God. Thus, for Strauss, the ministry of Jesus was oriented to futuristic events; that is, it was eschatologically conditioned.

Many of the events ascribed to the career of Jesus were myths, according to Strauss. In making such a declaration, Strauss opposed equally the supernaturalistic interpretation which accepted the miraculous events as narrated as historical occurrences and the rationalistic interpretation which sought to explain the events as either due to the misunderstanding of the disciples or to the operation of secondary causes. For Strauss, myth was "the clothing in historic form of religious ideas, shaped by the unconsciously inventive power of legend, and embodied in a historic personality" (Schweitzer, 79). It was a form of expression of religious faith. The mythological character of much of the Gospel tradition meant that the Gospels must be taken as primarily religious documents and not as biographical history.

The question of the origin and character of the Gospels, the eschatological orientation of Jesus' ministry and preaching, and the problem of the role of mythological thought in the portrayal of Jesus are Strauss' legacy to the subsequent course of New Testament studies, although in many ways he was continuing the work of Reimarus.

The nineteenth century saw the rise of thoroughgoing skepticism with regard to Jesus which went to the point of denying his historicity. Bruno Bauer (1809–82) was one of the first and most influential representatives of such a position. Bauer did not begin his studies with his skeptical view formulated; it was the product of his literary studies on the Gospels and other New Testament writings published between 1840 and 1877. Bauer began his studies on the Gospels with an investigation of the Gospel of John. The Fourth Gospel he concluded was the product of the creative reflection of its author who presented his theological views through the utilization of the *logos* concept. Bauer's subsequent investigations of the other Gospels led to a similar skepticism. The Gospels—even Mark which he considered the earliest—were literary products of their authors who projected back into a historical form the Christ of the Christian community. Many of the Gospel stories embody reflections of the early church's experiences and contain the church's explanations of its life and character. The Jesus of the Gospels was thus the product of the church and the Gospel writers' imagination, not the creator of Christianity. Bauer, in his last work, sought to explain the origin of the church by placing its beginning in the early days of the second century through the confluence of influences from Judaea, Greece, and Rome. It owed its origin to numerous factors: Stoicism, Neo-Platonism, the general resignation which characterized the Roman Empire in the second half of the first century, the Roman philosopher Seneca, and the Neo-Roman Jews, Philo and Josephus. Behind the Gospels' depiction of Jesus can be seen the shadowy influence of Seneca, Philo, and Josephus.

The nineteenth century saw numerous presentations of the historical Jesus, which may be designated liberal lives of Jesus. In some respects, these liberal lives of Jesus represent a continuation of the interests of the earlier rationalists. That is, their aim was to present a version of the life and teachings of Jesus which would be acceptable to modern man and at the same time challenge man's religious and ethical consciousness. Liberal scholars accepted the assumption that the Gospels are basically nonhistorical in their present form. However, liberalism felt that through a rigorous application of historical-critical study to the Gospels it was possible to discover the basic outline of the life of Jesus and the basic content of his teachings. On the basis of these, a reconstruction of the historical Jesus could be developed which could be distinguished from the Christ of faith. Liberal versions of the life of Jesus reached their apogee at the end of the nineteenth and the beginning of the twentieth century. An important contribution to this approach was the theological position of Albrecht Ritschl and his followers. Ritschl had argued that the concept of the kingdom of God which Jesus utilized in his preaching referred to the final and ideal goal of human life, a social goal which could be attained by moral and ethical endeavor and heroism on the part of mankind.

A classic example of the liberal presentation of Jesus is found in Adolf Harnack's *What Is Christianity?* Harnack argued that one must study the Gospels and Jesus in order to discover something useful for us in our age. In such a study, the basic aim is to distinguish "what is permanent from what is fleeting, what is rudimentary from what is merely historical." The essence of the preaching of Jesus, Harnack argued, has to be separated from the shell in which Jesus preached it. That is, the abiding Gospel must be separated from the eschatological and other-worldly language of Jesus which belongs to that which is merely historical. When this is done, Harnack concluded that "the Gospel in the Gospel is something so simple, something that speaks to us with so much power, that it cannot easily be mistaken" (15). This something so simple—the essentials of the teachings of Jesus—could be understood in terms of the kingdom of God and its coming, God the Father and the infinite value of the human soul, and the higher righteousness and the commandment of love. Speaking of these essentials, Harnack wrote:

To our modern way of thinking and feeling, Christ's message appears in the clearest and most direct light when grasped in connexion with the idea of God the Father and the infinite value of the human soul. Here the elements which I would describe as the restful and restgiving in Jesus' message, and which are comprehended in the idea of our being children of God, find expression. I call them *restful* in contrast with the impulsive and stirring elements; although it is just they that are informed with a special strength. But the fact that the whole of Jesus' message may be reduced to these two heads—God as the Father, and the human soul so ennobled that it can and does unite with him—shows us that the Gospel is in nowise a positive religion like the rest; that it contains no statutory or particularistic elements; *that it is, therefore, religion itself.* It is superior to all antithesis and tension between this world and a world to come, between reason and ecstasy, between work and isolation from the world, between Judaism and Hellenism. It can dominate them all, and there is no factor of earthly life to which it is confined or necessarily tied down (68-69).

DIFFICULTIES IN RECONSTRUCTING THE LIFE OF JESUS

How is it possible for conscientious, academically trained scholars, working with the same material and presumably seeking the same objectives, to arrive at such diverse interpretations of the historical Jesus and the content of his preaching and teaching? What were and are the problems which seem to make it impossible for academicians and scholars to reach a consensus on the nature and character of the historical life of Jesus? The problems seem to fall into three basic categories. First, there are the problems associated with the extent and character of the source materials. Second, there are the problems associated with the attempts to develop a methodology for approaching the issue of reconstructing the historical Jesus. And third, there are the problems involved in the presuppositions and objectives of the researcher.

The primary source material for any knowledge of the historical Jesus is of course the New Testament. There are some scattered references to the early church and to Jesus in ancient non-Christian sources. These include references found in Seutonius, Pliny, Tacitus, Josephus, the Talmud, and the Koran. Nothing of a historical value about Jesus can be gained from the first two. Tacitus who lived about A.D. 60-120 notes, in discussing the persecution of Christians under Nero, that the founder of the sect was Christus who "was executed at the hands of the procurator Pontius Pilate in the reign of Tiberius" (*Annales*, xv. 44). The authenticity of references in Josephus to Jesus is questioned since in one passage (*Antiquities*, xviii 63-64) he gives a good Christian confession about Jesus. Most scholars suspect a Christian interpolation. In the Slavonic version of Josephus' account of the Jewish war with Rome, several long passages appear which are not found in the Greek text (see below, pp. 154-55). The evidence about Jesus in the Talmud has been summarized in the following fashion by Joseph Klausner:

There are reliable statements to the effect that his name was Yeshu'a (Yeshu) of Nazareth; that he "practised sorcery" (*i.e.* performed miracles, as was usual in those days) and beguiled and led Israel astray; that he mocked at the words of the Wise; that he expounded Scripture in the same manner as the Pharisees; that he had five disciples; that he said that he was not come to take aught away from the Law or to add to it; that he was hanged (crucified) as a false teacher and beguiler on the eve of the Passover which happened on a Sabbath; and that his disciples healed the sick in his name.

There are statements of a tendencious or untrustworthy character to the effect that he was the bastard of an adulteress and that his father was Pandera or Pantere; that for forty days before his crucifixion a herald went out proclaiming why Jesus was to be put to death, so that any might come and plead in his favour, but none was found to do so; that there was doubt whether Jesus had any share in the world to come (*Jesus of Nazareth*, 46).

The Koran which dates from the seventh century A.D. contains several references to Jesus. In Islam, Jesus was accepted as one of the greatest of the prophets but not on an equal footing with Muhammad. The Koran accepted the tradition of the virgin birth but denied that Jesus was crucified. In Muslim tradition, someone else was put to death while Jesus was raised to heaven, a view held by some unorthodox groups in early Christianity.

There are numerous nonbiblical Christian traditions about Jesus. Over fifty different apocryphal Gospels are known or are referred to by the early church fathers. Most of these have survived, if at all, only in fragmentary form or in quotations. Some of the episodes about Jesus in these Gospels describe him as a miracle working child at the age of four and five or as a teacher of secret sayings. As a rule, these Gospels attempted to expand the traditions about Jesus or else to portray him as teaching a form of Christianity different from the orthodoxy of the second and third centuries.

When one turns to the New Testament, there are surprisingly few references to the historical career of Jesus outside of the four Gospels (see Galatians 1:19, 4:4; Romans 1:3; I Corinthians 7:10-11, 9:5, 14, 11:23-26, 15:4-8). A cursory reading of the four Gospels easily suggests the great differences which exist between Matthew, Mark, and Luke (the so-called Synoptic Gospels) on one hand and the Gospel of John on the other hand. In the synoptics, Jesus teaches in parables and short sayings; in John, he teaches in long allegorical speeches. In the synoptics, Jesus does not proclaim himself as messiah; in John, Jesus preaches himself as the messiah from the beginning of his ministry. In the synoptics, Jesus begins his career in Galilee after the arrest of John the Baptist; in John, he carries on a simultaneous ministry with the Baptist in Judah. In the synoptics, Jesus cleanses the temple during the last week of his career; in John, this event takes place at the beginning of his ministry. In the synoptics, Jesus was crucified on what is now called Good Friday; in John, the crucifixion occurs on Thursday. In the synoptics, Jesus goes to Jerusalem only once during his ministry; in John, he is in and out of Jerusalem on several occasions. In the synoptics, Jesus' ministry appears to be rather short; in John, it lasts for over three years. Much of the material in the synoptics has no parallel in John and vice versa. In other words, it is very difficult to reconcile the two portrayals of Jesus.

Even within the synoptic traditions, numerous differences exist. To take one example: All three Gospels report a visit to the tomb early one Sunday morning. In Mark 16:1-8, Mary Magdalene; Mary, the mother of James; and Salome go to the tomb, find the stone rolled away and a young man sitting in the tomb who tells about the resurrection. In Matthew 28:1-10, Mary Magdalene and Mary go to the tomb, an earthquake occurs, an angel descends and rolls away the stone, the guards tremble and fear, and the angel reports the resurrection. In Luke 24:1-11, Mary Magdalene; Joanna; Mary, the mother of James; and other women come to the tomb, find the stone rolled away, and two men in the tomb announce the resurrection to the women.

Study of the Synoptic Gospels has led to the conclusion that Mark was the first Gospel written and that Matthew and Luke are both dependent upon Mark plus a sayings source (referred to as "Q") not used by Mark. In addition, Matthew and Luke both contain some material unique to each Gospel. Thus the vast majority of scholars assume that behind the synoptics are four "sources" of which Mark and the sayings source are the most important.

The basic problem concerning the Gospel sources for the reconstruction of the historical Jesus centers on their character and reliability. Are the Gospels historical documents? Or biographical? How much influence have the individual authors and church tradition contributed to the portraits of Jesus in the Gospels? John 20:31 states that the Gospel was written to create belief in Jesus; that is, the Gospels were written as documents of faith or to stimulate faith and not to report mere historical facts. Luke, in the prologue, states that the Gospel was written with a particular perspective, to present "an orderly account." The author of Luke also notes that he is dependent upon previously written accounts as well as church tradition. The basic issues here are (1) how much the individual authors of the Gospels who wrote a generation or so after Jesus have utilized material or perhaps formulated traditions to support their individual purposes and (2) how much influence the church and its faith has had on the shape, content, and character of the traditions about Jesus.

Given the nature and character of the Gospels, is it possible to develop a methodology or approach which will allow one to reconstruct something of the outline of Jesus' career and his teaching? Is it possible, in other words, to determine what in the Gospels reflects the actual life of Jesus? Two extreme approaches to this question have been proposed. Some scholars argue that the Gospel traditions—events and sayings—should be accepted as authentically historical unless it is impossible to reconcile diverse traditions or unless there are overwhelming reasons to doubt a tradition. Others conclude that nothing should be accepted as authentic unless good reasons can be given to establish authenticity. Numerous variations, of course, exist between these two polar approaches. For the first position, the basic problem centers on the reconciliation of the differences between the

Gospels. For the latter position, the problem consists of developing criteria by which authenticity can be established. In attempting to establish authentic traditions, scholars have sought for "pillar passages"—that is, for passages whose historicity and genuineness seem assured. Some of the criteria which have been used are: appearance in more than one of the Gospel sources, occurrence of a saying in more than one form, reflection of an Aramaic linguistic background, reflection of Palestinian conditions, lack of any parallel in either Judaism or the early church, and various combinations of these.

The diversity in reconstructions of the historical Jesus are not only due to the character of the source materials and the methodological questions but also to the presuppositions and objectives of the researcher. Research without presuppositions is of course impossible. One's scientific assumptions about the world, for example, will influence the way in which the miracle stories are understood. If one assumes that nature is a closed continuum of cause and effect, this will certainly determine the manner in which the miraculous is evaluated. However, if one believes the universe to be open to the intervention of divine activity, this will color the treatment of the miraculous.

The religious convictions of the investigator are obviously a factor in one's research on the historical Jesus. A scholar who takes a decidedly antichurch attitude, as many of the earlier investigators did, will present a picture of Jesus quite different from one who seeks to support the church's faith through research.

One's sociocultural background and context can influence one's research. Frequently, current philosophical interests and cultural issues provide clues and approaches which scholars utilize in investigating the life of Jesus. Portraits of Jesus sometime seem to be a reflection of a present cultural or philosophical fad.

Even the personality and ego of the researcher may influence his investigations. Much research is based on the hope and excitement of new discovery and new perspectives.

Perhaps this drive to reveal the unknown is a greater factor in much historical research than we realize and more important to the personality and ego of the researcher than he imagines.

Many people have argued that the presuppositions and dispositions of researchers are the dominant factors in research on Jesus. Do all men find in Jesus what they wish to find or create him in their own image? This has frequently been proposed, but it certainly is an overstatement of the influence of one's convictions and presuppositions. Few scholars have taken such cavalier freedom with their treatments of the historical Jesus. For many, study of the historical Jesus has been not a support of their beliefs but a serious trial of their faith.

2. JESUS: THE CHRIST OF ORTHODOXY

Lord Jesus Christ, the only-begotten Son of God, begotten of the Father before all the ages, Light of Light, true God of true God, begotten not made, of one substance with the Father, through whom all things were made; who for us men and for our salvation came down from the heavens, and was made flesh of the Holy Spirit and the Virgin Mary, and became man, and was crucified for us under Pontius Pilate, and suffered and was buried, and rose again on the third day according to the Scriptures, and ascended into the heavens, and sitteth on the right hand of the Father, and cometh again with glory to judge living and dead, of whose kingdom there shall be no end. —*The Nicene Creed* (A.D. 325)

Throughout the centuries, Christian orthodoxy has held that the Jesus of history, the Christ of Christian faith, and the presentations of Jesus in the Gospels are, for all practical purposes, identical. The two works to be discussed in this chapter, though separated by decades and radically different in approach, reflect this position.

David Smith, in the preface to his widely popular work *The Days of His Flesh*, states that his two aims in discussing the historical Jesus were (1) "to vindicate the historicity of the evangelic records and adduce reason for believing, in opposition to an influential school of modern criticism, that they present Jesus as He actually lived among men, and not as He appeared to a later generation through a haze of reverence and superstition" and (2) "to justify the church's faith in Him as the Lord from Heaven." In these aims, one can see the faith and ambition of an orthodox interpretation of Jesus and the Gospels.

Smith's book opens with a discussion of the Gospels as sources for the life of Jesus. The preservation and transmission of the traditions about Jesus are related to the process by which rabbinical teachings were preserved and passed on through oral transmission. Reference is made to the efforts of the rabbis "directed to the immaculate transmission of the Oral Law" in which "disciples were drilled in the multitudinous precepts of that interminable tradition until they had them by heart. The lesson was repeated over and over till it was engraved upon their memories" (xiii). Among the disciples of the rabbis, "the study of the Law was thus a purely mechanical exercise, and the least disposition to originality would have been fatal to proficiency. The qualifications were a retentive memory and scrupulous adherence to the letter of the tradition. It must be handed on exactly as it had been received, *ipsissimis verbis* . . . and, if a disciple forgot a word . . . it was accounted to him as if he were guilty of death" (xiv). The same method of transmitting traditions was adopted in the early church: "It was at once natural and inevitable that the Apostles, being Jews, should follow it in recording the life and teaching of Jesus" (xv) and "it was the sacred duty of those to whose custody it had been committed to guard it no less faithfully than the Rabbis guarded the traditions of the elders" (xvi).

Between the time of the apostles and the writing of the Gospels, "there was a class of teachers in the primitive church whose function it was to go about instructing the believers in the oral tradition and drilling it into their minds in the fashion of the rabbinical schools. They were named the Catechisers and their scholars the catechumens" (xvii).

Smith describes the writing of the Synoptic Gospels in the following terms:

The oral tradition emanated from the Apostles, being their testimony to the things they had seen and heard. It was preserved and disseminated far and wide by the Catechisers; and when the Evangelists composed their narratives, they simply reduced the oral tradition to writing, each adopting the version of it which was current in his locality. The First Gospel represents the tradition as it circulated in Judaea, and though it was not written as it stands by Matthew, it was certainly derived from him and is stamped with his authority. The Second Gospel represents the tradition as it circulated in the Roman church, and it has this connection with Peter, that Mark was his companion and enjoyed the advantage of hearing his discourses. . . . The Third Gospel, composed by Luke, the physician of Antioch and the companion of Paul, represents the tradition as it circulated in Asia Minor and Achaia, and is pervaded by the spirit of the Apostle of the Gentiles (xvii-xviii).

The Synoptic Gospels thus exhibit close parallels and at times absolute verbal agreement but "each gospel is an independent reproduction of the apostolic tradition, and the differences are such variations as were natural and inevitable in the process of oral transmission" (xviii). The evangelists were therefore not so much authors as editors. In their editorial work, the editors had to omit much of the authentic tradition that was passed along to them. Some of this authentic material later shows up in quotes of the early church fathers and in additions to the Greek texts of the Gospels—although most of the additions to the biblical texts are worthless material and represent originally marginal annotations innocently inserted into the text.

The evangelists were not only forced to omit much of the oral tradition but they were also forced to exercise editorial freedom since in oral transmission, the original tradition had gotten broken up into sections with the chronological sequence being lost. Since the Catechisers repeated only so much of the tradition at a time, the material was generally passed along as "a large assortment of disconnected material. . . . To ascertain the historical sequence was, to a large extent, impossible; nor was it indeed any great matter to the Evangelists" (xx). The editors then arranged the material more topically than chronologically. Examples of this arrangement are the Sermon on the Mount (Matthew 5-7) and the Commission of the Twelve (Matthew 10). Thus the evangelists often introduced *logia* or sayings without the incidents to which they were originally connected or introduced incidents out of chronological order because they illustrated the theme at hand.

The oral transmission and recording of the tradition obviously allowed "sundry mishaps" to befall it. Among these, Smith notes: (1) slips of memory, (2) fusion of similar but really distinct passages, (3) emendation of what was deemed incredible or unintelligible, (4) mutilation of obscure *logia*, (5) modification of the tradition when an Old Testament prophecy found its fulfilment in some incident in Jesus' ministry, (6) confusion due to an erroneous presupposition in the minds of the editors, and (7) editorial comments inserted in the tradition as *logia* of Jesus. Such mishaps, however, are rather easy to detect and rectify (xxvi-xxxiv).

The Fourth Gospel was written to correct some of these mishaps as well as to supplement the Gospels of Matthew, Mark, and Luke. The Fourth Gospel was written by the disciple John who could, therefore, "in the fulness of his personal knowledge" (xxxii) make such corrections and supplementation. For example, John detailed Jesus' Judaean ministry because the synoptic traditions had originally been formulated under the apostles at Jerusalem where the incidents of the Judaean ministry were well known and needed no special mention. Another example is in the story of the cleansing of the temple where the Fourth Gospel has preserved the correct chronology.

The greatest differences among the Gospels are to be found, according to Smith, in the birth stories and the accounts of the resurrection. This is due to the fact that the apostolic tradition encompassed only the ministry of Jesus. The tradition therefore began with the public ministry of Jesus and concluded with the death of Jesus. Thus there were no birth and resurrection accounts in the transmitted tradition. The birth narrative in Matthew goes back to Joseph, a tradition which circulated in Jerusalem and Judaea and thus stressed Bethlehem as the home of Joseph and Mary. Luke's version represents Mary's account of the tradition; in fact Luke may have heard this story from Mary herself during Luke's visit to Jerusalem with Paul (xxxviii).

The diversity in the accounts of the resurrection is due, according to Smith, to three factors. First, "when the tradition took shape, the wonder of the Resurrection was at its height . . . an amazing and overwhelming fact which had happened but yesterday and was fresh in every mind." Second, exposition of the Resurrection in the tradition "was deemed all the more needless for as much as the Lord's Return was believed to be imminent." Third, "the Apostles always speak with a certain reticence about the Resurrection. They proclaim the fact, but they refrain from entering into particulars" (xxxix). Only after time passed and the Lord did not return did John, the last surviving eye witness, yield to the importunities of the believers and write the wondrous story. Therefore, the Gospel of John presented the resurrection narratives accurately thus correcting the synoptics who "agree only in their unfaltering and triumphant proclamation of the fact that Jesus rose and appeared to His disciples" (xl).

Thus the Gospels provide the reader with the apostolic tradition which was passed along in the church through the process of oral tradition with some disturbance and distortion of this tradition, but such as can be corrected. In so far as recovering the *ipsissima verba* of Jesus, however, Smith warns the reader to remember that the evangelists "wrote from memory" and thus "seldom, if ever, is it given us to quote a sentence and say: 'The Lord spoke these words.' The utmost that we can say is: 'He spoke after this manner.'" Yet, "one knows instinctively where Jesus ceases and the Evangelist begins. It is like passing into another atmosphere. . . . The words of Jesus shine on the pages of the Evangelists. It is indeed indubitable that they have suffered some measure of change and are not always written precisely as they came from His lips; but the change is generally inappreciable. As they stand on the sacred page, they attest their originality" (xlvi-xlvii).

Thus does Smith explain the origin of the Gospels and the historical reliability of the traditions.

In his discussion of the life of Jesus, Smith basically accepts as historical the accounts of the Gospels supplementing these with references to historical events contemporary to the time of Jesus and with references to Jewish and other

Near Eastern literature and practices. The preexistence of Jesus is accepted as well as his virgin birth, although Smith notes that Jesus' birth probably took place sometime between April and October, perhaps in 5 B.C. Jesus went through the normal Jewish childhood, was taught by his parents, received instruction in the Jewish elementary school, was taught the trade of carpentry by his father, absorbed much from his days in Nazareth amid his life with his brothers and sisters, and enjoyed "a sweet and happy childhood" (18).

Jesus became aware of his true person and mission during the Passover festival which he attended in Jerusalem at the age of twelve. "Nevertheless He quietly returned to Nazareth and resumed His simple and duteous life. For eighteen years He toiled with hammer and saw, knowing all the while Who He was and wherefore He had come, yet hiding the wondrous secret in His breast and never, until His hour arrived, revealing it by word or sign. . . . All the while He would be brooding over those Sacred Scriptures which spake of Him, foretelling His Advent and prefiguring His Redemption. And He would be looking abroad, with keen eye and sympathetic heart, upon the world which He had come to save" (23-24).

Jesus submitted himself to baptism at the hands of John the Baptist without guilt or fear, and "as John surveyed that serene form and that holy face radiant with the peace of God, his soul bowed in reverence and awe, and, like every mortal who ever came under the gaze of Jesus in the days of His flesh, he realised his own unworthiness" (31). Jesus thus submitted himself to a baptism of repentance just as "in His helpless infancy He endured the rite of circumcision" and later "paid year by year the Temple-tax, though as the Son of God whose House the Temple was, He might have claimed exemption" (31-32). The baptismal vision, experienced by John and Jesus, revealed to John the Baptist that Jesus was none other than the messiah (although John later became possessed of doubt about this).

"Impelled by the Holy Spirit, who had taken possession of Him at His Baptism and thenceforth dwelt in Him 'without measure,' Jesus retired" to the wilderness where he wrestled with the perplexities which crowded upon him (34). Smith explains the temptations in terms of Jesus' psychological struggle with the common expectations and desires of the Jewish people as well as with possible alternative patterns which his ministry might assume. Jesus, however, affirmed what he already knew: "He had not come to be welcomed and honoured but to be rejected and slain, a sacrifice for the sin of the world" (38).

The earliest disciples of Jesus were recruited, as noted in the Fourth Gospel, from the followers of John the Baptist since Jesus would not have chosen men whom he had not tested and approved. Jesus' basic designation for himself was Son of man, a title taken over from current Judaism where the term "sons of man" was employed to refer to "common folk." Smith suggests that this "nickname" was originally used by the people of Jesus as a "contemptuous epithet" and adopted by Jesus "as a continual protest against that secular ideal of the Messiahship which more than anything else hindered His recognition and acceptance; and in assuming it Jesus designed to make men think and perchance discover that the true Messianic glory was not what they conceived—not the glory of earthly majesty but the glory of sacrifice. And He had the further design of identifying Himself with the weak and despised, and thus revealing His grace" (50).

Jesus' public ministry was begun in Jerusalem at the Feast of Passover in A.D. 26. "Ever since His twelfth year He had gone up annually with the train of pilgrims from Galilee, but on this occasion it was not the mere custom of the Feast that took Him hither. He would go up as the Messiah. It was fitting that His public ministry should open in the sacred capital and His first appeal be addressed to the rulers of the Nation" (58). It was on this occasion that he cleansed the temple. This event perplexed the Jewish rulers who subsequently sought from him a sign and later sent their representative, Nicodemus, "to wait upon Him and ask what they [his miracles] meant. Of this much they had no doubt, that Jesus was a God-sent teacher, and they thought it probable that He was indeed the Messiah." Jesus did not answer directly but sought to show Nicodemus that the kingdom of God was "a spiritual order invisible to the eye of sense" and that "the Jews should be required to enter the Kingdom of Heaven by that door of humiliation [regeneration], on the self-same terms as the despised Gentiles" (65). Like the Jewish leaders, Nicodemus did not understand or could not accept the idea and "would go away in utter bewilderment. Yet the good seed had been sown in his heart, and after many days it sprang up and bore rich and abiding fruit" (68).

Jesus' first phase of ministry in Jerusalem ended with the arrest of John the Baptist and Jesus' desire not to precipitate at that time his final crisis with the Jewish leaders. Smith affirms, following the Gospel of John, a Samaritan ministry of Jesus, early in his career, that is, on his return to Galilee.

In discussing the miracles of Jesus, Smith accepts their historicity (with the exception of the story of the coin in the fish's mouth [Matt. 17:24-27], an incident in which he merely engaged in a little raillery with Peter). However, in discussing Jesus' exorcism of demons, he points out that Jesus did not believe in demons, yet "with gracious condenscension He accomodated Himself to the ignorance of men, but He did not share it" (108). To have shared the idea of demonical possession would have involved Jesus with the passing opinions of his day, and "He never entangled His teaching with contemporary ideas; He never made a statement which has been discredited by the progress of human knowledge" (106). "Jesus dealt with the demoniacs after the manner of a wise physician. He did not seek to dispel their hallucination. He fell in with it and won their confidence" (108).

The opposition to Jesus by the Jewish leaders was based on a number of factors: his actions on the Sabbath, his usurpation of the role of God, his identification of himself with God in the forgiveness of sin, and his association with the outcasts of society.

Smith understood the Sermon on the Mount, while recognizing that all this material was not spoken on one occasion, as part of the ritual of Jesus' ordination of the twelve instructing them on "how they should comport themselves as the heralds of His Kingdom." He was thus "not enunciating a general code of Christian ethics" nor setting out general rules of conduct for "literal and universal application" but outlining for the disciples "a loftier goodness" since "their vocation imposed upon them a peculiar necessity for self-abnegation and self-effacement" (161-62).

In sending out the Twelve, Jesus' instructions that they were to go only to the lost house of Israel, implies, according to Smith, that Jesus understood his ministry as inclusive of the Gentiles. Otherwise, why the instruction since "no Jew would have dreamed of preaching to Gentiles or Samaritans, and the idea would never have entered into the Apostles' minds had not Jesus, by His sympathy with aliens, set them the example" (217). Jesus' apparently harsh response to the Phoenician woman (Mark 7:24-30) was in actuality his proverbial response to her proverbial retort and in no way must be understood as reflecting Jesus' limitation of his ministry and teaching to the Jews (250-51).

The final confrontation between Jesus and the Jewish leaders which led to his arrest, trial, and crucifixion was due to the Sanhedrin's fear that such miracles as the raising of Lazarus "must procure Jesus a vast access of popularity; and, knowing the jealous surveillance which Rome exercised over turbulent Palestine, they dreaded the consequences, should the multitudes rally round Him and acclaim Him the Messianic King of Israel" (374). It was a question of removing Jesus rather than risk the national tragedy that might follow such popular acclamation.

Judas' betrayal of Jesus was due to disillusionment.

He was a disappointed man. He had attached himself to Jesus because he deemed Him the Messiah and expected reward and honour in the Messianic Kingdom. [Although Jesus had taught his disciples about the form his ministry must take and had predicted his resurrection, they, like

46

Judas had not understood.] Gradually the truth had come home to him, and he had discovered the vanity of expectation. His disillusionment was complete when he realised that what awaited Jesus was not a crown but a cross. He perceived that he had embarked on a ruinous enterprise, and to his worldly judgment it appeared the wisest policy to come out of it on the best possible terms. It may be also that he was actuated by a desire to be avenged on the Master who, as he deemed, had fooled him (436-37).

Jesus had, however, from the time of his call of Judas known of his ultimate betrayal and had seen in him a vehicle of the divine purpose.

For Smith, the trial of Jesus before the Sanhedrin was illegal, "a succession of flagrant illegalities" (469). Insufficient and disagreeing witnesses were used, the capital case was heard on a single day, and no written votes were cast: all acts prohibited by Jewish law regulated by the Talmudic tractate *Sanhedrin* (472). Pilate did the best he could under the conditions, but "when his position is understood, it appears that he was to a large extent the victim of circumstances, and may even claim a measure of pity" (477).

Over half a century of serious and critical New Testament study separates David Smith's *The Days of His Flesh* from Ethelbert Stauffer's *Jesus and His Story*. Nonetheless, Stauffer's view of the historical Jesus agrees with the confession embodied in the title to Smith's volume: "God himself had become man, more human than any other man in the wide expanse of history" (195).

Stauffer begins his discussion by agreeing with the opinion of many critical scholars concerning the New Testament Gospels upon which any reconstruction of the historical Jesus must draw.

Today we know that the theological and church-oriented bias in the traditions is much older than the Gospels themselves.
    Twenty-five years ago a prominent Protestant theologian [Hans Lietzmann] wrote: "The Passion of Jesus, as it unfolds before our eyes in the Gospels, must be counted among the most tremendous creations of religious fiction." Today we must ask ourselves whether this same verdict does not apply to everything the Gospels have to say about Jesus (vii-viii).

47

In spite of such a negative affirmation about the historical nature of the Gospel materials, Stauffer argues that it is still possible to provide a portrait of the historical Jesus although not in the sense envisioned by many of the nineteenth-century efforts.

The nineteenth-century ideal was a *biography* of Jesus—that is to say, a representation of the psychological development of Jesus, of his mind and his activities, rendered with narrative vividness, analytic insight, and plausibility. Whether this was a legitimate ideal is a moot question. At any rate, we know today that it was unattainable. What, then, may our ideal be, what ideal am I entitled to set up? I reply: a *history* of Jesus. By this term I mean something extremely modest. I mean a strict clarification of those facts which can be ascertained, possibly of a series of events, perhaps too of a number of casual relationships (xiii).

Stauffer's ambition is a "presentation of facts and casual relationships." In establishing such a presentation, Stauffer argues that the "Evangelists' interpretation of Jesus, the interpretation offered by the dogmas of the church, and even my personal interpretation of Jesus are barred" (xiii).

If the Gospel interpretation, church dogma, and researchers' bias are to be eliminated, how is it possible to isolate the "historical facts from the dogmatic bias" (viii). How can one go beyond "lives" of Jesus based solely on the Bible or on imaginative techniques and arrive at a pragmatic history of Jesus? How does one discover "Jesus' own interpretation of himself" (xiii)? His answer to this question is: "To open new sources unaffected by Christian tendencies" (viii).

In speaking of such sources, Stauffer divides them into indirect and direct sources. The indirect sources are those which provide the "contemporary testimony on the conditions, events, and personalities that played a part in the story of Jesus. In such testimony there is no mention of Jesus himself. For the most part, the authors of these documents knew nothing whatsoever about the existence of Jesus. Consequently, these writings are quite free of religious fiction or dogmatic bias" (viii). Stauffer is here speaking about those documents and remains which provide information about Palestinian conditions and Roman governmental administration and activities during the time contemporary with Jesus: "on personalities, Jewish politics, Palestinian geography, jurisprudence, taxation, penal code, familial law, religious law, liturgy, expectation of the Messiah, astronomy, and astrology" (6). Of special importance in this cateogry are "the Jewish legal provisions concerning heretics and the rules of trials. . . . When we train the rays of legal history upon the Gospels, we obtain a historical X-ray photograph. Upon it stands revealed the clear outline of the life of Jesus" (viii-ix). These indirect sources are of special importance, according to Stauffer, in arriving at a chronological synchronization of the life of Jesus.

The direct sources are those ancient sources which contain direct statements about Jesus. Some of these sources are Jewish, mentioning Jesus by name or under a code name. "Most of these texts are the work of the rabbinical authorities; a few spring from the movement that grew up around John the Baptist. There are not many; they are all very short, in many cases camouflaged and muddled; and in these texts, also, truth and fiction are closely intertwined." However, "in these brief notices lie concealed many an old tradition concerning Jesus, traditions perhaps reaching back to the days of Caiaphas, and at any rate back to the first and second centuries" (ix).

According to Stauffer, these Jewish sources, generally critical and polemical in nature, and the Christian Gospels as well, were the products of the early Jewish-Christian conflict. Both the Jewish texts on Jesus and the Christian Gospels were the products of "a passionate controversy centering around the interpretation and the meaning of Jesus of Nazareth. . . . The oldest and most important function of the traditions was polemical. They originated in the conflict over Jesus. . . . Out of these struggles emerged the Gospels and the rabbinical or Baptistic documents concerning Jesus" (xii). The origin of these conflicts Stauffer places back into the life of Jesus but it was the shape of the conflict after

Jesus' death that produced the final form of the traditions. "On the one side there were the groups around Peter, James, Matthew, Luke, and John. On the other side stood the scribes, the anti-Roman partisans, the desert sects, the disciples of John the Baptist, and the Samaritans" (xii). Stauffer argues that in these polemical Jewish and Christian texts there is testimony and countertestimony concerning Jesus. In these texts, one frequently finds that the "facts are employed in the one case to sustain faith in Christ, in the other to attack that faith." When such a "confrontation of witnesses yields statements that agree on some points, then these points must represent facts accepted by both sides" (x). These facts, according to Stauffer, provide the hope for writing a history of Jesus.

The direct Christian sources about Jesus are dated, according to Stauffer, in the following order: the speeches of Peter in Acts, the Epistles of Paul, the *Logia* (or Q) reconstructed from Matthew and Luke, the Synoptic Gospels which adhered most faithfully to the language of Jesus, the Fourth Gospel which clarified the chronology in the story of Jesus, Jewish-Christian books (apocryphal traditions) which have survived in fragmentary form and in quotations by early church fathers. Non-Christian sources include, in addition to the Roman authors, Josephus and the rabbinic traditions; the medieval Mandaean texts stemming from the oldest community of the followers of John the Baptist; Islamic texts including the Koran and the eleventh century writings of Al Ghazzali, which contain some material going back to an ancient Judao-Christian tradition; and two Chinese lives of Jesus written around A.D. 640 at the insistence of Emperor Tai-Tsung, which are based, according to Stauffer, on ancient Syrian traditions, some going back to non-Christian sources (3-5).

In outlining his "pragmatic history of Jesus," Stauffer stresses the importance of chronology. Confronted with the problem of the synoptic chronology which envisions a ministry of Jesus of about a year and a half, according to Stauffer (in Mark 2:23 it is springtime and in Mark 14:1 it is spring again), and the Gospel of John which has Jesus' ministry span four years, Stauffer argues: "There is no fitting the chronological structure of the Gospel of John within the narrow span of the Synoptic account. But it is possible to fit the Synoptic frame into John's structure. This is important as evidence for the correctness of the Johannine chronology." Thus chronologically, "the Fourth Evangelist corrects and integrates the Synoptic account and treats the entire period of Jesus' ministry, the early phase under the Baptist, and the concluding, climactic phase" (7). Dating the beginning of the ministry of John the Baptist to A.D. 28 (see Luke 3:1-2), Stauffer arrives at the following chronology for the ministry of Jesus:

Spring of 28: Baptism of Jesus. Passover of 29: cleansing of the Temple. November 29: northward journey through Samaria. December 29 to the autumn of 30: ten quiet months. Autumn of 30: arrest of John the Baptist. October 30: Feast of Tabernacles in Jerusalem. Late autumn of 30: fresh beginning in Galilee. Spring of 31: Passover in Galilee. October 31: Feast of Tabernacles in Jerusalem. Passover of 32: Passover of death (8).

Was Jesus a son of David? To this question Stauffer can answer an assured yes since Joseph was a member of this family line. Support for this premise is deduced not from the New Testament evidence but from other traditions. Firstly, Jewish evidence from the time shows that many Jews preserved lists of Jewish families which were officially supervised and "were of the highest importance in legal matters concerning marriage, property, occupation and religion" (14). Secondly, Stauffer points to the fact that

Domitian, in connection with his persecution of the former Jewish royal dynasty, called to Rome two great-grandsons of Joseph (grand-nephews of Jesus) by the names of Zachariah and James, because they had been denounced to him as Davidites. The two "confessed" their Davidic origins without ifs or buts, but were released on the grounds that they were completely non-political. Under Trajan, however, the aged

Bishop Simeon (cousin of Jesus and successor of James the Just) was condemned to death as a "Davidite and Christian" (14-15).

"In both the major Gospels (Matthew and Luke) Jesus is accounted the son of the Virgin Mary. Is the miraculous birth of Jesus a historical fact" (15)? Stauffer answers yes and then adduces his evidence both from Christian and anti-Christian testimony which agree on the matter and therefore substantiate the fact. Stauffer finds a belief in the virgin birth of Jesus in all four Gospels and the earlier *Logia*. At the marriage festival in Cana where Jesus turned the water into wine (John 2:1-11), John reports the incident so that "with Mary already counting upon Jesus' power to work miracles, he [the author] appears to take it for granted that the mother knows from the beginning the secret of her son" (16). In the *Logia,* Jesus' opponents berate him for being a glutton and drunkard, a particular insult which was "flung at a person born of an illegitimate connection who betrayed, by his mode of life and his religious conduct, the stain of his birth. This was the sense in which the Pharisees and their fellows employed the phrase against Jesus. Their meaning was: he is a bastard" (16). In Mark 6:3, the countrymen of Jesus refer to him as "son of Mary," as do the Samaritan, Mandaean, and Koranic texts, a practice followed only when the father was unknown. A rabbinic tradition, dated as before A.D. 70 by Stauffer, speaks of Jesus as "the bastard of a wedded wife" while later Jewish texts claimed he was the illegitimate son of the Roman Panthera. All these lines of evidence are asserted as proof of Jesus' virgin birth. "Jesus was the son of Mary, not of Joseph. That is the historical fact, recognized alike by Christians and Jews, friends and adversaries" (18).

Other facts associated with Jesus' birth which are authenticated, according to Stauffer, by direct and indirect sources, are his birth at Bethlehem (Matthew 2:1-5, Luke 2:4), the census reported by Luke (Luke 2:1-5), the miraculous star (Matthew 2:2-11), and the massacre of the children by Herod (Matthew 2:16). Jesus' membership in the

Davidic family, whose ancestral home was Bethlehem, and the fact that Jewish writings never deny his birth there, while later playing down any connection of the messiah with Bethlehem, lead Stauffer to affirm the conclusion of the ancient church historian Origen: "Jewish polemicists could not deny the birth of Jesus at Bethlehem and therefore expurgated any mention of Bethlehem [see Micah 5:2] in connection with Messianic prophecies, in order not to foster belief in Jesus, the child of Bethlehem" (20).

Since D. F. Strauss, many scholars have argued that the census referred to in the Lucan infancy narrative was the census taken in A.D. 6/7 when the Romans took direct control over Judaea after Archelaus, the son of Herod the Great, was deposed. Josephus, the ancient Jewish historian refers to a census at this time but not to one during the reign of Herod which would be required by the Lucan text if Jesus was born before the death of Herod in 4 B.C. Stauffer argues that a "wealth of inscriptions, papyri, and other original documents on ancient taxation laws has come to light" which refutes Strauss' conclusions (22). Stauffer draws from Egyptian papyri and other references reflecting Roman taxation practices, inscriptional references to Quirinius, and the fact that King Herod came under Augustus' displeasure in 8 B.C. to argue the following: "In the autumn of 12 B.C. Quirinius took charge of Oriental affairs and commenced the census in the Roman East. In 8 B.C. Herod the Great was demoted. In 7 B.C. the *apographa* [a systematic listing of all taxable persons and property] in Palestine began. At this time Joseph probably journeyed to Bethlehem with Mary. In A.D. 7 the work of the census was completed with the *apotimesis*" [the official assessment of taxes] (31). Josephus' reference to a census during this time is therefore to the final phase. Stauffer realizes that there is no definite reference to the 7 B.C. *apographa* but argues that all the circumstantial evidence supports Luke at this point. Thus Jesus was born in 7 B.C. and began his public ministry at the age of about thirty-three. Stauffer declares Luke 3:13, which states that Jesus began his ministry at about thirty years of age, to be useless for purposes of chronology since thirty was considered in antiquity as the "age when a man stood at the peak of his powers," and anyway Luke only says he was *about* thirty years old (7).

In the seventeenth century, the astronomer "Kepler ascribed the star of Bethlehem to the unique orbit of the planet Jupiter in the year 7 B.C." During this year, there was a conjunction of Jupiter and Venus in the spring, and in the summer and autumn, the planet "encountered the planet Saturn in the Sign of the Fishes—this being the extremely rare Great Conjunction that takes place in this form only once every 794 years" (32). Stauffer argues that throughout the ancient world, the year 7 B.C. was predicted by astronomers, on the basis of astronomical calculations, to be a very propitious and apocalyptic year. Stauffer notes the Berlin Planetary Tablet, the Celestial Almanac, and the tradition associating Jupiter with Augustus as pointing to this expectation. The Berlin Planetary Tablet from Egypt (copied in A.D. 42) lists the movements of the planets for the years 17 B.C. to A.D. 10, while the Celestial Almanac, a cuneiform tablet from Sippar, "The Greenwich of Babylonia," predicts the positions of the planets for the year 7 B.C. and notes in particular the conjunction of Saturn and Jupiter in the Fishes. In Rome, "Augustus was regarded as Jupiter in human form. . . . Venus was considered the star of the Julian family, and Saturn the symbol of the Golden Age. In these circumstances the extraordinary path of Jupiter in 7 B.C. could only be taken as referring to the career of the Emperor Augustus" (34). Thus the world was anticipating the phenomenal year 7 B.C. In the East, "Saturn was considered to be the planet of Palestine. . . . Jupiter was regarded as the star of the ruler of the universe, and the constellation of the Fishes as the sign of the last days. . . . The clay tablet of Sippar may be regarded as the astronomical pocket-almanac with which the wise men set out from the East" (33-34). Thus the Eastern Magi set out for Jerusalem and witnessed the star of Bethlehem as a historical fact.

The historicity of Herod's massacre of the innocents is

confirmed for Stauffer on the basis of Matthew 2, references to the characters of Herod and Augustus, and passages from Josephus and the apocalyptic work called the *Assumption of Moses* (dated by Stauffer to A.D. 6–15). The passage in the *Assumption of Moses* (chapter 6) speaks in a prophecy after the event (or a "diatribe . . . in the nature of a literal report" [38]) of a ruler (Herod) who would follow the Hasmonaeans (whose reign ended in 63 B.C.) and who would slaughter the old and young without mercy as was done at the time of the Exodus in Egypt. Stauffer relates this reference to a passage by Josephus which, in describing the slaughter of the babies in Egypt at Moses' birth, spoke of the announcement of a king to be born among the Hebrews following which the pharoah issued his edict to destroy every male child. The testimony to Herod, Augustus' brutality, and especially Herod's numerous exterminations of family and enemies in the year 7 B.C. convince Stauffer that "Herod's massacre of the innocents is a historical fact, no matter what fable-making was at work" (41).

Although Stauffer admits that we are told very little about Jesus' life from 7 B.C. to A.D. 27, he accepts as historical the flight to Egypt and the trip to the temple for Passover at the age of twelve, in A.D. 6, the year Archelaus was deposed— when the "occupation troops of the Roman procurator were marching through the streets of the city for the first time" (54). From Jewish sources describing Palestinian life and religion, Stauffer seeks to fill in the hidden years of Jesus stressing his education in the law and holy scriptures and his knowledge of the apocryphal materials—in their preedited form—and especially texts dealing with martyrology. Jesus read the Bible like any of his Jewish contemporaries, but he read them knowing—like a son—the love of God the father. Jesus spoke Aramaic and Greek and knew Hebrew and Latin as well.

On the basis of Jewish texts, Stauffer is able to describe Jesus' physical appearance. "In rabbinical theory, the reflection of the divine presence could descend only upon a man of tall and powerful stature. Evidently Jesus was able to meet this physical standard, for otherwise his adversaries would surely not have missed the chance to attack him on such grounds" (59). "His voice must have had a unique resonance, and his manner of speech a unique gracefulness" (60). The long years of waiting

"may have been years of temptation, for Jesus and his mother. . . . The excitement that had surrounded his birth had to remain concealed in order not to cast suspicion upon the grown man and bring down upon him the bloodhounds of Herod [Antipas] and the Romans. Jesus, too, held his peace. He could only wait. It was as if the millennial expectations of mankind and of all creation, the ancient hopes of the people of Israel, were concentrated and raised to their peak in those decades that Jesus of Nazareth spent in waiting" (62).

Jesus' public ministry was inaugurated with his baptism by John the Baptist, whom he had known from childhood. For a time he had functioned as a member of the movement of John—a fact recognized by rabbinical and Mandaean sources—where he engaged in baptizing respondents and was "considered by the public, and by the disciples of John as well, to be no more than the Baptist's favorite disciple, the most successful of his messengers" (65). Jesus was aware of his divine sonship, as was his mother, and after the wedding in Cana, the "disciples guessed it" (66). Jesus performed miracles as his opponents during his lifetime recognized and as later rabbinical sources admitted; in fact, "Jesus himself considered it of the greatest importance that his miracles should be observed, checked, and confirmed by outsiders and opponents" (9).

Jesus' cleansing of the temple was an "absolute rigorous application of the rabbinical precepts" against priestly corruption, and "since Jesus was as concerned with preserving the holiness of the temple as the most scrupulous Pharisee . . . he even had many sympathizers in the ranks of the Great Sanhedrin" (67). The cleansing of the temple won Jesus the enmity of the higher priesthood and the Sadducees; his disregard of the Sabbath laws and customs won him the enmity of the rabbinate and the Pharisees.

Jesus: The Christ of Orthodoxy

Following the Passover of A.D. 31, Jesus was placed under close scrutiny by his adversaries and a "new swarm of emissaries from the Sanhedrin arrived in Galilee. There were signs of intensified counter-propaganda. Curses were called down upon the head of the blasphemer" (84). "Lawyers from Jerusalem were already arriving in Capernaum to look into Jesus' miracles on the spot" (85). Jesus was judged to be preaching apostasy and performing demonic miracles, and for a time it appeared that the whole city of Capernaum might be officially declared a "seduced city"—guilty of apostasy (see Deuteronomy 13:12-18).

The events following the beginning of this open opposition between Jesus and the religious establishment have to be seen, according to Stauffer, in the light of Jewish law regarding heretics which provides an objective tool to reconstruct the subsequent events, since it was the "provisions against heresy which dictated each successive phase in the prosecution of Jesus" as a violator of the Torah and a preacher of apostasy. This "inevitable conflict that had to end in a verdict of death" explains "Jesus' early conviction that death would be his lot; . . . the attitude of Judas, the fears of Jesus' mother, his kindred, his disciples, and sympathizers; . . . and the rigid consistency of the Great Sanhedrin" (77). Jesus became a fugitive. The Sanhedrin set out to arrest and convict this heretic.

The basic charge of the Sanhedrin against Jesus was his use of the expression "I am He," an expression originating in the Old Testament where it is a formula used by the deity in speaking of himself. It was thus a theophanic formula and in using it and calling for a "confession of faith in this 'I am He' as the prerequisite for the forgiveness of sins" (91), it "was the purest, the boldest, and the profoundest declaration by Jesus of who and what he was. . . . This meant: where I am, there God is, there God lives and speaks, calls, asks, acts, decides, loves, chooses, rejects, suffers, and dies. Nothing bolder can be said, or imagined. It was the profoundest declaration" (194). The Sanhedrin took action to remove this heretical apostate.

The first effort to excommunicate Jesus by the Sanhedrin failed because of the opposition of Nicodemus. The Sanhedrin later "came to the unanimous decision to excommunicate anyone who . . . declared his faith in Jesus" (92). Jesus' sermon about himself as the good shepherd at the Festival of Dedication (Hanukkah) in December, 31 (John 10:22-39), greatly angered the Sanhedrin, and they sought to arrest him, but he escaped. "There are sundry indications that stones were already flying through the air as Jesus escaped the fanatics like a bird fleeing the nets of the fowler" (98). Jesus fled from Judaean territory taking refuge in Transjordan. After Jesus raised Lazarus from the dead, the Sanhedrin took definite action: "The result was that the Great Sanhedrin decided to condemn Jesus to death. A proclamation of outlawry was issued, reminding all Jews faithful to the Torah of their obligation to denounce the criminal" (103). Stauffer sees in the Talmudic statement that before Jesus was crucified on the eve of the Passover a herald had gone forth and announced the sentence and called for witnesses for forty days, a confirmation of this verdict of the Sanhedrin. The forty days are to be taken as an approximately correct round figure, but the "passage enables us to date the proclamation of outlawry mentioned in John 11:57— sometime in February of A.D. 32" (104).

Jesus withdrew from his pursuers and returned north for a short time, only leaving his hiding place to return later to Jerusalem. Why did he follow this course: "Jesus wished to die on the Passover" (105). After Jesus' return to and entry into Jerusalem, it was only a matter of time before the Sanhedrin would arrest him; but it had to pick its time, since "it was impossible to capture Jesus in the midst of his massed bodyguards" (111). The Sanhedrin sought to arrest Jesus and execute him before Passover so that peace and public order might be preserved as far as possible. But the Sanhedrin needed help, for it was hard to find and seize Jesus. "The final struggle between Jesus and Caiaphas must have been in actuality far more dramatic than the accounts of the Evangelists suggest" (112). Here Judas enters the picture since it was he who betrayed the Master and offered the Sanhedrin its opportunity. But why did Judas do this deed: "It may be that Judas, the non-Galilean, had for months been a secret agent of the Jerusalem Sanhedrin assigned to work among the Galilean's disciples. At any rate, he regarded the capture of the man who had been proclaimed a blasphemer and pseudo-prophet as his bounden duty. For he took an oath pledging himself to commit the betrayal—an oath that may well have included a curse upon himself should he fail to carry out the task he had undertaken" (112).

The trial of Jesus by the Sanhedrin ended in a unanimous vote against the blasphemer who in his trial had again used the theophanic formula "I am" (Mark 14:62). Since the Sanhedrin had been deprived in A.D. 30 of its jurisdiction over capital crimes (209), the Sanhedrin had to secure a condemnation and execution from Pilate. Before Pilate, Jesus was indicted on political charges as "instigator of unrest, a partisan, a messianic king" (128). Pilate wished to avoid the execution but was pushed by Caiaphas the high priest and "on the eve on the Passover Jeshu of Nazareth was executed" as the rabbinical texts say and the Fourth Gospel states (143).

The story of the empty tomb is historical—"even Jesus' opponents reluctantly—and therefore all the more credibly—bear witness to the fact of the empty tomb" (144). Stauffer supports this claim not only by the New Testament witness but by rabbinical claims that the disciples stole the body or the gardener removed it. Further confirmation is found in a Roman inscription discovered in Nazareth in 1878 and published in 1930. This inscription is a summary of an imperial edict directed against the robbery of corpses and the desecration of graves. "Perhaps it is based upon a rescript of Emperor Tiberius, and may possibly be the Emperor's reply to Pontius Pilate's report on Jesus, the empty tomb, and the rumors that the body had been stolen" (146).

The appearances of the risen Christ are historical events. The absence of any reference to the women as recipients of appearances from Paul's list in I Corinthians 15 is due to that fact that according to Jewish law "women were not qualified to bear witness" (151). The later Jewish opponents did not seek to deny the resurrection and the appearances, they merely sought to discredit the account. "They contended that Jesus had always practiced magical raisings from the dead, and that his own 'resurrection' was nothing but a necromantic trick" (152).

3. JESUS: THE APOCALYPTIC VISIONARY

> As of old Jacob wrestled with the angel, so German theology wrestles with Jesus of Nazareth and will not let Him go until He bless it—that is, until He will consent to serve it and will suffer Himself to be drawn by the Germanic spirit into the midst of our time and our civilisation. But when the day breaks, the wrestler must let Him go. He will not cross the ford with us. Jesus of Nazareth will not suffer Himself to be modernised. As an historic figure He refuses to be detached from His own time. —Albert Schweitzer, *The Quest of the Historical Jesus* (p. 312)

The Quest of the Historical Jesus by Albert Schweitzer has to be considered one of the most influential books of the twentieth century. Insofar as New Testament scholarship is concerned, it probably has to be classified as the most important work of modern times. The book, like the man himself, has cast its shadow across our times, a shadow not confined to the academic world, a shadow touching directly or indirectly every intellectual attempt to come to grips with the Jesus of history.

In the narrowest sense, the work is a survey of the research on the life of Jesus since the time of Reimarus. Its focus, however, centers primarily on Protestant German scholarship. In page after page, Schweitzer presents scholarly research on the subject interspersed with a sharp, incisive critique of the methodologies employed and the conclusions drawn. But the book is more than a history and a presentation of the research of others. It contains Schweitzer's own understanding of the historical Jesus and his relationship to the twentieth century.

61

In his delineation of the contours of Jesus research, Schweitzer focused on the three basic either/or problems which had developed in nineteenth-century research. "The first was laid down by Strauss: *either* purely historical *or* purely supernatural. The second had been worked out by the Tübingen school and Holtzmann: *either* Synoptic *or* Johannine. Now came the third: *either* eschatological *or* non-eschatological" (238). In other words, first, was the life of Jesus to be understood in historical terms or in supernatural categories? Was it to be understood in terms of a rigorous historical critical analysis or in terms of a faith acceptance of the supernatural? Secondly, in discussing the historical Jesus, are the synoptic or the Johannine perspectives and traditions to be the basic point of departure? Thirdly, was Jesus' teaching and life dominated by and oriented to the eschatological future?

Before moving to an analysis of Schweitzer's portrait of the historical Jesus, we should note two works published just prior to Schweitzer's survey since they pose many of the issues with which he was concerned. The first of these is Johannes Weiss' *The Preaching of Jesus Concerning the Kingdom of God* (1892). The second is Wilhelm Wrede's *The Messianic Secret in the Gospels: A Contribution toward the Understanding of the Gospel of Mark* (1901). The first of these, by Weiss, forced upon scholars the alternative of discounting the eschatological in Jesus and his message or else taking the matter with absolute seriousness. In describing the clarity of Weiss' presentation, which he called "thoroughgoing eschatology," Schweitzer wrote:

In passing . . . to Johannes Weiss the reader feels like an explorer who after weary wanderings through billowy seas of reed-grass at length reaches a wooded tract, and instead of swamp feels firm ground beneath his feet, instead of yielding rushes sees around him the steadfast trees. At last there is an end of "qualifying clause" theology, of the "and yet," the "on the other hand," the "notwithstanding"! The reader had to follow the others step by step, making his way over every footbridge and gang-plank which they laid down, following all the meanderings in which they indulged, and must never let go their hands if he wished to come safely through the labyrinth of spiritual and eschatological ideas which they supposed to be found in the thought of Jesus.

In Weiss there are none of these devious paths: "behold the land lies before thee" (238).

The basic theses of Weiss' book are the following: (1) All modern ideas read into the concept of the kingdom of God must be eliminated. (2) The kingdom of God was for Jesus a transcendental reality, without political expectations, and still in the future and was spoken of as present only as a cloud may be said to be present by casting its shadow upon the earth. (3) Jesus did not establish the kingdom; he only proclaimed its coming and waited its establishment by supernatural means. (4) As Jews under the kingdom, penitence was necessary for the kingdom's coming, but since sufficient penitence did not show itself, Jesus offered his own death as the ransom price. (5) Jesus died believing that he would return again in splendor and glory after his death. (6) The ministry of Jesus and that of John the Baptist differ only in Jesus' consciousness of being the messiah—that is, his consciousness that he would exercise the messiahship in the future beyond death at his return. (7) The ethic of Jesus was an ethic to set men free from the world so they might be prepared to enter unimpeded into the kingdom. Schweitzer saw in Weiss the first scholar since Reimarus who had taken seriously the eschatology in the preaching of Jesus.

For Schweitzer, Wrede represented what he called "thoroughgoing skepticism." Wrede challenged the opinion, commonly held at the time, that Mark, the earliest Gospel, provided the means to arrive at a historical view of Jesus. The Marcan motif of the messianic secret was for Wrede unhistorical, and its dominance in the Gospel shows that the Gospel is a product of the church's faith, a chapter in the history of dogma rather than an historical representation of the life of Jesus. The narrative of Mark arose from the impulse of the church to give a messianic form to the otherwise nonmessianic earthly life of Jesus. Thus the structure and interconnections between the individual units in Mark were attributed to a secondary development and were not a reflection of the historical ministry of Jesus. Schweitzer summarizes the implications of Wrede in the following terms:

> Formerly it was possible to book through-tickets at the supplementary-psychological-knowledge office which enabled those travelling in the interests of Life-of-Jesus construction to use express trains, thus avoiding the inconvenience of having to stop at every little station, change, and run the risk of missing their connexion. This ticket office is now closed. There is a station at the end of each section of the narrative, and the connexions are not guaranteed (333).

Schweitzer accepted the positions of Weiss in his emphasis on the eschatological form of Jesus' message. Wrede's arguments were partially adopted. Schweitzer agreed that the Gospel of Mark could no longer be used as was common in nineteenth-century research—that is, as a reliable foundation document in reconstructing the historical life of Jesus.

In formulating his version of the historical Jesus, Schweitzer worked with the following general overall assumptions. (1) In spite of critical and skeptical study of the Gospels, these documents still reflect the historical Jesus and the course of his career in a sufficient form to warrant a reconstruction of this history. This is especially the case with the Gospel of Matthew and to a lesser degree the Gospel of Mark. "The Life of Jesus cannot be arrived at by following the arrangement of a single Gospel, but only on the basis of the tradition which is preserved more or less faithfully in the earliest pair of Synoptic Gospels" (394). (2) Not only Jesus' preaching but also his teaching and the actual course of his ministry were eschatologically or apocalyptically determined. (3) The secret of the messiahship of Jesus was truly a secret. Jesus understood himself as the messiah but sought to guard this belief from his followers and disciples.

For Schweitzer, the ministry of Jesus lasted perhaps for one year at the most. His contact with John the Baptist

probably occurred during one Passover season—the following Passover he was dead. It was a year dominated by Jesus'
belief in his own messiahship in which Jesus' acted on the
basis of this dogmatic belief concerning his messiahship. The
erratic character of the Gospel traditions is due to the erratic
dogmatic actions of Jesus and not to the church's reconstruction of his actions. "His life . . . was dominated by a 'dogmatic
idea' which rendered Him indifferent to all else" (353).

"The chaotic confusion of the narratives ought to have
suggested the thought that the events had been thrown into
this confusion by the volcanic force of an incalculable
personality, not by some kind of carelessness or freak of the
tradition" (351). The dogmatic element is thus not the faith
of the church which was imposed upon the traditions, the
dogmatic element goes back to Jesus himself. Even the
closest disciples of Jesus did not understand the incoherent
shape of his life.

Even its most critical moments were totally unintelligible to
the disciples who had themselves shared in the experiences,
and who were the only sources for the tradition. They were
simply swept through these events by the momentum of the
purpose of Jesus. That is why the tradition is incoherent. The
reality had been incoherent too, since it was only the secret
Messianic self-consciousness of Jesus which created alike
the events and their connexion. Every life of Jesus remains
therefore a reconstruction on the basis of a more or less
accurate insight into the nature of the dynamic self-
consciousness of Jesus which created the history (395).

Jesus' public ministry centered on his pronouncement of
the immediacy of the eschatological, supermundane kingdom of God. Jesus did not understand himself as a teacher.
When a successful and happy work as a teacher opened itself
to him, Jesus abandoned at that moment the people anxious
to learn and eager for salvation.

His action suggests a doubt whether He really felt Himself to
be a "teacher." If all the controversial discourses and sayings
and answers to questions, which were so to speak wrung
from Him, were subtracted from the sum of His utterances,

65

how much of the didactic preaching of Jesus would be left over?

But even the supposed didactic preaching is not really that of a "teacher," since the purpose of His parables was, according to Mark iv. 10-12, not to reveal, but to conceal, and of the Kingdom of God He spoke only in parables (Mark iv. 34). . . . Jesus, whenever He desires to make known anything further concerning the Kingdom of God than just its near approach, seems to be confined, as it were by a higher law, to the parabolic form of discourse. It is as though, for reasons which we cannot grasp, His teaching lay under certain limitations. It appears as a kind of accessory aspect of His vocation. Thus it was possible for Him to give up His work as a teacher even at the moment when it promised the greatest success (353-54).

Behind Jesus' hesitancy to be a teacher lay the influence of the idea of predestination. Jesus did call for repentance on the part of the people and understood their repentance as forcing the kingdom of God or taking it by force; but Jesus also believed and proclaimed that "many are called, but few are chosen." The Beatitudes, for example, are not to be understood as exhortations or admonitions "but as a simple statement of fact: in their being poor in spirit, in their meekness, in their love of peace, it is made manifest that they are predestined to the Kingdom. By the possession of these qualities they are marked as belonging to it. In the case of others (Matt. v. 10-12) the predestination to the Kingdom is made manifest by the persecutions which befall them in this world. These are the light of the world, which already shines among men for the glory of God (Matt. v. 14-15)" (355).

If Jesus' function was not that of a teacher, how then does one explain the Sermon on the Mount? It was a special ethic, an interim ethic, applicable only to the time between the proclamation of the coming kingdom and its arrival. "There is for Jesus no ethic of the Kingdom of God, for in the Kingdom of God all natural relationships, even, for example, the distinction of sex (Mark xii. 25 and 26), are abolished. Temptation and sin no longer exist. All is 'reign,' a 'reign' which has gradations—Jesus speaks of the 'least in the

66

Kingdom of God'—according as it has been determined in each individual case from all eternity, and according as each by his self-humiliation and refusal to rule in the present age has proved his fitness for bearing rule in the future Kingdom" (365-66).

In proclaiming the apocalyptic end of history, Jesus spoke of the mystery of the kingdom of God. What was the mystery of the kingdom?

It must consist of something more than merely its near approach, and something of extreme importance; otherwise Jesus would be here indulging in mere mystery-mongering. The saying about the candle which He puts upon the stand, in order that what was hidden may be revealed to those who have ears to hear, implies that He is making a tremendous revelation to those who understand the parables about the growth of the seed. The mystery must therefore contain the explanation why the Kingdom must now come, and how men are to know how near it is. For the general fact that it is very near had already been openly proclaimed both by the Baptist and by Jesus. The mystery, therefore, must consist of something more than that (355-56).

The mystery or secret of the kingdom was its analogical and temporal connection with the harvest. In Matthew 9:37-38, Jesus spoke of the harvest as plentiful and the laborers as few. This reference to the harvest was, according to Schweitzer, directly related to the actual harvest at hand in the Palestinian fields. In the parables of the kingdom, Jesus compared the kingdom to the sowing and planting and the ultimate harvest. The initial fact in the parable is the sowing. The point of importance is not the sower but the fact that the sowing has taken place. The sowing was present or already past—it had taken place in the "movement of repentance evoked.. by the Baptist and now intensified by His own preaching. ... That being so, the Kingdom of God must follow as certainly as harvest follows seed-sowing. ... Any one who knows this sees with different eyes the corn growing in the fields and the harvest ripening, for he sees the one fact in the other, and awaits along with the harvest the heavenly, the revelation of the Kingdom of God" (356). In other words, Jesus believed the coming of the kingdom would occur in conjunction with the harvest already ripening in the fields. "The harvest ripening upon earth is the last" (357). This was the true secret of the kingdom.

Jesus' actions and his expectations regarding the coming of the kingdom, Schweitzer finds reflected in Matthew 10-11. "Without Matt. x. and xi. everything remains enigmatic" (360). These two chapters contain Jesus' commissioning of his disciples, his sending them forth to proclaim the coming kingdom, and narratives about Jesus' actions in their absence. How and why are these two chapters so important in understanding the course of Jesus' ministry?

Jesus expected the coming of the kingdom at harvest time. Before sending out his disciples, Jesus "charged" them. "He tells them in plain words (Matt. x. 23), that He does not expect to see them back in the present age. The Parousia of the Son of Man, which is logically and temporally identical with the dawn of the Kingdom, will take place before they shall have completed a hasty journey through the cities of Israel to announce it. That the words mean this and nothing else, that they ought not to be in any way weakened down, should be sufficiently evident. This is the form in which Jesus reveals to them the secret of the Kingdom of God" (358-59). The disciples went forth and preached but the prediction was not fulfilled, the kingdom of God had not arrived, the Son of man had not come! "The disciples returned to Him; and the appearing of the Son of Man had not taken place. The actual history disavowed the dogmatic history on which the action of Jesus had been based. An event of supernatural history which must take place, and must take place at that particular point of time, failed to come about. That was for Jesus, who lived wholly in the dogmatic history, the first 'historical' occurrence, the central event which closed the former period of His activity and gave the coming period a new character" (359).

In order to understand the significance of this failure of the

arrival of the kingdom for Schweitzer's view of the reconstruction of the course of Jesus' life, it is necessary to point to
a few other elements in Matthew 10 and how Schweitzer
interpreted these in terms of Jesus' apocalyptic expectations.
It should, in this respect, be emphasized that Schweitzer
viewed the discourse in Matthew 10 as "historical as a whole
and down to the smallest detail" (363).

In his discourse, Jesus spoke of the suffering which would
confront the disciples in their mission and the disrupted
relationships which would result—it would be a sword not
peace that Jesus' coming would bring (Matthew 10:34).
These sufferings were the messianic woes which were
immediately to precede the arrival of the kingdom. In
conjunction with their mission, Jesus believed, the Spirit of
God would be given, fulfilling Joel 3:13, and the disciples
would be granted divine knowledge to make known the
mystery of the kingdom.

A kind of supernatural illumination will suddenly make
known all that Jesus has been keeping secret regarding the
Kingdom of God and His position in the Kingdom. This
illumination will arise as suddenly and without preparation
as the spirit of strife.

And as a matter of fact Jesus predicts to the disciples in the
same discourse that to their own surprise a supernatural
wisdom will suddenly speak from their lips, so that it will be
not they but the Spirit of God who will answer the great ones
of the earth (362).

In other words, Jesus believed that the coming of the Son of
man—the arrival of the kingdom—would take place in the
midst of the disciples' mission, and the suffering and gift of
the Spirit would fulfill the requirements of the messianic
dogma about the suffering events preceding the end.
According to Schweitzer, Jesus believed that he would be the
Son of man. During the preaching mission of the disciples,
he believed that he would be revealed as the heavenly Son of
man. "That Jesus of Nazareth knew himself to be the Son of
Man who was to be revealed is for us the great fact of His
self-consciousness" (367).

The nonoccurrence of the kingdom's arrival divided Jesus' ministry into two halves. The first half was oriented to the coming of the kingdom at that year's harvest time; the second half was characterized by Jesus' actions in light of the failure of this apocalyptic vision. The significance of this failure for the course of Jesus' ministry is hard to overemphasize in Schweitzer's reconstruction.

The whole history of "Christianity" down to the present day, that is to say, the real inner history of it, is based on the delay of the Parousia, the non-occurrence of the Parousia, the abandonment of eschatology, the progress and completion of the "de-eschatologising" of religion which has been connected therewith. It should be noted that the non-fulfilment of Matt. x. 23 is the first postponement of the Parousia. We have therefore here the first significant date in the "history of Christianity"; it gives to the work of Jesus a new direction, otherwise inexplicable (360).

The second half of Jesus' career must not be seen however as a time in which Jesus was no longer acting on his beliefs concerning the eschatological end. The nonrealization of the kingdom's arrival reoriented some elements in his views, but he still acted as the apocalyptic visionary on the basis of his messianic and kingdom dogmas. From beginning to end, "Jesus' purpose is to set in motion the eschatological development of history, to let loose the final woes, the confusion and strife, from which shall issue the Parousia, and so to introduce the supra-mundane phase of the eschatological drama" (371). Neither Jesus nor John the Baptist were borne along by the current of an external eschatological movement or enthusiasm.

They themselves set the times in motion by action, by creating eschatological facts. . . . The Baptist appears, and cries: "Repent, for the Kingdom of Heaven is at hand." Soon after that comes Jesus, and in the knowledge that He is the coming Son of Man lays hold of the wheel of the world to set it moving on that last revolution which is to bring all ordinary history to a close. It refuses to turn, and He throws Himself upon it. Then it does turn; and crushes Him. Instead of

70

bringing in the eschatological conditions, He has destroyed them. The wheel rolls onward, and the mangled body of the one immeasurably great Man, who was strong enough to think of Himself as the spiritual ruler of mankind and to bend history to His purpose, is hanging upon it still. That is His victory and His reign (370-71).

Before we examine Schweitzer's discussion of Jesus' final effort to turn the wheel, we should note his discussion of the messianic secret, which Jesus had not intended to reveal, and how this came to be known in the days following the first delay of the Parousia.

Two events are of special importance with regard to this question—the Transfiguration (Mark 9:2-13) and the confession of Jesus as the messiah by Peter at Caesarea Philippi (Mark 8:27-33). How are these to be understood? In the first place, Schweitzer argues that although Jesus acted throughout his ministry with the full knowledge that he was the messiah, "He had never had the intention of revealing the secret of His Messiahship to the disciples. Otherwise He would not have kept it from them at the time of their mission, when He did not expect them to return before the Parousia" (386). The secret was discovered by the inner circle of three disciples at the Transfiguration and revealed to the others by Peter at Caesarea Philippi. Here it should be noted that Schweitzer rearranges the order of these events. In the Gospels, the confession of Peter precedes the Transfiguration. Schweitzer argues that for them to be understood properly, the order must be reversed.

After the return of the disciples from their mission, Jesus' overwhelming desire was to get away from the people. He and his disciples withdrew to Bethsaida (Mark 8:22), and it is this context to which the Transfiguration belongs. The Transfiguration was, in fact, "the revelation of the secret of the Messiahship to the three who constituted the inner circle of the disciples. And Jesus had not Himself revealed it to them; what had happened was, that in a state of rapture common to them all, in which they had seen the Master in a glorious transfiguration, they had seen Him talking with

Moses and Elias and had heard a voice from heaven saying, 'This is my beloved Son, hear ye Him.' . . . Even at the transfiguration the 'three' do not learn it from His lips, but in a state of ecstasy, an ecstasy which He shared with them" (385-86).

At Caesarea Philippi, the secret of Jesus' messiahship was made known to the other disciples by Peter. So Jesus did not reveal to his disciples and certainly never to the general public that he was the messiah. "Jesus did not voluntarily give up His messianic secret; it was wrung from Him by the pressure of events" (386). Jesus did however reveal to his disciples, at Caesarea Philippi, the secret of his forthcoming suffering.

Jesus' journey to Jerusalem was undertaken "solely in order to die there" (391). Why did Jesus choose this course? Jesus had "placed his Parousia at the end of the pre-Messianic tribulations" at the time of the disciples' mission (388). After the suffering and his Parousia did not occur, Jesus reached the conclusion that he must undergo the tribulation and suffering himself; it would not begin of itself. "That was the new conviction that had dawned upon Him. He must suffer for others . . . that the Kingdom might come" (389). Jesus then came to associate the suffering of the messianic prelude to the coming of the kingdom with an historic event, with his own death: "He will go to Jerusalem, there to suffer death at the hands of authorities. . . . He no longer speaks of the general tribulation" (388). Jesus was now to force the kingdom and undergo the suffering; "another of the violent must lay violent hands upon the Kingdom of God. The movement of repentance had not been sufficient" to force the kingdom (389). Jesus must die for the many who were predestined for the kingdom and in his death compel its coming. Jesus had reached this last conclusion on the basis of the prophecy of the suffering servant spoken of in the book of Isaiah (see especially Isaiah 53). So "for Jesus the necessity of His death is grounded in dogma, not in external historical facts" (392). Schweitzer interpreted Jesus' understanding of the death of the suffering servant in the following manner: "The mysterious description of Him who in His humiliation was despised and misunderstood, who, nevertheless bears the guilt of others and afterwards is made manifest in what He has done, points, He feels, to Himself. And since He found it there set down that He must suffer unrecognised, and that those for whom He suffered should doubt Him, His suffering should, nay must, remain a mystery" (390). Thus Jesus felt no obligation nor need to make clear his understanding of his death, in fact, he felt exactly the reverse.

Jesus' activity in Jerusalem was calculated to bring about his suffering and death. In the events which led up to his death, according to Schweitzer, Jesus was the "sole actor" intent upon the "deliberate bringing down of death upon Himself." He "thinks only how he can so provoke the Pharisees and the rulers that they will be compelled to get rid of Him. That is why He violently cleanses the Temple, and attacks the Pharisees, in the presence of the people, with passionate invective" (392).

In Jerusalem, no one except Jesus and the disciples knew the secret of his messiahship. "The entry into Jerusalem was . . . Messianic for Jesus, but not for the people" (394). Then the High Priest suddenly showed himself in possession of the secret. The finger pointed to Judas as the betrayer of the secret.

For a hundred and fifty years the question has been historically discussed why Judas betrayed his Master. That the main question for history was *what he betrayed* was suspected by few and they touched on it only in a timid kind of way. . . .

In the betrayal . . . there were two points, a more general and a more special: the general fact by which he gave Jesus into their power, and the undertaking to let them know of the next opportunity when they could arrest Him quietly, without publicity. The betrayal by which be brought his Master to death, in consequence of which the rulers decided upon the arrest, knowing that their cause was safe in any case, was the betrayal of the Messianic secret. Jesus died because two of His disciples had broken His command of silence: Peter when he made known the secret of the

Messiahship to the Twelve at Caesarea Philippi; Judas Iscariot by communicating it to the High Priest (396).

In Jesus' trial before Pilate, the multitude was there only to ask for the release of a prisoner according to the custom. But they were a threat to the priests who had hoped to have Jesus crucified before anyone knew what was happening. They might have asked for Jesus' release, since they considered him an honored prophet. The priests however went among the crowd "telling them why he was condemned, by revealing to them the Messianic secret" (397).

That makes Him at once from a prophet worthy of honour into a deluded enthusiast and blasphemer. That was the explanation of the "fickleness" of the Jerusalem mob which is always so eloquently described, without any evidence for it except this single inexplicable case.

At midday of the same day—it was the 14th Nisan, and in the evening the Paschal lamb would be eaten—Jesus cried aloud and expired. He had chosen to remain fully conscious to the last (397).

Schweitzer had no doubt about the ability to discover the historical Jesus. He also had no doubt about the liberals' reconstructed historical Jesus' irrelevance for modern man.

Those who are fond of talking about negative theology can find their account here. There is nothing more negative than the result of the critical study of the Life of Jesus.

The Jesus of Nazareth who came forward publicly as the Messiah, who preached the ethic of the Kingdom of God, who founded the Kingdom of Heaven upon earth, and died to give His work its final consecration, never had any existence. He is a figure designed by rationalism, endowed with life by liberalism, and clothed by modern theology in an historical garb.

This image has not been destroyed from without, it has fallen to pieces, cleft and disintegrated by the concrete historical problems which came to the surface one after another, and in spite of all the artifice, art, artificiality, and violence which was applied to them, refused to be planed down to fit the design on which the Jesus of the theology of the last hundred and thirty years had been constructed, and were no sooner covered over than they appeared again in a new form (398). . . .

The study of the Life of Jesus has had a curious history. It set out in quest of the historical Jesus, believing that when it had found Him it could bring Him straight into our time as a Teacher and Saviour. It loosed the bands by which He had been riveted for centuries to the stony rocks of ecclesiastical doctrine, and rejoiced to see life and movement coming into the figure once more, and the historical Jesus advancing, as it seemed, to meet it. But He does not stay; He passes by our time and returns to His own. What surprised and dismayed the theology of the last forty years was that, despite all forced and arbitrary interpretations, it could not keep Him in our time, but had to let Him go. He returned to His own time, not owing to the application of any historical ingenuity, but by the same inevitable necessity by which the liberated pendulum returns to its original position (399).

If such negative results for theology result from the study of the historical Jesus, this did not mean the end of Christianity for Schweitzer. If the Jesus of history could not be brought with meaning into the present, the same could not be said for "Jesus."

Jesus of Nazareth will not suffer Himself to be modernised. As an historic figure He refuses to be detached from His own time. He has no answer for the question, "Tell us Thy name in our speech and for our day!" But He does bless those who have wrestled with Him, so that, though they cannot take Him with them, yet, like men who have seen God face to face and received strength in their souls, they go on their way with renewed courage, ready to do battle with the world and its powers (312). . . .

We are experiencing what Paul experienced. In the very moment when we were coming nearer to the historical Jesus than men had ever come before, and were already stretching out our hands to draw Him into our own time, we have been obliged to give up the attempt and acknowledge our failure in that paradoxical saying: "If we have known Christ after the flesh yet henceforth know we Him no more" [II Corinthians 5:16]. And further we must be prepared to find that the historical knowledge of the personality and life of Jesus will not be a help, but perhaps even an offence to religion.

But the truth is, it is not Jesus as historically known, but Jesus as spiritually arisen within men, who is significant for our time and can help it. Not the historical Jesus, but the spirit which goes forth from Him and in the spirits of men strives for new influence and rule, is that which overcomes the world.

It is not given to history to disengage that which is abiding and eternal in the being of Jesus from the historical forms in which it worked itself out, and to introduce it into our world as a living influence. It has toiled in vain at this undertaking. As a water-plant is beautiful so long as it is growing in the water, but once torn from its roots, withers and becomes unrecognisable, so it is with the historical Jesus when He is wrenched loose from the soil of eschatology, and the attempt is made to conceive Him "historically" as a Being not subject to temporal conditions. The abiding and eternal in Jesus is absolutely independent of historical knowledge and can only be understood by contact with His spirit which is still at work in the world. In proportion as we have the Spirit of Jesus we have the true knowledge of Jesus.

Jesus as a concrete historical personality remains a stranger to our time, but His spirit, which lies hidden in His words, is known in simplicity, and its influence is direct. Every saying contains in its own way the whole Jesus. The very strangeness and unconditionedness in which He stands before us makes it easier for individuals to find their own personal standpoint in regard to Him (401). . . .

He comes to us as One unknown, without a name, as of old, by the lake-side, He came to those men who knew Him not. He speaks to us the same word: "Follow thou me!" and sets us to the tasks which He has to fulfil for our time. He commands. And to those who obey Him, whether they be wise or simple, He will reveal Himself in the toils, the conflicts, the sufferings which they shall pass through in His fellowship, and, as an ineffable mystery, they shall learn in their own experience Who He is (403).

4. JESUS: THE CONSTANT CONTEMPORARY

> So often we have added to the word, "he was in the world," the seemingly pious and proper theological conclusion, "but he was not of the world," that we have actually come to believe it. So we have looked for someone who was not there and missed the one who was. —Morton S. Enslin, *The Prophet from Nazareth* (p. 7)

A number of studies on the historical Jesus have sought to focus on the permanent relevance of the historical Jesus. Many of these works have been thoroughly historical and critical in their approach to the sources for a life of Jesus but have attempted in the process to lay hold of some distinctive feature or features in the life and teachings of Jesus which will address and challenge modern man. There is, in other words, no mere interest in the historical Jesus simply for the sake of antiquarian information about this person in the past. This perspective, of course, embodies one of the fundamental interests of the rationalistic lives of Jesus without being directly influenced by any particular rationalistic reconstruction. Simultaneously, the search for a historical Jesus relevant to modern man embodies the ambitions of the nineteenth-century liberal quest. It should be noted that frequently when the nineteenth-century liberal scholars and their twentieth-century counterparts sought for a Jesus relevant to their times, they were not necessarily thinking of relevance only with regard to the church and Christians. The search was for a Jesus relevant to modern man whether Christian or otherwise. And in fact, some of these portraits of the historical Jesus have frequently appealed to many who would not and perhaps could not describe themselves as Christian. Other scholars within the same general stream sought for a historical Jesus who could form the ground of Christian faith over against the orthodox Christ confessed and preached by the church. Thus they sought to construct an alternative route to Christian faith different from traditional expressions.

Various aspects or features in the life of the historical Jesus have occupied the concerns of scholars searching for a Jesus relevant and contemporary to modern man. Some have pointed to the life of Jesus as a pattern or paradigm of human existence to be imitated in the present. Others have pointed to the personality of Jesus or the person of Jesus as a basis of faith. Still others have focused on the inner life of Jesus as the ground and basis for communion with God. Some have pointed to the religious life of Jesus, and others focused on his theological understanding of God. Many had examined the teachings of Jesus as the embodiment of a style of life or an approach to existence.

In this chapter, we shall examine three studies which, although not representing every perspective, display a representative selection of approaches.

The first work is the book by Bruce Barton entitled *The Man Nobody Knows*. This volume, described by its publisher as the "most popular and successful religious book of our age," has experienced a wide distribution having sold over 600,000 copies in hardcover form.

The intent and interest of the author in writing this book can be seen in his introduction. He describes his feelings of repulsion when as a lad he was presented by the church and Sunday school with a Jesus who was a "pale young man with no muscle and a sad expression" and red whiskers. Jesus was encountered as a sissified lamb of God, a physical weakling, a kill-joy, a man of sorrows, and as a nonfighter in the battle of life.

Barton then set out to present a true picture of the historical Jesus based on a reading of the New Testament Gospels which would counter and offer an alternative to this typical Jesus of Sunday school theology. In painting his portrait of Jesus, Barton wishes to "take the story just as the simple narratives give it—a poor boy, growing up in a peasant family, working in a carpenter shop; gradually feeling His powers expanding, beginning to have an influence over His neighbors, recruiting a few followers, suffering disappointments, reverses and finally death. Yet building so solidly and well that death was only the beginning of His influence" (19).

Barton begins with what he calls the "eternal miracle" which happens to all men of power; that is, the "awakening of the inner consciousness of power" (20). When did Jesus become aware of this power and become conscious of his divinity? When did he realize that "he was larger than the limits of a country town, that his life might be bigger than his father's?" One cannot be certain but the "consciousness of His divinity must have come to Him in a time of solitude, of awe in the presence of Nature. . . . Somewhere, at some unforgettable hour, the doing filled his heart. He knew He was bigger than Nazareth" (21). Perhaps at his baptism by John, Jesus realized that "He was going to do the big things which John had done; He felt the power stirring in Him: He was all eager to begin" (22). Jesus' enthusiasm soon was clouded with doubt, and he struggled to affirm his initial feeling. "In the calm of that wilderness there came the majestic conviction which is the very soul of leadership—the faith that His spirit was linked with the Eternal, that God had sent Him into the world to do a work which no one else could do, which—if He neglected it—would never be done. . . . The youth who had been a carpenter stayed in the wilderness; a man came out. . . . Men who looked on Him from that hour felt the authority of one who has put his spiritual house in order and knows clearly what he is about" (23-24).

Jesus' basic characteristics of leadership which gave him power over men were threefold. (1) He possessed the quality of conviction which begets loyalty and commands respect. (2) He possessed the powerful gift of picking men and recognizing hidden capacities in them. "He had the born leader's gift for seeing powers in men of which they themselves were often almost unconscious" (27). He brought together an unknown group of men who had never accomplished anything—a "haphazard collection of fishermen and small-town businessmen, and one tax collector"— and out of them built an organization. Take Matthew, for example: the "crowd saw only a despised taxgatherer. Jesus saw the potential writer of a book which will live forever" (28). (3) In training his organization, Jesus manifested an unending patience. For three years he struggled to teach them, to lead them to an understanding knowing "that the way to get faith out of men is to show that you have faith in them" (29).

In leadership qualities Jesus was successful, whereas John was a miserable failure.

John the Baptist . . . could denounce, but he could not construct. He drew crowds who were willing to repent at his command, but he had no program for them after their repentance. They waited for him to organize them for some sort of effective service, but he was no organizer. So his followers drifted away, and his movement gradually collapsed. The same thing might have happened to the work of Jesus. He started with much less than John and a much smaller group of followers. He had only twelve, and they were untrained, simple men, with elementary weakness and passions. Yet because of the fire of His personal conviction, because of His marvelous instinct for discovering their latent powers, and because of His unwavering faith and patience, He molded them into an organization which carried on victoriously. Within a very few years after His death, it was reported in a far-off corner of the Roman Empire that "these who have turned the world upside down have come hither also." A few decades later the proud Emperor himself bowed his head to the teachings of this Nazareth carpenter, transmitted through common men (30-31).

Jesus must be understood as having been physically strong. When he spoke of building a house upon a rock he knew what he was talking about. His fellow townsmen had frequently "seen Him bending His strong clean shoulders to deliver heavy blows; or watched Him trudge away into the woods, His ax over His shoulders, and return at nightfall with a rough-hewn bean" (36). When he cleansed the temple he showed the stuff he was made of. "As His right arm rose and fell, striking its blows with that little whip, the sleeve dropped back to reveal muscles hard as iron. No one who watched Him in action had any doubt that He was fully capable of taking care of Himself. The evidence is clear that no angry priest or money-changer cared to try conclusions with that arm" (35). When Jesus spoke to the sick man upon his pallet, his command and his appearance solicited confidence.

"Walk!" Do you suppose for one minute that a weakling, uttering that syllable, would have produced any result? If the Jesus who looked down on that pitiful wreck had been the Jesus of the painters, the sick man would have dropped back with a scornful sneer and motioned his friends to carry him out. But the health of the Teacher was irresistible; it seemed to cry out, "Nothing is impossible if only your will power is strong enough." And the man who so long ago had surrendered to despair, rose and gathered up his bed and went away, healed—like hundreds of others in Galilee—by strength from an overflowing fountain of strength (39).

Something of the person of Jesus can be seen in the fact that whereas men followed him, "women worshiped Him" (40).

The important, and too often forgotten, fact in these relationships is this—that women are *not* drawn by weakness. The sallow-faced, thin-lipped, so-called spiritual type of man may awaken maternal instinct, stirring an emotion which is half regard, half pity. But since the world began, no power has fastened the affection of women upon a man like manliness. Men who have been women's men in the finest sense have been vital figures of history (41). . . .

All His days were spent in the open air—this is the third outstanding testimony to His strength. On the Sabbath He was in the synagogue because that was where the people were gathered, but by far the greater part of His teaching was done on the shores of His lake, or in the cool recesses of the hills. He walked constantly from village to village; His face was tanned by the sun and wind. Even at night He slept outdoors when He could—turning His back on the hot walls of the city and slipping away into the healthful freshness of the Mount of Olives. He was an energetic outdoor man. The vigorous activities of His days gave His nerves the strength of steel. As much as any nation ever, Americans understand and respect this kind of man (43).

When Jesus stood before the Roman procurator, "in the face of the Roman were deep unpleasant lines; his cheeks were fatty with self-indulgence; he had the colorless look of indoor living. The straight young man stood inches above him, bronzed and hard and clean as the air of His loved mountain and lake." Surely no painter could ever have produced a truer picture than the words that "dissipated cynical Roman cried: 'Behold the man!'" (45).

Christian theology has done Jesus tremendous harm in failing to stress that he was a very sociable man. "The friendliest man who has ever lived has been shut off by the black wall of tradition from those whose friendship He would most enjoy. Theology has reared a graven image and robbed the world of the joy and laughter of the Great Champion" (46-47). Jesus loved a crowd. He was the type of man whom you would have chosen as a companion on a fishing trip. "No other public figure even had a more interesting list of friends. It ran from the top of the social ladder to the bottom" (53).

Jesus' message of God portrays God as a great companion. It announced a "happy God, wanting His sons and daughters to be happy" (56).

That was the message of Jesus—that God is supremely better than anybody had ever dared to believe. Not a petulant Creator, who had lost control of His creation and, in wrath, was determined to destroy it all. Not a stern Judge dispensing impersonal justice. Not a vain King who must be flattered and bribed into concessions of mercy. Not a rigid Accountant, checking up the sins against the penances and striking a cold hard balance. Not any of these . . . nothing like these; but a great Companion, a wonderful Friend, a kindly indulgent, joy-loving Father (61-62).

Jesus hoped through the instrumentality of his small band of disciples to carry his message to the world. Soon his organization would succeed, and his message would conquer. "It conquered not because there was any demand for another religion but because Jesus knew how, and taught His followers how, to catch the attention of the indifferent, and translate a great spiritual conception into terms of practical self-concern" (71).

Jesus was a master teacher, always complete master of the situation. His teaching in parables avoided the unattractive generality. His teachings were marvelously condensed, simple ("all the great things in human life are one-syllable things"), with sincerity illuminating every word, every sentence he uttered, and they are repeatable.

And whoever feels an impulse to make his own life count in the grand process of human betterment can have no surer guide for his activities than Jesus. Let him learn the lesson of the parables: that in teaching people you first capture their interest; that your service rather than your sermons must be your claim on their attention; that what you say must be simple and brief and above all *sincere*—the unmistakable voice of true regard and affection (99).

In Jesus' works and his relations with people, one can see his philosophy which Barton summarizes in three prepositions:

1. Whoever will be great must render great service.
2. Whoever will find himself at the top must be willing to lose himself at the bottom.
3. The rewards come to those who travel the second, undemanded mile (109).

One of the final tests of man's life is how he bears up under disappointment. In this test, Jesus shows his true greatness. Jesus' hometown turned against him, his brothers deserted him, his best friend died doubting him, the people forsook him, his disciples fled from him, and yet when Jesus was dying upon the cross he "so bore Himself that a crucified felon looked into His dying eyes and saluted him as King" (133).

Morton Enslin, in his *The Prophet from Nazareth,* provides a search for the "real Jesus" of history and for a Jesus who "was never placed in any tomb, but has lived in the hearts and lives of the millions of men and women to whom he is endlessly calling, demanding that they follow with him to the only goal" (217).

The basic theses of Enslin's book are:

(1) All who heard Jesus understood him. His enemies sent him to the cross, not because they did not know what he meant but because they did. His first followers braved the same opposition which had cost him his life and sounded his word at home and abroad because they knew what he had meant and had accepted it as the very word of God. (2) While we cannot write a biography, we can know the man, can see him engaged in a life-and-death struggle, in the midst of real men, enemies and friends alike, not lifeless puppets seeming to move on the silver screen of an altogether-other Cinerama *in vacuo theologico.* (3) Far from being dispensable, a figure cavalierly to be dismissed as inconsequential then, irrelevant now, he stands ever demanding from his followers the same commitment and devotion to their tasks which he brought to his (14).

What can be known about this real Jesus? Enslin suggests that the material about the early life of Jesus—the birth narratives and the story of his visit to the temple at the age of twelve—are "charming stories," a "lovely part of the Christian tradition," perhaps "closer to poetry than to unedited prose." They, especially the stories of the virgin birth, reflect a class of stories like those told of "many heroes who have achieved fame in the past, as Romulus, the elder Scipio, Augustus, Sargon, Cyrus, Alexander the Great, Pythagoras, and Plato. It was as natural to the ancient world to explain unusual prowess or achievement as due to a divine parent as it is to us to style one superlatively great of 'more than human clay' " (38). Nevertheless something may be said of Jesus' early life: "With confidence, we must ascribe his birth, as well as early years, to the little Galilean town of Nazareth" (39).

Enslin sees selected verses from the synoptics (Luke

4:17-21, 7:39; Mark 1:15, 6:3, 12:37, 14:55, 15:15) as revealing the "basic facts in the story" of Jesus.

And these facts, when set down simply are: a man completely convinced that God had revealed to him that at long last the promised time of triumph was at hand, the period of testing and trial was momentarily to pass, the new age to dawn. Convinced himself, he was able to convince others, and they gladly harkened. To those in positions of authority and power the man and his message were alike an outrage and a menace and had to be suppressed at any cost. And with little difficulty they were able to convince the resident governor of the necessity of quenching the blaze before it was too late (37).

What triggered the public ministry of Jesus? "What led one who had hitherto been a Galilean carpenter to assume the role of a prophet of God?" (41). It was perhaps not the activity of John the Baptist, since the two were probably never associated and the "two movements were originally quite unrelated." Jesus first became associated with John the Baptist in church tradition which "sought to bring a later generation of followers of the Baptist into their ranks by the claim that John had been but the conscious forerunner of their crucified Lord and that his one function had been to designate his greater successor" (42). Why Jesus suddenly began his career can no longer be determined, but Enslin argues that it may have been triggered by one of the altercations between the Jews and Pilate or some local Galilean episode.

For Enslin, Jesus was a prophet not unlike the Old Testament prophetical figures. He was the herald of the new age about to dawn, and, as a prophet, he announced the will of God which had been supernaturally revealed to him. In announcing the nearness of the kingdom, Jesus was declaring that God's purpose and intent are inevitable.

The kingdom comes of itself. It is in consequence of God's initiative. It is not that Jesus brings it. Instead, God has appointed him to announce its approach. . . . To that extent it may be said that the kingdom has brought Jesus. It comes of itself, unobserved, impossible to detect by outward signs or clues, and quite apart from man's efforts. In soberest reality it is the act of God, not the deed of any man (74). . . .

Thus few things would seem more certain than that Jesus believed passionately in the near approach of the universal sovereignty of God, which, as he viewed it, was the apocalyptic "age to come." This was the good news which he so insistently proclaimed (79).

In his proclamation, Jesus was clearly understood by his audience, attracted common people who heard him gladly, and it was this acceptance of the proclamation of Jesus that lived on in spite of his later death. One must see this confidence which his followers had that he was indeed a prophet sent by God as the basis of the later missionary work of the church.

Had not his companions become convinced—perhaps more deeply than some of them at the moment realized—of the rightness of his claim to be a prophet sent by God, it is highly improbable that they would have seen him on the Easter morning. . . . The later conventional stories of the Resurrection—supernatural appearances, resuscitated body, empty tomb—were the *result* of this all-central confidence, not its *cause*. To fail to see this is to strip Jesus of his true significance and to make of him but one more puppet in an otherworldly drama (91).

Jesus' proclamation of the coming kingdom with its note of radical change, economically and otherwise, attracted the economically oppressed and the religiously scorned, the common people. "In a word, to those at the bottom of the wheel, whichever way the wheel were to turn, it could not fail to bring an improvement" (108). But this aroused the establishment, the wealthy and those in positions of power. Jesus' apocalyptic views aroused the suspicions of the educated for whom the law embodied true religion. "The way his word was accepted," by the humble, poor, and uneducated, "led to his appearing the understanding and sympathizing 'friend of publicans and sinners,' the caustic and unsympathetic foe of those in positions of wealth and power" (110).

In his preaching, Jesus was no exponent of social change. The demands he laid upon his hearers and would-be followers were "for the sake of the man himself, not for the alleviation and betterment of society and the world at large" (123). The ethics which Jesus proclaimed demanded a sort of conduct which would continue after the coming of the new world and the new age. "It may very well be that in the eyes of Jesus there was nothing radically new in such a way of life. Rather, it was the way men have lived in their earlier innocence before they had allowed themselves by their new traditions to vitiate and change the ways ordained by God" (125). "In the last analysis, it would seem that for Jesus the ideal life, which God had ordained from the beginning and which would be demanded by his final judge at the coming Final Judgment, was the sort of life and conduct which appealed to him personally" (126). In other words, the words of Jesus on the ideal life "come from a man who is accustomed to a direct and common-sense view of what is 'obviously' fair and sensible and who is equally accustomed to express himself in the homeliest and simplest way" (127).

Part of the attractiveness of Jesus—both to his contemporaries and to moderns—was the fact that Jesus lived up to what he taught as the ideal. It was his "personality"—"that amazing and babbling congeries of gifts and abilities"— which convinced many (128).

The qualities, essence, or whatever other terms be used to attempt to classify and interpret "personality," quite elude the scales and camera. But it is they which constitute the real person, and it is they which constituted the real Jesus. And *this* was not put into any grave. It had been built by that strange alchemy of life into those with whom he had been in contact. Had this not been the case, it is highly unlikely that they would have "seen" him in the days following Easter (129).

Enslin argues that behind some of the miraculous cures and exorcisms attributed to Jesus may lie a kernel of historical truth. "Granted the belief that the word was

87

freighted with power, there is little ground for wonder that on occasion the effect was realized" (152). Most of the miracles are not to be rationalized nor stripped of their miraculous quality to reveal some historical nucleus. Such "explanations which are harder to credit than the difficulties which they seek to explain are to most academic disciplines suspect, even if to the theologian they are attractive and convincing" (158). Many of the miracle stories were the result of reading Old Testament texts and episodes and applying these to Jesus by creating events which reflect the text. For example, probably behind the story of the stilling of the storm lie such Old Testament passages as Psalms 107:23-30; 89:9.

When Jesus went to Jerusalem—to continue his work—his fate was sealed. "Rumors of the rabble-rousing, demon-possessed prophet with his message of the overthrow of law and order—exaggerated and garbled rumors and their credence by those in authority are no invention of the modern world—had preceded him" (173). For the religious leaders, "Jesus' easy pronouncements and judgments . . . were . . . the insolent and outrageous mouthings of an ignorant and untrained peasant, who not only was unforgivably destitute of the knowledge which God himself had enjoined upon all men as their chief duty, but who also blindly attacked them for doing what they knew was in strictest accord with God's clearly revealed will" (176). The clash, in other words, partially centered on the issue of a simple, common sense, prophetic approach versus a religious system founded on the strict observance of the law and its interpretation as the final will of God. Simultaneously, the actions of Jesus confirmed to the religiously and educationally elect that he was a friend of sinners. "His careless hobnobbing at table with publicans and harlots gained for him the name, 'a gluttonous man and a winebibber' [Matthew 11:19], that is, he ate too heartily, drank too freely, and kept very disreputable company" (176).

Jesus' actions in cleansing the temple was an "enacted parable" reflecting his disgust with the religious life of the temple.

Surely the sweating hosts of pilgrims surging through its courts, the lowing and bellowing of terrified cattle in the pens and on the slabs for slaughter; the billowing clouds of smoke and the nauseous stench from burning fat and meat; the cries of hawkers and money-changers—all this might have seemed to an even less sensitive observer than the prophet from Nazareth, little accustomed to such tumult and superficial piety, a strange answer to the age-old query of a Micah [see Micah 6:6-8]. . . .

To the outraged eyes of the prophet from Nazareth he was but once more joining the ranks of the host of the earlier prophets whom God had raised up, as he uttered his blasts against this sorry perversion of Israel's greatest obligation and privilege (180).

The prompt action by the religious leaders against Jesus and his speedy trial and condemnation were "occasioned by Jesus' passionate avowal that the axe was already laid at the root of the tree and that the end of the present order was at hand, for this in the eyes of the authorities was a direct attack upon both state and temple. And the fact that he was no remote or solitary figure—no voice of one crying in the wilderness—but had come, as they were convinced, with a throng of followers to Jerusalem for the express purpose of inciting the mob of pilgrims to violence, only added to their fears and fury" (182). "That Jesus was arrested and speedily remanded to the Roman governor for condemnation and execution as a man whose words and actions were dangerous to the state would seem as certain as the elaborating details are obscure" (200).

So Jesus was condemned, crucified, and buried. But his movement and message did not die. It found continued embodiment in the Easter experience. But how is this experience to be understood?

The usual—to many the natural—understanding of the Easter hope . . . is in terms of a changed Jesus. To me there appears a far profounder change, without which our hopes would be dead: Not a changed Jesus, but changed disciples. Jesus was the same. He had sown his seed, had lived his life, had built himself into the lives of those with whom he had lived and worked. . . . The change was not in any physical transformation of the body he had tenanted, but in the outlook and convictions of the men and women whom he had touched (209-10).

His followers realized that the one they had followed could not but yet be alive for he was even then living in them. "The real Jesus was not the flesh and blood and the bone and the skin, but that something which had the power to reproduce itself in them, that lived in them" (212). Like to his first century companions so to us in the modern world, "there stands the figure of the Prophet from Nazareth, who by his life has left us both the proof that men, however heedless, however blind they may be, do have sufficient of the divine insight to see in such a life the very impress of God himself, and the challenge to do in our day an equivalent of what he did in his" (216). "Not the body which walked the Palestinian hills, but that essence of the divine that made Jesus Jesus; that quality which drew men to him, which transformed them, which enabled them to see aright the kind of life God wished them to live—that still lives. Jesus is not dead, can never die" (217).

In *Jesus on Social Institutions,* Shailer Mathews provides an interpretation of Jesus and argues for the relevancy of his life and teachings for modern man. For Mathews, Jesus and his teachings must be viewed and understood against the revolutionary spirit of his time. The background and context of Jesus' ministry must be viewed through the means of social psychology and particularly the psychology of revolution.

All revolutions are preceded by and spring from the same social attitudes. A new class consciousness is evoked by a sense of political, economic, and social inequality; propaganda arouses a spirit of revolt; a sense of injustice breeds the desire for revenge; an enthusiasm for some abstract ideal provokes a series of outbreaks that attempt to realize the hopes and avenge the wrongs of an oppressed group (13).

Jesus: The Constant Contemporary

The Roman Empire which had brought many advances to ancient men had, in the process of its domination, suppressed nationalism. For many, this provided no real problem, but the Jews, in spite of the derived blessings received and the special religious privileges granted them, were the one people who refused to be repressed and nurtured within their culture a revolutionary spirit.

Instead of the peace and municipal growth, the Jews could see only the policeman and the soldier. Instead of prosperity, they could only see the tax collector. Instead of freedom of worship, they could see only the Temple guard of Roman soldiers who kept them from religious massacres. Instead of cities like Caesarea, and Samaria, Tiberias, and those of the Decapolis, they could see only the standards of the foreign power. Their suppressed nationalism turned to the praise of their past, the glorification of David, and the hope for the reëstablishment of a Davidic dynasty through the aid of their God. This was revolution in the making (16).

Only a small segment of Jewish society directly profited from Roman rule. The masses were subjected to extreme taxation, economic inequality, and political repression. These pent-up frustrations and surging hopes produced a revolutionary eschatological hope, a messianic expectation.

Its really significant elements are simple: (1) the defeat of Satan by God; (2) the defeat of the Romans by God's aid given to the Jews; (3) the complete establishment of the will of God in the Jewish people by observance of the Mosaic law, as a preparation for the divinely established Jewish kingdom; (4) the reliance upon force, violence, and massacre to being about this social order (28).

It is against this background that one must understand the teachings of Jesus. In such revolutionary thoughts and hopes "lay human values that needed to be reinterpreted rather than opposed. To accomplish this proved to be the task and opportunity of Jesus" (28). "For, without leading revolt, he was to live and teach in the atmosphere of revolution, use the language of revolution, make the revolutionary spirit the instrument of his message, and organize a movement composed of men who awaited a divinely given new age" (12).

Jesus' mission was that of reshaping the "revolutionary hopes in the crucible of his own individuality" (32).

Jesus found in his own experience a censor of the psychology which he shared and to which he appealed. He looked to God as the ultimate basis of all future blessing, and God he knew as a father rather than a king. This conviction, born of the study of the prophets and reënforced by his own experience, prevented his full acceptance of the revolutionary hopes of those who followed him. The defeat of Satan could be shown in cures, but the reign of God was to be established by God himself. Human effort would not bring it in. Ideals need not be adjusted, therefore, to social processes. The passionate desire on the part of the people for a better social order with better institutions and better authority could be analyzed by Jesus because he felt within himself the spirit of the Heavenly Father. All elements in the hopes of his times that were inconsistent with this filial experience he rejected (38).

Jesus repudiated the role of violence in bringing about the kingdom of God—the perfect order of society. In fact, "He was not seeking to establish the kingdom of God but to prepare men to enter it" (60). He sublimated the social passion of the revolutionary hopes transforming the "revolutionary spirit into a new moral attitude pregnant with social implications" (42). "God's will will not be done on earth, until men love their enemies and are determined rather to be just than to oppress, to be brothers rather than masters" (39). "Jesus was far less interested in the rights than in the obligations of men." "His gospel was not a new Declaration of Rights but a Declaration of Duties" (73).

The essential content of the teaching of Jesus is described by Mathews in a number of ways: "love as a dominating force in nature and history," "sacrificial social-mindedness," "heroic sacrifice," "social coöperation in which the coöperating parties treat each other as persons," "brotherliness," and "social goodwill." Although Jesus anticipated the speedy arrival of the kingdom, his ethical imperatives were not anchored in this eschatological perspective but rather in the character and will of God. "In the character of God lies the justification of goodwill and love on the part of those who await the kingdom" (51). "Love, as the characteristic of God, was the indispensable characteristic of those who would enjoy his reign" (37-38).

Jesus was a revolutionary and an agitator, but he did not set out to destroy the established institutions and create new ones. "He was endeavoring to inculcate attitudes in the individual soul rather than to organize a new state or to urge political reform" (107). Nonetheless, the effort of the individual to express goodwill and love in society would lead to the transformation of society and its institutions. Jesus was not a legislator; therefore he proposed no legislation as the means to transform society; he was no economist, so he offered no economical system for men preparing for the kingdom; but he was an "expounder of attitudes for the group preparing for the kingdom" (84).

Jesus taught that love is a practicable basis upon which to build human relations. Once let humanity actually believe this and the perspective of values will be changed. Giving justice will replace fighting for rights; the democratizing of privilege will replace the manipulation of social advantages; the humanizing of necessary economic processes will replace the exploiting of human life in the interests of wealth or pleasure (155).

5. JESUS: THE JEW
FROM GALILEE

Jesus was not a Christian: he was a Jew. He did not proclaim a new faith, but taught men to do the will of God. According to Jesus, as to the Jews, generally, this will of God is to be found in the Law and the other canonical Scriptures. —Julius Wellhausen, *Einleitung in die drei ersten Evangelien* (p. 113)

The twentieth century has witnessed a sharp upsurge of interest in Jesus by Jews. Literary discussions of Jesus by Jewish writers are now commonplace. One element in this Jewish concern with Jesus is the renewed interest in recovering the Jewish past fostered by the existence of the Israeli state in Palestine. A second factor is the more ecumenical atmosphere existing worldwide between Jews and Christians. Sympathetic treatments of Jesus by several Jewish scholars, especially that by Martin Buber, have encouraged open and frank discussion of the issues.

This Jewish interest in Jesus has been described in the following way by Rabbi David Polish: "Ever since new Israel began, a special interest in Jesus has been manifested. This does not indicate, as some Christian theologians have wishfully stated, a turning toward Christianity. It does, however, show that in the free atmosphere of Israel, a new approach towards Jesus, removed from the realm of polemics or interpretation common to medieval Judaism, is taking place. It is to be expected that in the land where Jesus lived and from which the Christian message went forth, a deep interest should be stirred among Jews" (*The Eternal Dissent,* 207).

Some analogies between the life and fate of German Jews during World War II and that of Jesus have been noted as a factor contributing to this interest in Jesus. "The Nazarene's fervour, his love of his country and people and his tragic death have endeared him particularly to Jewish thinkers of the Auschwitz generation" (Pinchas E. Lapide, *Journal of Theology for Southern Africa,* V [Dec., 1973] 51).

The sense of kinship with Jesus can be seen in this evaluation by Martin Buber contained in the preface to his *Two Ways of Faith:* "Since early youth I have sensed in Jesus my great brother. That Christendom considers him God and Saviour, I always deemed a fact of supreme importance which I must seek to comprehend for his sake and for my own. . . . I am more certain than ever that he deserves a place of honour in the religious history of Israel, and that this place cannot be defined by any of the customary categories." In his recent book, *Brother Jesus,* Schalom Ben-Chorin has written: "For this our brother Jesus has been dead for us, and has now come back to life." Of this kinship with Jesus, Buber has written further: "We Jews know Jesus in a way—in the impulses and emotions of his essential Jewishness—that remains inaccessible to the Gentiles subject to him" (*Werke,* III, 957).

Several Jewish authors have written novels about Jesus, among them Scholem Asch, Ahoron A. Kabak, and Max Brod. Asch's book, *The Nazarene,* met with rather mixed Jewish reaction partially due to its highly favorable portrait of Jesus and partially due to its portrayal of the Jewish role in the death of Jesus.

Courses on Jesus and Christianity are now offered at the Hebrew University in Jerusalem and other Israeli institutions of higher learning where they enjoy popularity. But instruction about Jesus is not limited to the upper educational levels. Exposure to the life and teachings of Jesus is now a commonplace for the average Israeli student.

In assessing the importance of this Jewish interest in Jesus, Pinchas E. Lapide has written: "One may say that while the Israeli books on Jesus of one or two decades ago merely expressed academic or historic curiosity, those since the late '60's show a growing self-identification of their authors with the life, thought and fate of their Galilean compatriot. At a time when Christianity's Christ is being demoted by Paul Tillich to 'essential manhood in existence;' when Gerhard Ebeling obfuscates him into 'the basic situation of man as word-situation;' when Rudolf Bultmann and his school seem bent on demythologizing him out of all reality, it is refreshing to see the Jesus of Judaism take on new substance and credibility in the literature of his native land" (*Journal of Theology for Southern Africa*, 56).

In this chapter, we can discuss at length only two major Jewish treatments of Jesus—the first major scholarly study of the twentieth century and the most recent presentation. However, two other works on Jesus should be mentioned at this point: the first is David Flusser's *Jesus* published in 1969. Flusser says he wrote his book primarily "to show that it is possible to write the story of Jesus' life." For Flusser, Jesus was a religious genius whose personality makes it impossible to explain him purely on the basis of the psychological and cultural influences exerted upon him. Jesus was the great preacher, unique in Jewish thought, whose call to unconditional love went beyond anything found in the contemporary Judaism of his day.

Israeli Supreme Court Justice Haim Cohn has written a book, *The Trial and Death of Jesus*, which explores the issue most troubling to Jewish-Christian relationships throughout the centuries. Cohn argues that the Gospel accounts which depict a trial and condemnation of Jesus by the Sanhedrin on the night before the crucifixion cannot be historical. Cohn concludes that many factors argue against the historicity of the trial as depicted. (1) It is doubtful if the Sanhedrin would have undertaken any investigation on behalf of the hated Pontius Pilate. (2) A trial after sundown is most unlikely especially on the eve of Passover when Jews would have been busy with ritual preparations for the celebration. (3) Any condemnation would have required two truthworthy witnesses. Cohn contends that the Jewish leadership was not interested in securing Jesus' death. "There can, I submit, be only one thing in which the whole Jewish leadership of the day can have been, and indeed was, vitally interested: and that was to prevent the crucifixion of a Jew by the Romans, and, more particularly, of a Jew who enjoyed the love and affection of the people" (115). The high priest and the Sadducean Sanhedrin set out, according to Cohn, to support and save the widely popular Jesus from the Romans in order to help salvage their own sagging reputations among the people. Thus the Sanhedrin's actions with Jesus were intended to save him. It first examined witnesses to find men who could testify in his favor before the Romans. Finding none, it sought to persuade Jesus to plead not guilty before Pilate, but he refused. When Jesus refused to cooperate and bow to the authority of the Sanhedrin, there was nothing that could be done to prevent the Roman trial from taking its course and Jesus from being condemned for the political crime of sedition.

The first major objective, scholarly study of Jesus by a Jewish academian was Joseph Klausner's *Jesus of Nazareth: His Life, Times, and Teaching*, first published in Hebrew in 1922. The English translation appeared in 1925. His statement of the purpose in writing the book is worth quoting in part.

Above all things, the writer wished to provide in Hebrew for Hebrews a book which shall tell the history of the Founder of Christianity along the lines of modern criticism, without either the exaggeration and legendary accounts of the evangelists, or the exaggeration and the legendary and depreciatory satires of such books as the *Tol'doth Yeshu.* . . . Of the necessity for such a book it is needless to speak at length: it is enough to say that there has never yet been in Hebrew any book on Jesus the Jew which had not either a Christian propagandist aim—to bring Jews to Christianity, or a Jewish religious aim—to render Christianity obnoxious to Jews (11).

Klausner first provides a thorough examination of all the ancient sources about Jesus—Jewish, Roman, Christian—analyzing them in terms of bias and historicity. He examines their origin, their nature, and intent. Just as he notes the Christian tendencies and theologizing in early Christian traditions about Jesus, so he points out the tendencies and unreliability of much in the Jewish references, and especially so in the medieval Jewish accounts and narratives about Jesus.

The author's survey of the history of the study of the life of Jesus is an admirable historical essay. Though briefer than that of Schweitzer, it is more comprehensive in the number of scholars surveyed, especially with regard to Jewish writings about Jesus, an area almost totally neglected by Schweitzer.

Klausner then surveys the political, economic, religious, and intellectual conditions of the period from Pompey's conquest of Jerusalem till the destruction of the temple (63 B.C.–A.D. 70). It is a survey still worth the reading.

In describing the childhood and youth of Jesus, Klausner argues that "Jesus was as legitimate as any Jewish child in Galilee . . . [and] there is scant support for the theory . . . that Jesus may have been of Gentile origin" (232-33). Klausner was refuting the idea widely discussed in German literature at the turn of the century, namely, that Jesus was of Aryan extraction and therefore Gentile. The genealogical references in Matthew and Luke, Klausner argues, were the product of the church's desire to claim that Jesus was the messiah from the stock of Jesse. The virgin birth stories are the product of the later church's desire to present Jesus as the divine Son of God. Although his father died when Jesus was still young, Klausner claims "that his father's memory was more precious to him than his living mother, who did not understand him and whom he turned away when she and his brothers came to take possession of him" (235).

The natural environment of Galilee and Nazareth exerted the first great influence on Jesus.

Jesus: The Jew from Galilee

There, cut off by mountains from the great world, wrapped up in natural beauty, a beauty tender and peaceful, sorrowful in its peacefulness, surrounded by peasants who tilled the soil, with few necessities in life—there, Jesus could not help being a dreamer, a visionary, whose thoughts turned not on his people's future (he was far removed from their political conflicts), nor on the heavy Roman yoke (which had scarcely touched him); his thoughts turned, rather, on the sorrows of the individual soul and on the "Kingdom of Heaven," a kingdom not of this world. . . . This Nazareth, tightly enclosed within its hills, hearing but a faint, distant echo of wars and conflicts, a charming corner, hidden away and forgotten, could create only a dreamer, one who would reform the world not by revolt against the power of Rome, not by national insurrection, but by the kingdom of heaven, by the inner reformation of the *individual* (236-37).

A second influence on the youthful Jesus was the Hebrew scriptures.

His was an active mind and a fervid imagination, and the study (by his own reading or from the lips of others) of the books of the Prophets set his spirit aflame. The stern reproofs of the "First Isaiah," the divine consolations of the "Second Isaiah," the sorrows of Jeremiah, the soaring vision and stern wrath of Ezekiel, the sighs and laments of the Psalms, the promises foreseen in Daniel (and, perhaps, the *Book of Enoch*), together with those portions of the Pentateuch, full of the love of God and the love of man—all moved him to rapture and enthusiasm, penetrated his soul and enriched his spirit (237).

A third influence on Jesus was the life of the Galileans. Following the death of Herod and the census of Quirinius, Galilee became a "boiling cauldron of rebels, malcontents and ardent 'seekers after God.' " As the result of taxation, rebellions, and disease the people lived a hard life. They looked forward to the messianic age when there would be an end to all sorrows and pains, all servitude and ungodliness.

Jesus, who was one of the people and lived among them, knew their distress and believed too in the prophetic promises and consolations, certainly meditated much on

99

present conditions, and his imagination pictured for him in glowing colours the redemption, both political and spiritual.

As one of the "meek upon earth," the prevailing element with him was the spiritual side of the messianic idea, that of redemption (237).

At the baptism—the most decisive event in his life—Jesus came to believe he was the messiah. "Was there any reason why he, great and imaginative dreamer that he was, he who felt himself so near to God, he who was so filled with the spirit of the prophets, he who felt with his every instinct that what above all things was wanted was repentance and good works—was there any reason why *he* should not be the imminent Messiah? Perhaps his very name 'Jesus,' 'he shall save,' may have moved this simple villager to believe that he was the redeemer" (252).

Certain differences separated Jesus, the Galilean itinerant, from the Rabbis and homilists of his day. (1) The main purport of his teaching was the near approach of the messiah and the kingdom of heaven. For them, this was secondary. (2) The Pharisees taught the observance of the ceremonial laws. Jesus taught scarcely anything beyond the moral law and this generally in parables. (3) Jesus relied but slightly on scriptures in his teaching, whereas for the Pharisees, the basic teaching method was exposition of the scriptures and their interpretation. (4) Jesus was a worker of miracles; for him teaching and miracles possessed equal importance (264-67).

Jesus always called himself the "Son of man," that is, "simple flesh and blood." Jesus did, in using this term of himself, partially divulge his messiahship, especially for those who were familiar with the Son of man passages in Daniel and Enoch (256-57).

The miracles of Jesus are divided by Klausner into five types: (1) "Miracles due to a wish to fulfil some statement in the Old Testament or to imitate some Prophet"; (2) "Poetical descriptions which, in the minds of the disciples, were transformed into miracles"; (3) "Illusions;" (4) "Acts only apparently miraculous"; and (5) "The curing of numerous 'nerve cases' " (267-71).

In his life, "Jesus remained steadfast to the old *Torah:* till his dying day he continued to observe the ceremonial laws like a true Pharisaic Jew" (275). "Although Jesus never ventured wholly to contradict the Law of Moses and the teaching of the Pharisees, there yet was in his teaching the nucleus of such a contradiction" (248). The activity of Jesus and his disciples did, however, raise some doubt about his total obedience to the demands of the Torah. "The Pharisees and the local authorities were ... displeased by his consorting with 'publicans and sinners,' and by his disciples' abstention from fasting and their frequenting the publicans' banquets" (277). His healing on the Sabbath when life was not endangered was an "important landmark in Jesus' career." The Pharisees, the leaders of Jewish democracy, viewed such action with disfavor and "instilled into the people a dislike for Jesus" (279).

Jesus selected close disciples, first four (260) and then perhaps twelve to be associated with him. His sending out of the disciples to preach the coming of the kingdom and the need for repentance and good works was due to the fact that his enemies had become numerous and "Jesus felt the fatigue of constant teaching" (285).

Jesus' final break with the Pharisees came when he taught his disciples that there is nothing from without that could defile a man. "Thus Jesus would abrogate not only fasting, and decry the value of the washing of hands in the 'tradition of the elders' or in current traditional teaching, but would even permit (though he does this warily and only by hints) the foods forbidden in the Law of Moses" (291). The Pharisees came to view Jesus as a "sorcerer, a false prophet, a beguiler and one who led men astray (as the *Talmud* describes him), and it was a religious duty to put him to death. He was compelled to escape" (293).

In withdrawal, at Caesarea Philippi, Jesus' made known his messiahship to his disciples but taught them that he must suffer. He realized his coming suffering because he had seen the fate of John the Baptist, because he was presently being persecuted and opposed, and because he must undergo the messianic pangs. The idea of a messiah who should be put to death was incomprehensible to the Jews and to Jesus; therefore Jesus may have spoken of his sufferings to the disciples but not of his death. He went to Jerusalem where he believed "he should suffer greatly but would, in the end, be victorious and be recognized by the crowds of people who had come up to the Passover, as the Messiah" (302). The final revelation of his messiahship must "be done in Jerusalem, the Holy City, where the greatest publicity was possible, and not in an out-of-the-way corner such as Upper Galilee" (303).

Jesus revealed himself as the messiah in the gates of the city in his entry into Jerusalem and sought a dramatic means to reveal his messiahship within the city. "What public-religious deed could better secure publicity than some great deed in the Temple, the most sacred of places, which now, in the days immediately before the Passover, was crammed with Jews from every part of the world? Jesus resolves, therefore, to purify the Temple" (313). In doing so, Jesus was forbidding much of what the Mishnah forbade when it denounced using the temple as a shortcut; in other words, his act had some legal basis. "Both the act and the sentiment gained the approbation of the people; but the priests were enraged" (315). When Jesus and his disciples left Jerusalem after cleansing the temple, they "were satisfied with what they had accomplished in, or near the Temple: they had aroused popular indignation against their leaders, they had won popular approval and created an impression" (316).

Jesus, however, was shortly to lose his popular support. How? In his response to the question of paying tribute to Caesar, Jesus convinced the people that he "was not their expected redeemer who would free them from the Roman-Edomite yoke" (318). In other words, he failed to fulfill the political expectations of messiahship.

It was Judas' disappointment with Jesus and his desire to

turn the "deceiver" over to his just reward that led him to betray Jesus. As Klausner describes Judas' sentiments, these seem to be a reflection of the rejection of Jesus by the general population intensified by Judas' repudiation of his previous commitments.

He was gradually convinced that Jesus was not always successful in healing the sick; that Jesus feared his enemies and persecutors, and sought to escape and evade them; that there were marked contradictions in Jesus' teaching. One time he taught the observance of the Law in its minutest detail, ordaining the offering of sacrifices and submitting to priestly examination, and so forth; while at other times he permitted forbidden foods, paid little respect to Sabbath observance and the washing of hands, and hinted that "the new wine must be put in new bottles." One time he deferred to public opinion and paid the Temple half-shekel, and refused to countenance or discountenance the payment of tribute to Caesar; while another time he inveighs against the Temple and the best of the nation and the nation's rulers. One time he says, "Whosoever is not against us is for us," and another time, "Every one who is not with me is against me." One time he ordains, "Strive not against evil," while another time he himself rises up against the traffickers and moneychangers in the Temple and takes the law into his own hands. One time he says that a man must give all his goods to the poor, and another time he allows himself to be anointed with oil of myrrh, worth three hundred dinars.

What was more, this "Messiah" neither would nor could deliver his nation, yet he arrogated to himself the role of "the Son of man coming with the clouds of heaven," asserting that he should sit at the right hand of God in the Day of Judgment, daring to say of the Temple, the most sacred place in the world, that not one stone of it should remain upon another and, actually, that he would destroy it and in its place raise up another after three days!

Judas Iscariot became convinced that here was a false Messiah or a false prophet, erring and making to err, a beguiler and one who led astray, one whom the Law commanded to be killed, one to whom the Law forbade pity or compassion or forgiveness. Till such time as Jesus divulged his messianic claims to the disciples at Caesarea Philippi, Judas had not thought to find in Jesus more than might be found in any Pharisaic Rabbi or, at the most, in a Jewish prophet. But after this revelation to the disciples at Caesarea, and to the entire people at Jerusalem, Judas expected that in the Holy City, the centre of the religion and the race, Jesus would demonstrate his claims by mighty works, that he would destroy the Romans and bring the Pharisees and Sadducees to naught; then all would acknowledge his messianic claims and all would see him in his pomp and majesty as the "final saviour."

But what, in fact, did Judas see? No miracles (Matthew alone tells how Jesus healed the blind and lame in the temple, matters unknown to Mark), no mighty deeds, no one is subdued by him, the mighty Messiah escapes nightly to Bethany; except for "bold" remarks against the tradition of the elders and vain arrogance, Jesus reveals no plan by which he will effect the redemption. Was it not, then, a "religious duty" to deliver up such a "deceiver" to the government and so fulfil the law: Thou shalt exterminate the evil from thy midst [Deut 13:2-12] (324-25).

The death of Jesus took him by surprise. He had no foreknowledge of his impending death and did not anticipate it. He sensed he needed armed protection against his enemies and thus "prepared himself and his disciples for armed opposition in the time of need" (see Luke 22:36-38). "He dreaded suffering and persecution and like everyone of delicate susceptibilities he had a deeply disturbing premonition of impending trouble" (331). When the attempt at armed resistance in the garden failed to do more than wound one of the police, the disciples were seized with fear and fled. Jesus was taken to the high priest for "trial."

The trial of Jesus before the Sanhedrin, according to Klausner, was not a trial proper but only a preliminary examination which led to his being turned over to Pilate for trial. This hearing was conducted by only a few of the priestly caste—the aristocratic Sadduccees—and much of their action was taken out of fear of Pilate. Being practical politicians they took into account the national danger involved in not turning over Jesus.

There was no real justice in the case: neither the Sanhedrin nor Pilate probed deeply enough to discover that Jesus was no rebel; and a Sadducaean Court of law would not pay scrupulous regard to the fact whether or not Jesus was a "blasphemer," or "false prophet," or an inciter to idolatry, in the Biblical or *Mishnaic* sense. But when or where *has* ideal justice prevailed!

Of the two charges which the Sanhedrin brought against Jesus—blasphemy and Messianic pretensions—Pilate took account of the second only. Jesus was the "King-Messiah" and so, from Pilate's standpoint (since he could have no notion of the spiritual side to the Hebrew messianic idea), he was "king of the Jews." This was treason against the Roman Emperor for which the *Lex Juliana* knew but one punishment—death; and the prescribed death of rebel traitors was—crucifixion (350).

How does one explain the empty tomb and the resurrection appearances? Certainly deception on behalf of the disciples is no answer. The church was not founded on trickery and fraud. Klausner explains the events as follows:

Deliberate imposture is not the substance out of which the religion of millions of mankind is created. We must assume that the owner of the tomb, Joseph of Arimathaea, thought it unfitting that one who had been crucified should remain in his own ancestral tomb. Matthew alone tells us that the tomb was new, hewn out of the rock specially for Jesus the Messiah (just as the ass's colt on which Jesus rode was one on which none other had ever sat). Joseph of Arimathaea, therefore, secretly removed the body at the close of Sabbath and buried it in an unknown grave; and since he was, according to the Gospels, "one of the disciples of Jesus," or "one who was looking for the kingdom of God," there was some measure of truth in the report spread by the Jews, though it was, in the main, only the malicious invention of enemies unable to explain the "miracle."

The fact of the women going to anoint the body is proof that neither they nor the other disciples expected the resurrection, and that Jesus had not told them beforehand that he would rise again. Mark, the oldest of the Gospels, says that the women were *afraid* to say that they had found the tomb empty and that an angel had appeared to them. It should also be remembered that one of those who saw the angel was Mary Magdalene "from whom Jesus cast out seven devils," *i.e.*, a woman who had suffered from hysterics to the verge of madness. In the end she could not restrain herself and told what she had seen.

105

Then the Apostles, with Peter at their head, remembered Jesus' words, that "he would go before them to Galilee." Judas Iscariot, of course, had left them. Matthew reports that he repented his treachery, returned the thirty pieces of silver, and, like Ahitophel, hanged himself. Another account tells how he did not commit suicide but died a horrible death "at the hands of heaven.". . .

After his death, and after the women had, at last, related the vision which they had seen, first Peter and then the other disciples also saw Jesus in a vision (as did Paul later), when they went to the appointed mountain in Galilee. . . . It is impossible to suppose that there was any conscious deception; the nineteen hundred years' faith of millions is not founded on deception. There can be no question but that some of the ardent Galilaeans saw their Lord and Messiah in a vision. That the vision was spiritual and not material is evident from the way Paul compares his own vision with those seen by Peter and James and the other apostles. . . . Consequently the vision seen by the disciples, a vision which Paul deliberately compares with his own, was a spiritual vision and no more. This vision became the basis of Christianity; it was treated as faithful proof of the Resurrection of Jesus, of his Messiahship, and of the near approach of the kingdom of heaven. But for this vision the memory of Jesus might have been wholly forgotten or preserved only in a collection of lofty ethical precepts and miracle stories.

Could the bulk of the Jewish nation found its belief on such a corner-stone? (357-59).

Klausner concludes his work with a discussion of the teachings of Jesus and why Christianity was found unacceptable to the Jews of his day. Klausner stresses the fact that Jesus was always a "Jew to his fingertips." His mission was only to Jews. His teachings were Jewish. "In all this Jesus is the most Jewish of Jews, more Jewish than Simeon ben Shetah, more Jewish even than Hillel" (374). Yet in Jesus, one finds an exaggerated Judaism, a stress on the moral ideals in the form of such an extremist and individualistic ethic that neither society nor nation could endure their implementation. Jesus' attitude toward the ceremonial laws was such as to make them of secondary importance and almost to nullify them. But no people, no nation can endure without them. "The nation as a whole could only see in such public ideals as those of Jesus, an abnormal and even dangerous phantasy." Jesus' teachings in this exaggerated form—this radicalization of ethics—would have had the effort of negating "everything that had vitalized Judaism; . . . it brought Judaism to such an extreme that it became, in a sense, *non-Judaism*. . . . Judaism brought forth Christianity in its first form (the teaching of Jesus), but it thrust aside its daughter when it saw that she would slay the mother with a deadly kiss" (376).

Secondly, Jesus possessed an exaggerated sense of near-ness to God which gave the impression that there was one man with whom God was exceptionally intimate beyond any other. Such a view of intimacy with God by one man Judaism could not accept. In addition, Jesus spoke of God as if all—good and evil—are of the same worth in God's sight. Such a view destroys the idea of God as a God of justice, as a God of history. This Judaism could not accept.

Judaism is a national life, a life which the national religion and human ethical principles (the ultimate object of every religion) embrace without engulfing. Jesus came and thrust aside all the requirements of the national life; it was not that he set them apart and relegated them to their separate sphere in the life of the nation; he ignored them completely; in their stead he set up nothing but an ethico-religious system bound up with his conception of the Godhead.

In the self-same moment he both annulled *Judaism* as the *life-force* of the Jewish nation, and also the nation itself as a nation. For a religion which possesses only a certain conception of God and a morality acceptable to *all* mankind, does not belong to any special nation, and, consciously or unconsciously, breaks down the barriers of nationality. This inevitably brought it to pass that his people, Israel, rejected him. In its deeper consciousness the nation felt that then, more than at any other time, they must not be swallowed up in the great cauldron of nations in the Roman Empire, which were decaying for lack of God and of social morality (390).

Finally there was the "self-abnegation" taught by Jesus. Jesus was not an ascetic like John the Baptist, but he adopted, after the beginnings of his persecution by the Pharisees and the Herodians, a negative attitude toward the life of this present world. But Judaism assumed a life-affirming attitude. Jesus' belief in the nearness of the end led to this extremist ascetic system. "He cared not for reforming the world or civilisation" (397). To adopt such a negating attitude would have led Judaism to remove itself from the whole sphere of ordered national and human existence, to give up its national world outlook. Judaism could not accede to such a monastic, ascetic ideal which to it has ever been foreign. Klausner concludes with a positive appreciation of Jesus' ethical teachings and of him as a teacher.

Jesus is, for the Jewish nation, *a great teacher of morality and an artist in parable*. He is *the* moralist for whom, in the religious life, morality counts as—everything. Indeed, as a consequence of this extremist standpoint his ethical code has become simply an ideal for the isolated few, a "Zukunfts-Musik," an ideal for "the days of the Messiah," when an "end" shall have been made of this "old world," this present social order. It is no ethical code for the nations and the social order of to-day, when men are still trying to find the way to that future of the Messiah and the Prophets, and to the "kingdom of the Almighty" spoken of by the *Talmud*, an ideal which is of "this world" and which, gradually and in the course of generations, is to take shape in this world.

But in his ethical code there is a sublimity, distinctiveness and originality in form unparalleled in any other Hebrew ethical code; neither is there any parallel to the remarkable art of his parables. The shrewdness and sharpness of his proverbs and his forceful epigrams serve, in an exceptional degree, to make ethical ideas a popular possession. If ever the day should come and this ethical code be stripped of its wrappings of miracles and mysticism, the Book of the Ethics of Jesus will be one of the choicest treasures in the literature of Israel for all time (414).

Professor Geza Vermes, in his *Jesus the Jew,* has developed a rather new approach to the question of Jesus' relationship to the Judaism of his day and to the issue of the typological category most useful in understanding Jesus within the Jewish life and culture of his day. Scholars have seen Jesus as a Rabbi, a Pharisee, a Prophet, an Essene, a Zealot, a Teacher, an apocalyptic visionary, or as a member of the *am-ha-aretz*—the people of the land. For Vermes, Jesus did not belong among the Pharisees, Essenes, Zealots, or Gnostics, but was one of the holy miracleworkers of Galilee. In other words, Jesus is best seen and understood against the background of a charismatic Judaism of the first century. "Everything combines, when approached from the viewpoint of a study of first-century A.D. Galilee, or of charismatic Judaism, or of his titles and their development, to place him in the venerable company of the Devout, the ancient Hasidim" (223). For Vermes then three lines of approach contribute to this view of Jesus: the character of first-century Galilean life and culture, the resemblances between the words and works of Jesus and those of some of the Hasidim, and the titles which were most likely applied to him during his lifetime either by himself or others.

First, how does Jesus fit into the context of first-century Galilean life from which he came? Galilee, in the period before the destruction of the temple, was a territory *sui generis.* "Not only did it have its own peculiar past, but its political, social and economic organization also contributed to distinguish it from the rest of Palestine. The conflict between Jesus and the religious and secular authority outside Galilee was at least in part due to the fact that he was, and was known to have been, a Galilean" (43-44).

Geographically, Galilee, the northernmost district of Palestine, was a "little island in the midst of unfriendly seas." It was basically an "autonomous and self-contained politico-ethnic unit" surrounded by Gentiles and heathen on the East, North, and West and separated from Judaea on the south by the Samaritans and the Hellenistic territory of Scythopolis, a Greek city-state of the Decapolis. Galilee's overwhelming Jewishness was a recent historical phenomenon. Only after the final triumph of the Maccabeans at the end of the second century B.C., were the Galileans annexed to the Jewish state and issued an ultimatum to "be circumcised and to live in accordance with the laws of the Jews" (44).

Governmentally, Galilee at the time of Jesus was still ruled by a descendant of Herod and was spared the humiliation of direct rule by the Romans. Galilee was reasonably populous and wealthy with a "self-sufficiency which, with the legacy of its history and the unsophisticated simplicity of its life, is likely to have nourished the pride and independence of its inhabitants" (46).

Galilee was also a hotbed of revolutionary and rebel movements. The struggle against the Roman Empire was a "full-scale Galilean activity in the first century A.D." (47). The major Jewish revolts against the Romans were led by Galileans but in particular by the members of one Galilean family, that of Ezekias who first led a revolt against Herod's rule in about 47 B.C. and whose descendants were prime movers in the revolt of A.D. 66. Thus in the first century, the word "Galilean" had taken on the dark connotation of revolutionary. In addition to being strong nationalists, the Galileans were "quarrelsome and aggressive among themselves" but were ones who "preferred honour to financial gain" (48).

In rabbinical sources, the portrait of a northerner— Galilean—shows him "as a figure of fun, an ignoramus, if not both" (52). The Galilean did not speak correct Aramaic, was generally a religiously uneducated person, and was rather loose in his attitudes toward such matters as temple sacrifices and offerings, levitical laws of cleanness and uncleanness, and to the rabbinic code of proper behavior. Pharisees were not a dominant element in Galilee, and in fact it seems that the Pharisaic presence and impact on Galilee postdates the first century or at least the time of Jesus' ministry. The Pharisees with whom Jesus is shown in conflict must therefore have been foreign—that is, Judaean. Thus Jerusalem and southern opposition to Jesus was due to the fact that as a Galilean he was a political suspect and a religious nonconformist; that is, he was a victim "to a sentiment of superiority on the part of the intellectual *élite* of the metropolis towards unsophisticated provincials" (57). Could anything good come out of Galilee?

Secondly, how is Jesus related to the charismatic Judaism of his day? Vermes analyzes the texts which discuss two such charismatic holy men—Honi, called the Circle-Drawer by the rabbis and the Righteous by Josephus, a first century B.C. saint, and Hanina ben Dosa who lived before the fall of Jerusalem in A.D. 70. Both of these were probably Galilean; the first not absolutely for sure but the latter undoubtedly.

Honi was a man to whom tradition and his contemporaries ascribed power over natural phenomenon; he possessed among other things, the power to cause rain. Hanina was a holy man possessed by the power to cure, even from a distance, to deliver people in physical peril, and to influence natural phenomena. Hanina gave expression to the Hasidic piety with its detachment from possessions, a lack of interest in legal and ritual affairs, and an exclusive concentration on moral questions. These Hasidim spoke of their relationship to God in terms of father-son and could be and were called sons of God. They were also understood as prophetic figures, heirs to an ancient prophetic tradition possessing powers which came from their immediate contact with God. As authoritative figures, they were addressed as "lord." As popular figures, the "image of the charismatic was inseparable from the figure of Elijah."

That a distinctive trend of charismatic Judaism existed during the last couple of centuries of the Second Temple is undeniable. These holy men were treated as the willing or unsuspecting heirs to an ancient prophetic tradition. Their supernatural powers were attributed to their immediate relation to God. They were venerated as a link between heaven and earth independent of any institutional mediation.

Moreover, although it would be forcing the evidence to argue that charismatic Judaism was exclusively a Northern phenomenon because Jesus, Hanina ben Dosa, and possibly Abba Hilkiah were Galileans, this religious trend is likely to have had Galilean roots. It is, in any case, safe and justifiable to conclude that the unsophisticated religious ambiance of Galilee was apt to produce holy men of the Hasidic type, and that their success in that province was attributable to the simple spiritual demands of the Galilean nature, and perhaps also to a lively local folk memory concerning the miraculous deeds of the great prophet Elijah (79-80).

The longest section of Vermes' book is a discussion of the titles applied to Jesus in the Synoptics Gospels in light of the use of these titles in first-century Judaism and particularly in a Galilean milieu. The object of this effort is to determine what Jesus' contemporaries thought of him and perhaps what Jesus thought of himself. The title "prophet," which is frequently applied to Jesus in the Synoptics, is considered an authentic title ascribed to Jesus during his ministry: "It seems to have been the description he himself preferred" (99). "The belief professed by his contemporaries that Jesus was a charismatic prophet rings so authentic, especially in the light of the Honi-Hanina cycle of traditions, that the correct historical question is not whether such an undogmatic Galilean concept was ever in vogue, but rather how, and under what influence, it was ever given an eschatological twist" (90). The eschatological twist is related, by Vermes, to the expectation of a prophetic revival hinted at in I Maccabees (4:46; 14:41) and Josephus, to the belief in the return of the prophet Elijah, and to the expectation of a coming prophet like Moses (Deuteronomy 18:18). Jesus' celibacy is explained on the basis of the general incompatibility between prophecy and marriage, a factor referred to in several rabbinic texts. The title prophet with regard to Jesus was not developed very intensively in early Christianity, in spite of its authenticity with reference to Jesus' career, because it could not be exploited in dogmatic terms and secondly because of the great number of pseudoprophets who appeared in conjunction with the first Jewish revolt against Rome.

The term "lord" is also assumed to be authentic in light of its usage in Aramaic sources. In fact, it appears to have been a frequent title utilized in the earliest Christian traditions. "In Jewish Aramaic the designation, '(the) lord,' is appropriate in connection with God, or a secular dignitary, or an authoritative teacher, or a person renowned for his spiritual or supernatural force" (121). "The title primarily links Jesus to his dual role of charismatic Hasid and teacher, and if the stress is greater in the earlier strata of the tradition, that is no doubt due to the fact that his impact as a holy man preceded that of teacher and founder of a religious community" (127).

Of the title "messiah" as applied to Jesus, Vermes writes: "Since the figure of the Messiah appears not to have been central to the teaching of Jesus, and since no record has survived of any hostile challenge concerning his Messianic status before his last days in Jerusalem; since, moreover, he deliberately withheld his approval of Peter's confession and, in general, failed to declare himself to be the Christ, there is every reason to wonder if he really thought of himself as such" (149). Such an argument does not deny that "Jesus' denial of Messianic aspirations failed to be accepted by his friends as well as his foes" (154). Vermes understands the early church's emphasis on Jesus as the messiah as due "to its psychological and polemical value in the Jewish-Christian debate" (155).

The importance of the title "Son of man" has dominated New Testament scholarship for generations. Vermes' analysis of the evidence offers a radical departure from previous research.

To sum up, there is no evidence whatever, either inside or outside the Gospels, to imply, let alone demonstrate, that "the *son of man*" was used as a title. There is, in addition, no valid argument to prove that any of the Gospel passages directly or indirectly referring to Daniel 7:13 may be traced back to Jesus. The only possible, indeed probable, genuine utterances are sayings independent of Daniel 7 in which, in accordance with Aramaic usage, the speaker refers to himself as the *son of man* out of awe, reserve or humility. It is this neutral speech-form that the apocalyptically-minded Galilean disciples of Jesus appear to have "eschatologized" by means of a midrash based on Daniel 7:13 (185-86).

Thus, according to Vermes, Jesus did not understand himself as nor refer to a Son of man figure who would appear as the apocalyptic judge or as a redemptive suffering one.

The use of the term "Son of God" in the Old Testament and rabbinic literature shows a wide range of usage: of angels, of the Israelite king, of Israelites or the people as a whole, of just men, and of the messiah as an epithet. Thus Vermes argues that there is no reason to deny the title to the historical Jesus but there, it "derives from his activities as a miracle-worker and exorcist, and from his own consciousness of an immediate and intimate contact with the heavenly Father" (211).

Thus for Vermes, Jesus was a first century Galilean Hasid, a miracle-worker, healer, and exorcist, who was referred to and known as a prophet, lord, and son of God. But he was more than an ordinary charismatic Hasid: "no objective and enlightened student of the Gospels can help but be struck by the incomparable superiority of Jesus" (224).

Second to none in profundity of insight and grandeur of character, he is in particular an unsurpassed master of the art of laying bare the inmost core of spiritual truth and of bringing every issue back to the essence of religion, the existential relationship of man and man, and man and God.

It should be added that in one respect more than any other he differed from both his contemporaries and even his prophetic predecessors. The prophets spoke on behalf of the honest poor, and defended the widows and the fatherless, those oppressed and exploited by the wicked, rich and powerful. Jesus went further. In addition to proclaiming these blessed, he actually took his stand among the pariahs of his world, those despised by the respectable. Sinners were his table-companions and the ostracised tax collectors and prostitutes his friends (224).

6. JESUS: THE PROCLAIMER
CALLING TO DECISION

> The earliest Church resumed the message of Jesus and through its preaching passed it on. So far as it did only that, Jesus was to it a preacher and prophet. But Jesus was more than that to the Church: He was also the Messiah; hence that Church also proclaimed him, himself—and that is the essential thing to see. He who formerly had been the *bearer* of a message was drawn into it and became its essential *content. The proclaimer became the proclaimed.*—Rudolf Bultmann, *Theology of the New Testament,* Volume I (p. 33)

The most influential school in German New Testament scholarship during the twentieth century has centered around Rudolf Bultmann and his students. Bultmann repudiated the quest of the historical Jesus declaring it historically an impossibility and theologically an irrelevancy. However, out of Bultmann's circle of students there developed, during the 1950s, a so-called new quest of the historical Jesus. In this chapter, we will examine Bultmann's position as well as that of the new quest by the so-called post-Bultmannians.

In order to understand and appreciate Bultmann's position, several developments in New Testament studies and in philosophy and theology need to be noted since these form a background for Bultmann's approach.

The first of these is the development of New Testament form criticism. As a discipline, modern form criticism developed near the end of the nineteenth century, being first applied to classical and Germanic literature and then to the Old and New Testaments. Form criticism is an attempt to classify and study literature on the basis of genre analysis. That is, literary materials, on the basis of their form, structure, mood, and content, are divided into various genres and analyzed with regard to their use and function. Behind and involved in the concerns of genre analysis is the question of the genres' use and employment within the community which preserved them.

With regard to the New Testament Gospels, the following conclusions were drawn from the results of form critical studies: (1) The traditions in the Gospels originally circulated in the church as independent and unconnected units. Therefore the connections between the units (with the possible exception of the passion story) are not indigenous to the earliest form of the traditions. (2) The traditions that now make up the Gospels were preserved because they could be utilized by the church in its preaching, teaching, worship, and dialogue with non-Christians. (3) The traditions have been influenced by and are expressive of the faith of the early church in Christ the risen redeemer. (4) In the process of transmission, the traditions were sometimes molded, changed, and transformed by the faith of the church or the Gospel writers. (5) Traditions were sometimes created by the church or borrowed from non-Christian sources and baptized into the church's tradition. Bultmann was not only influenced by form critical studies but was also one of the main participants in development of the movement and methodological approach to the Gospels. His work, *The History of the Synoptic Traditions,* published in its first edition in 1921, represents in many ways the culmination of form critical study of the Gospels.

A second development reflected in Bultmann's approach was the revival of Reformation theology which is generally designated with the rubrics, neo-orthodoxy or dialectical theology. Karl Barth, the Swiss theologian, is generally considered the father of this theological movement and was certainly its most significant exponent. The rise of neo-orthodoxy is frequently associated with the publication of Barth's commentary on Romans published in 1919 against the background of World War I in Europe. In several ways, many of the conclusions concerning the historical Jesus which have characterized the neo-orthodox position were already articulated by Martin Kähler in a book published in Germany in 1892 and translated into English with the title *The So-Called Historical Jesus and the Historic, Biblical Christ*. Kähler argued against the possibility of rediscovering the Jesus of history and thus attacked and repudiated the nineteenth-century quest. Among other reasons, he argued that the kerygmatic nature of the Gospels, that is their preaching and confessional character, made it impossible to use the materials for biographical purposes. In this he anticipated the later conclusions of form criticism. Secondly, Kähler argued that the proper object of Christian faith is not the Jesus of history but the Christ of faith as preached in the church. Thirdly, he contended that to try to construct Christian faith around the historical Jesus or a Jesus reconstructed on the basis of a historical-critical study of the Gospels was to attempt to base faith on historical facts, a denial of the Reformation principle of salvation or justification by faith alone. Faith based on the historical Jesus would not be Christian faith but a Jesusology indistinguishable from idolatrous hero worship.

A third development was the rediscovery of the eschatological-apocalyptic orientation of Jesus' life and preaching. Johannes Weiss and Albert Schweitzer among others stressed the central importance of this perspective for any interpretation of the historical Jesus and his message. Bultmann took this emphasis seriously and sought to interpret the eschatological dimension in terms relevant to his understanding of modern man.

A fourth factor which contributed to Bultmann's interpretation of the New Testament was the rise of existentialist philosophy. The origin of existentialism is generally traced back to the thought of the Danish theologian Søren Kierkegaard. Bultmann was directly dependent, however, upon the thought of the German existentialist philosopher Martin Heidegger. Existentialist philosophy stresses man's need to affirm his authentic existence through decision and commitment by abandoning all security in an unreserved openness to the future. Bultmann claimed that existentialist philosophy and the New Testament are in this regard saying the same thing independently.

Bultmann's *Jesus and the Word* was originally published in Germany in 1926 but reflects an approach to Jesus which Bultmann has continued to hold throughout his teaching and preaching career. Being primarily an exposition of the teachings of Jesus, this work contains little discussion of the historical Jesus. So we shall turn to some other of Bultmann's writings for his statements about the historical Jesus.

Behind the kerygmatic Christ of the Gospels—the Christ of faith—stands a "concrete figure of history—Jesus of Nazareth. His life is more than a mythical event; it is a human life which ended in the tragedy of crucifixion" ("New Testament and Mythology," 34). If one asks Bultmann what might be known about the activity of the historical Jesus, he responds: "With a bit of caution we can say the following concerning Jesus' activity: Characteristic for him are exorcisms, the breech of the Sabbath commandment, the abandonment of ritual purifications, polemic against Jewish legalism, fellowship with outcasts such as publicans and harlots, sympathy for women and children; it can also be seen that Jesus was not an ascetic like John the Baptist, but gladly ate and drank a glass of wine. Perhaps we may add that he called disciples and assembled about himself a small company of followers—men and women" ("The Primitive Christian Kerygma," 22-23). How Jesus may have understood events in his own life is not open for our understanding. For example, the "Gospels furnish us with no biographical data on the basis of which one can decide what was in Jesus' mind when he went to his death" ("Is Jesus Risen as Goethe?" 233).

Why was Jesus drawn to Jerusalem at the end of his career? If the assumption is correct that "first and foremost his journey to Jerusalem was undertaken in order to confront the people there, in the holy city, with the message of the kingdom of God, and to summon them at the eleventh hour to make their decision"; if it is correct that "only on the journey with his followers to Jerusalem and the temple did Jesus seek the final decision," then he scarcely reckoned on execution at the hands of the Romans, but only on the imminent appearing of the kingdom of God. But these are all assumptions. What is certain is merely that he was crucified by the Romans, and thus suffered the death of a political criminal. This death can scarcely be understood as an inherent and necessary consequence of his activity; rather it took place because his activity was misconstrued as a political activity. In that case it would have been—historically speaking—a meaningless fate. We cannot tell whether or how Jesus found meaning in it. We may not veil from ourselves the possibility that he suffered a collapse ("The Primitive Christian Kerygma," 24).

To attempt an understanding of how Jesus may have viewed his death represents, for Bultmann, an illegitimate psychologizing of Jesus. Nonetheless, Bultmann does say in regard to the death of Jesus that "he knew himself to be sent by God and therefore also understood his destiny as determined by God" ("Is Jesus Risen as Goethe?" 233).

"Events" associated with Jesus, such as the virgin birth and the resurrection, must be understood as legendary. The virgin birth is the "legendary expression for faith's claim that the source of the meaning of the person of Jesus is not to be seen in his natural this-worldly origin. . . . The divine sonship of Christ consists in the fact that Jesus, in obedience to God as the Father . . . and in authority, proclaimed the Word of God which still encounters us today as his Word" ("Is Jesus Risen as Goethe?" 230). With regard to the resurrection, Bultmann says: "Both the legend of the empty tomb and the appearances insist on the physical reality of the risen body of the Lord," but a "corpse cannot come back to life or rise from the grave" (*Myth and Christianity*, 60). "An historical fact which involves a resurrection from the dead is utterly inconceivable" ("New Testament and Mythology," 39). "The reports of a bodily resurrection of Jesus are legends. But with that it is by no means said that the resurrection of Jesus is only the legendary concretization of an idea. The resurrection reports are the legendary concretization of the faith of the first Christian community in the risen Lord, the faith that God has exalted the crucified one as Lord" ("Is Jesus Risen as Goethe?" 237). "The real Easter faith is faith in the word of preaching which brings illumination. If the event of Easter Day is in any sense an historical event additional to the event of the cross, it is nothing else than the rise of faith in the risen Lord, since it was this faith which led to the apostolic preaching" ("New Testament and Mythology," 42). "Jesus is risen in the message of the church" ("Is Jesus Risen as Goethe?" 238).

Bultmann suggests that Jesus did not believe himself to be the messiah, but he considered this to be a matter of "secondary importance." "When we are dealing with the life and portrait of Jesus, we can only say of his preaching that he doubtless appeared in the consciousness of being commissioned by God to preach the eschatological message of the breaking-in of the Kingdom of God and the demanding but also inviting will of God. We may thus ascribe to him a prophetic consciousness, indeed, a 'consciousness of authority'" ("The Primitive Christian Kerygma," 23). "Jesus' preaching had 'kerygmatic' character. He did not appear as a teacher or rabbi, but as a prophet with an eschatological message, though he may also have made use of the doctrine and forms of rabbinic teaching for an interpretation of the will of God, the proclamation of which is intimately connected with the eschatological message" (27). Jesus' preaching however is not identical with the early kerygma of the church. Jesus did not preach the Christ-kerygma. Jesus' preaching must therefore be understood within the context of Judaism.

Over against the reproach that I conceive of Jesus as a Jew and assign him to the sphere of Judaism I must first of all simply ask: Was Jesus—the historical Jesus!—a Christian? Certainly not, if Christian faith is faith in him as the Christ. And even if he should have known that he was the Christ ("Messiah") and should actually have demanded faith in himself as the Christ, then he would still not have been a Christian and ought not to be described as the subject of Christian faith, though he is nevertheless its object (19).

In his book, *Primitive Christianity in its Contemporary Setting,* Bultmann discussed the proclamation of Jesus as a part of his discussion of Judaism.

Bultmann has described the preaching of Jesus in the following terms: "The preaching of Jesus is the eschatological message of the coming—more, of the breaking-in of the Kingdom of God. . . . For Jesus the eschatological proclamation goes hand in hand with the proclamation of the will of God, with the call to radical obedience to God's demands culminating in the commandment of love" ("The Primitive Christian Kerygma," 16).

Bultmann claims that for the early church's kerygma, only the "that" of the historical Jesus was of any importance. With this Bultmann's theology is in agreement. That is, the historicity of Jesus is of importance but not in terms of a portrait of or reconstructed Jesus of history.

Paul and John, each in his own way, indicate that we do not need to go beyond the "that." Paul proclaims the incarnate, crucified, and risen Lord; that is, his kerygma requires only the "that" of the life of Jesus and the fact of his crucifixion. He does not hold before his bearer's eyes a portrait of Jesus, the human person, apart from the cross (Gal. 3:1), and the cross is not regarded from a biographical standpoint but as saving event. . . . The eschatological and ethical preaching of the historical Jesus plays no role in Paul. John gives all due emphasis to the humanity of Jesus, but presents none of the characteristics of Jesus' humanity which could be gleaned, for example, from the Synoptic Gospels. The decisive thing is simply the "that" ("The Primitive Christian Kerygma," 20).

The really decisive thing is the *that* of Jesus' coming, not the *what,* that is, not the historical verifiable data of his life and work. Now it is uncontestable that in Paul and in the rest of the New Testament, except in the Synoptic Gospels, only the *that,* and not the *what,* plays a role. In the assertion of the *that,* the paradox is maintained that a historical figure, the person of Jesus of Nazareth, is at the same time the eschatological figure, the Lord Jesus Christ ("Is Jesus Risen as Goethe?" 231).

In Bultmann, one can see the full acceptance of three basic conclusions which had slowly developed out of the New Testament research and the quest for the historical Jesus in the nineteenth and the early part of the twentieth century as these found expression in critical scholarship. These general conclusions were: (1) The Gospel materials are kerygmatic, not biographical in nature; they have been influenced by and reflect the post-Easter faith of the early church. Therefore no biography or real presentation of the historical Jesus is possible even if this should be desirable. (2) The eschatological orientation of the early church and the preaching of Jesus cannot be ignored but must be confronted head on. Bultmann sought to preserve this eschatological emphasis but in terms of an existentialist reinterpretation. In the preaching of the word (the kerygma), man is confronted with the decisive eschatological event in the radical call to decision and authentic existence. "The proclamation of the church is an eschatological phenomenon in which Christ encounters us as present, and as final if this proclamation encounters us for the last time" ("Is Jesus Risen as Goethe?" 238). (3) Much of the New Testament is mythological reflecting an outmoded world view and a cosmological eschatology. To meet this issue, Bultmann proposed a hermeneutical approach called "demythologization." Such a methodology sought to preserve the kerygmatic message by interpreting the mythology in existential terms. "Whereas the older liberals used criticism to *eliminate* the mythology of the New Testament, our task today is to use criticism to *interpret* it" ("New Testament and Mythology," 12). The following statements illustrate Bultmann's view of myth, its importance, and its reinterpretation.

The cosmology of the New Testament is essentially mythical in character. The world is viewed as a three-storied structure, with the earth in the centre, the heaven above, and the underworld beneath. Heaven is the abode of God and of

122

celestial beings—the angels. The underworld is hell, the place of torment. Even the earth is more than the scene of natural, everyday events, of the trivial round and common task. It is the scene of the supernatural activity of God and his angels on the one hand, and of Satan and his daemons on the other. These supernatural forces intervene in the course of nature and in all that men think and will and do. Miracles are by no means rare. Man is not in control of his own life. Evil spirits may take possession of Him. Satan may inspire him with evil thoughts. Alternatively, God may inspire his thought and guide his purposes. He may grant him heavenly visions. He may allow him to hear his word of succour or demand. He may give him the supernatural power of his Spirit. History does not follow a smooth unbroken course; it is set in motion and controlled by these supernatural powers. This aeon is held in bondage by Satan, sin, and death (for "powers" is precisely what they are), and hastens towards its end. That end will come very soon, and will take the form of a cosmic catastrophe. It will be inaugurated by the "woes" of the last time. Then the Judge will come from heaven, the dead will rise, the last judgment will take place, and men will enter into eternal salvation or damnation (1-2). . . .

The real purpose of myth is not to present an objective picture of the world as it is, but to express man's understanding of himself in the world in which he lives. Myth should be interpreted not cosmologically, but an-thropologically, or better still, existentially (10). . . .

The importance of the New Testament mythology lies not in its imagery but in the understanding of existence which it enshrines (11). . . .

To de-mythologize is to deny that the message of Scripture and of the Church is bound to an ancient world-view which is obsolete (*Jesus Christ and Mythology*, 36).

Now to return to Bultmann's *Jesus and the Word*. As we have seen, Bultmann claimed that the preaching of Jesus centered in his eschatological message of the coming and breaking-in of the kingdom of God and his proclamation of the will of God. In *Jesus and the Word*, Bultmann discusses Jesus' message in terms of his teachings on the coming of the kingdom, the will of God, and God the remote and the near. By the message of Jesus, Bultmann was referring to what he called "the oldest layer of the synoptic tradition." This oldest layer is reached, according to Bultmann, by peeling away the later tradition. "Everything in the synoptics which for reasons of language or content can have originated only in Hellenistic Christianity must be excluded as a source for the teaching of Jesus." This brings one to the "Aramaic tradition of the oldest Palestinian community," but here again there are layers of traditions which reflect the interests of the church and its later development which must be removed to expose the oldest tradition. But here again some uncertainty remains, since one cannot be absolutely certain how far that tradition and "community preserved an objectively true picture of him and his message." However, "no sane person can doubt that Jesus stands as the founder behind the historical movement whose first distinct stage is represented by the oldest Palestinian community" (13).

As Bultmann expounds the teaching of Jesus on the kingdom of God, his emphasis fell upon the inauguration of the kingdom. "His message is based on the certainty: *the Kingdom of God is beginning, is beginning now!*" (30). Thus Bultmann does not accept the thoroughgoing eschatology of Weiss and Schweitzer in which the kingdom for Jesus was an event still entirely future though absolutely imminent.

The future Kingdom of God . . . is not something which is to come in the course of time, so that to advance its coming one can do something in particular, perhaps through penitential prayers and good works, which become superfluous in the moment of its coming. Rather, the Kingdom of God is a power *which, although it is entirely future, wholly determines the present*. It determines the present because it now compels man to decision; he is determined thereby either in this direction or in that, as chosen or as rejected, in his entire present existence. Future and present are not related in the sense that the Kingdom begins as a historical fact in the present and achieves its fulfillment in the future; nor in the sense that an inner, spiritual possession of personal attributes or qualities of soul constitutes a present hold on the Kingdom, to which only the future consummation is lacking. Rather the Kingdom of God is genuinely future, because it is not a metaphysical entity or condition, but the future action of God, which can be in no sense something given in the present. None the less this future determines man in his present, and exactly for that reason is true future—not merely something to come "somewhere, sometime," but destined for man and constraining him to decision.

The coming of the Kingdom of God is therefore not really an event in the course of time, which is due to occur sometime and toward which man can either take a definite attitude or hold himself neutral. Before he takes any attitude he is already constrained to make his choice, and therefore he must understand that just this necessity of decision constitutes the essential part of his human nature. Because Jesus sees man thus in a crisis of decision before God, it is understandable that in his thought the Jewish Messianic hope becomes the absolute certainty that in this hour the Kingdom of God is coming. If men are standing in the crisis of decision, and if precisely this crisis is the essential characteristic of their humanity, then every hour is the last hour, and we can understand that for Jesus the whole contemporary mythology is pressed into the service of this conception of human existence. Thus he understood and proclaimed his hour as the last hour (51-52).

The kingdom confronts man with the ultimate either-or and calls man to repentance and readiness for self-sacrifice in which every other interest disappears before the exclusiveness of the demand of God. The kingdom is proclaimed as eschatological deliverance. In his preaching, Jesus rejected the whole content of apocalyptic speculation, the calculation of the time and the watching for signs. For Jesus, the coming of the kingdom was for the benefit of the Jewish people though he stressed that the Jew as such has no claim before God.

Jesus was not only an eschatological prophet of the kingdom of God, he *"actually lived as a Jewish rabbi,"* teaching in the synagogue, gathering around him a circle of pupils, disputing along the same lines as Jewish rabbis, using the same methods of argument and the same turns of speech, and coining proverbs and parables (58). Jesus, in teaching the will of God, "conceived radically the idea of obedience" (73) and "demanded obedience without any secondary motive," such as rewards (79).

The will of God is then for Jesus as little a social or political program as it is either an ethical system which proceeds from an ideal of man and humanity or an ethic of value. He knows neither the conception of personality nor that of virtue; the latter word he does not even use, it is found first in Hellenistic Christianity. As he has no doctrine of virtue, so also he has none of duty or of the good. It is sufficient for a man to know that God has placed him under the necessity of decision in every concrete situation in life, in the here and now. And this means that he himself must know what is required of him, and that no authority and no theory can take from him this responsibility (108). . . .

Jesus thought of love neither as a virtue which belongs to the perfection of man, nor as an aid to the well-being of society, but as an overcoming of self-will in the concrete situation of life in which a man encounters other men. Hence Jesus' requirement of love cannot be more nearly defined in content, or be regarded as an ethical principle from which particular concrete requirements can be derived, as would be possible with the humanistic command of love, which depends on a well defined ideal of humanity. *What* a man must do in order to love his neighbor or his enemy is not stated. It is assumed that everyone can know that, and therefore Jesus' demand for love is no revelation of a new principle of ethics nor of a new conception of the dignity of man (112-13).

Jesus as the eschatological prophet proclaimed the coming kingdom and called for repentance and decision. Jesus as the Jewish rabbi preached radical obedience to the will of God. "How is the preaching of Jesus concerning the will of God related to his proclamation of the coming of the Kingdom? Or, as it could be phrased, how are Jesus the rabbi and Jesus the prophet related?" (120-21). Bultmann provides the following answer to this question, an answer which illustrates his existentialist interpretation of Jesus' message:

The one concern in this teaching was that man should conceive his immediate concrete situation as the decision to which he is constrained, and should decide in this moment for God and surrender his natural will. Just this is what we found to be the final significance of the eschatological message, that man *now* stands under the necessity of decision, that his "Now" is always for him the last hour, in which his decision against the world and for God is demanded, in which every claim of his own is to be silenced. Since, then, the message of the coming of the Kingdom and that of the will of God point men *to the present moment as the final hour* in the sense of the hour of decision, the two do form a unity, each is incomplete without the other (131).

In describing what he was doing in *Jesus and the Word*, Bultmann has said: "If I desire an encounter with the Jesus of history, it is true that I must rely on certain historical documents. Yet the study of those documents can bring us to an encounter with Jesus only as a phenomenon of past history. That was the aim and method of my *Jesus and the Word*. The Jesus of history is not kerygma, any more than my book was. For in the kerygma Jesus encounters us as the Christ—that is, as the eschatological phenomenon *par excellence*. . . . I am deliberately renouncing any form of encounter with a phenomenon of past history, including an encounter with the Christ after the flesh, in order to encounter the Christ proclaimed in the kerygma, which confronts me in my historic situation" ("A Reply," 117). Bultmann thus does here, as in other of his writings, admit some possibility of knowledge about the historical Jesus but denies anything beyond the "that" of Jesus to be of any significance for Christian faith. "It is therefore illegitimate to go behind the kerygma, using it as a 'source,' in order to reconstruct a 'historical Jesus' with his 'messianic consciousness,' his 'inner life' or his 'heroism.' That would be merely 'Christ after the flesh,' who is no longer. It is not the historical Jesus, but Jesus Christ, the Christ, preached, who is the Lord" ("The Historical Jesus and the Theology of Paul," 241).

Accepting such hypotheses, the Bultmann circle engaged in no quest for the historical Jesus until the mid-1950s. In 1953, Ernst Käsemann delivered a lecture in which he called for a renewed interest in the earthly Jesus arguing that this was not only possible but also necessary if the church was to avoid finding itself committed to a mythological lord unrelated to the historicity of Jesus. For him, the issue is the question of whether there was continuity between the preaching of Jesus and the preaching faith of the early church.

Out of the obscurity of the life story of Jesus, certain characteristic traits in his preaching stand out in relatively sharp relief, and . . . primitive Christianity united its own message with these. The heart of our problem lies here: the exalted Lord has almost entirely swallowed up the image of the earthly Lord and yet the community maintains the identity of the exalted Lord with the earthly. . . . The question of the historical Jesus is, in its legitimate form, the question of the continuity of the Gospel within the discontinuity of the times and within the variation of the kerygma ("The Problem of the Historical Jesus," 46).

Käsemann thus stresses the continuity of the preaching of Jesus with the preaching of the early church—thus a point of contact between the kerygma of the early church and that of Jesus.

Ernst Fuchs suggested a second line of approach to the problem of the continuity between the earthly Jesus and the Christ of faith. Fuchs claims that in the actions of Jesus as well as in his message, Jesus' conduct manifests implicitly his own eschatological understanding of his person which became explicit in the preaching of the church. The church's kerygma and faith thus made explicit what was already implicit in Jesus' actions and words.

The first major study of the historical Jesus emanating from the Bultmann circle was Günther Bornkamm's *Jesus of Nazareth*. Bornkamm recognizes the difficulty of penetrating the Gospel traditions to discover something of the historical Jesus. "We possess no single word of Jesus and no single story of Jesus, no matter how incontestably genuine they may be, which do not contain at the same time the confession of the believing congregation or at least are embedded therein. This makes the search after the bare facts of history difficult and to a large extent futile" (14).

In spite of this interblending of the church's faith in the narration of Jesus' history, Bornkamm argues that two apparently conflicting characteristics are to be seen in the Gospels: "an incontestable loyalty and adherence to the word of Jesus, and at the same time an astonishing degree of freedom as to the original wording" (17). The degree of freedom exercised by the Gospel writers is evident in their "believing interpretation of the history and person of Jesus." The words of Jesus "spoken while he was here on earth . . . soon took on a post-Easter form." In addition, "words spoken by the Risen Christ" originally "declared to the Church by her inspired prophets and preachers" have been read back into the tradition and "became words of the earthly Jesus" (19). The task of the interpreter is "to seek the history *in* the Kerygma of the Gospels, and in this history to seek the Kerygma" (21). In spite of the formation of the traditions in the light of the post-Easter faith, the Gospels show an interest in the pre-Easter Jesus for the church "made herself contemporary with her earthly pre-Easter Lord. . . . She made herself one with those who did not already live by faith, but who at the beginning were called to obedience and faith by the word of Jesus" (23-24). In telling the story of Jesus in brief anecdotes, the church gave expression to the person and history of Jesus in each unit. Understood as expressive of the person and history of Jesus, the "primitive tradition of Jesus is brim full of history" (26).

Bornkamm can proceed to speak of the "historically indisputable traits" and the "rough outlines of Jesus' person and history" (53). The birth narratives cannot be used as the basis for historical assertions. Jesus' home was semipagan, despised Galilee. His native town was Nazareth. His family belonged to the Jewish part of the population of Galilee. Jesus' father was a carpenter, and possibly he was himself. We know the names of his parents and his brothers who were not originally believers. Jesus' mother tongue was Aramaic. As a Jewish rabbi, Jesus was certainly acquainted with

Hebrew, and he and his disciples may have had some knowledge of Greek. His baptism by John the Baptist is "one of the most certainly verified occurrences of his life." Jesus began his work in Galilee, like John, as a prophet of the coming kingdom of God, but unlike John did not practice baptism but relied on "spoken word and helping hand." There is no certainty about the length of his ministry. People flocked to him; disciples followed him; and enemies arose to oppose him. The last decisive turning point in his life was the "resolution to go to Jerusalem with his disciples in order to confront the people there with his message in face of the coming kingdom of God. At the end of this road is his death on the cross." Bornkamm recognized the meager character of this outline but suggested that "it contains most important information about the life story of Jesus and its stages" (53-55).

Bornkamm considers Jesus' activity and preaching under the rubrics "rabbi" and "prophet." Jesus however superceded the normal category of prophet since he "never speaks of his calling, and nowhere does he use the ancient, prophetic formula" (Thus says the Lord) (56). Jesus was also a rabbi "who proclaims the divine law, who teaches in synagogues, who gathers disciples, and who debates with other scribes in the manner of their profession and under the same authority of scripture" (57). But Jesus differed from the ordinary rabbi in that he taught not just in synagogues, had followers who differed from ordinary rabbinic disciples, and taught with an immediacy and authority to which nothing in contemporary Judaism corresponds. Jesus' directness and authority were part of the mystery of his personality and influence, the mystery of making present the reality of God which signifies the end of the world in which it takes place.

Was Jesus the messiah, and did he so understand himself? In confronting this issue, Bornkamm says "Jesus does not directly make this claim, but lets it be absorbed in his words and works without justifying either in virtue of some office well known to his hearers, and without confirming the authority which the people are willing to acknowledge in him" (170). "There is in fact not one single certain proof of Jesus' claiming for himself one of the Messianic titles which tradition has ascribed to him." "We should, therefore not speak about Jesus' non-Messianic history before his death, but rather of a movement of broken Messianic hopes, and of one who was hoped to be the Messiah, but who not only at the moment of failure, but in his entire message and ministry, disappointed the hopes that were placed in him" (172). Bornkamm claims "that the Messianic character of his being is contained *in* his words and deeds and *in* the unmediatedness of his historic appearance." "The secret of his being could only reveal itself to his disciples in his resurrection" (178). With regard to whether Jesus understood himself as the Son of man, Bornkamm writes: "Although the historical Jesus spoke most definitely of the coming Son of man and judge of the world in the sense of the contemporary apocalyptic hope, and did so with the amazing certainty that the decisions made here with regard to his person and message would be confirmed at the last judgment, nevertheless he did not give himself the title Son of man. Also we can hardly assume that the earthly Jesus saw himself as destined to be the heavenly judge of the world" (177).

Jesus' basic preaching centered on the kingdom of God. The proclamation of the kingdom announced that God will reign—a message which Jesus preached with authority. Was this kingdom conceived of as present or future? "For Jesus calls: the shift in the aeons is here, the kingdom of God is already dawning." "It is happening now in Jesus' words and deeds" (67). "God's victory over Satan takes place in his words and deeds, and it is in them that the signs of this victory are erected" (68). Jesus proclaimed a call to repentance "to lay hold on the salvation which is already at hand, and to give up everything for it" (82). This preaching of the kingdom and the call to repentance manifest Jesus' prophetic function.

As a rabbi, Jesus taught the will of God. In his teaching, Jesus assumed an attitude of freedom over against the law.

"For Jesus, . . . the will of God is present in such immediate fashion that the letter of the law may be gauged by it" (100). The will of God, as preached by Jesus, demanded "obedience right in the heart of the actual deed itself" (106) that is, concrete obedience. His commandment to love "puts the other person in the centre" (112).

Jesus' disciples must be distinguished as a more intimate group from his followers in the wider sense. Bornkamm accepts the historicity of the twelve disciples who were "scarcely the creation of the post-Easter Church" (150).

For Bornkamm, the turning-point in Jesus' life was the decision to go to Jerusalem. For Bornkamm, the purpose of this decision is clear.

The reason why Jesus sets out with his disciples on his journey to Jerusalem cannot be doubted. It was to deliver the message of the coming kingdom of God in Jerusalem also, Jerusalem which Jesus himself calls the city of God, "the city of the Great King" (Mt. v. 35). As for every Jew, Jerusalem is also for Jesus not only the capital, but also the place which is in a special way connected with Israel's destiny. . . . The sources do not tell us clearly at what moment his readiness to accept death—a readiness which Jesus, as we know, demanded from his disciples too—turned into the certainty of his imminent end. We may, however, assume that first and foremost his journey to Jerusalem was undertaken in order to confront the people there, in the holy city, with the message of the kingdom of God, and to summon them at the eleventh hour to make their decision (154-55).

Jesus' last supper took place near the time of the Passover festival, but, according to Bornkamm, it is doubtful that this supper was itself held as a Passover meal. Many of the elements which made up the Passover celebration ritual are missing from the accounts, and Paul no where associates the Lord's Supper and Passover. The association of the two goes back to the early Christians and the first three Gospel writers (162).

The fixed point concerning Jesus' trial is the fact that he was put to death by the Romans and crucified, an act which was the exclusive right of the Roman court and by a form of death which was instituted for political crimes. Pilate's portrayal as an involuntary instrument of the public may reflect authentic tradition. "It is most probably authentic and not the invention of later poetic imagination that Pilate tried to extricate himself by offering to pardon Jesus, but that the incited people insisted upon the liberation of the Zealot Barabbas instead of Jesus—Barabbas who was rightly sentenced for the crime of which Jesus was wrongly accused" (164).

Speaking of the resurrection, Bornkamm says "there would be no gospel, not one account, no letter in the New Testament, no faith, no church, no worship, no prayer in Christendom to this day without the message of the resurrection of Christ" (181). "The miracle of the resurrection does not have a satisfactory explanation in the inner nature of the disciples, nor . . . does it have an analogy in the eternal dying and rebirth in nature" (185). "According to the interpretation of the early church, Easter is above all else God's acknowledgement of this Jesus, whom the world refused to acknowledge, and to whom even his disciples were unfaithful. It is at the same time the intervention of God's new world in this old world branded with sin and death, the setting up and beginning of his kingdom" (184). However, "the event of Christ's resurrection from the dead, his life and his eternal reign, are things removed from historical scholarship. History cannot ascertain and establish conclusively the facts about them as it can with certain other events of the past. The last historical fact available to them is the Easter faith of the first disciples" (180).

7. JESUS: THE MESSIANIC SUFFERING SERVANT

The historian is dealing in the end with an historical figure fully conscious of a task which had to be done, and fully conscious also that the only future which mattered for men and women depended upon the completion of his task. The future order, which it was the purpose of Jesus to bring into being, depended upon what he said and did, and finally upon his death. This conscious purpose gave a clear unity to his words and actions, so that the actions interpret the words and the words the actions.

Jesus acted as he did act and said what he did say because he was consciously fulfilling a necessity imposed upon him by God through the demands of the Old Testament. He died in Jerusalem, not because the Jews hounded him thither and did him to death, but because he was persuaded that, as messiah, he must journey to Jerusalem in order to be rejected and to die. —Edwyn Hoskyns and Francis Noel Davey, *The Riddle of the New Testament* (pp. 172, 115)

In this chapter, we shall examine the dominate description of the historical Jesus as he has been depicted in what may be called the mainstream of British and American scholarship from the 1930s until the 1960s. Among the many scholars who would fit within this mainstream are T. W. Manson, William Manson, C. H. Dodd, Vincent Taylor, A. M. Hunter, W. D. Davies, and J. W. Bowman. In German academic circles, Joachim Jeremias and Oscar Cullmann and to a lesser degree W. G. Kümmel and Eduard Schweizer are counterparts to this strand in English language scholarship.

A number of characteristics are held in common by most of the above named scholars. First of all, these scholars make a rather reserved use of form criticism especially with regards to the conclusions to be drawn about the importance of the church in the formation and transmission of the traditions. In much German New Testament study, deductions drawn from the results of form critical studies have frequently produced radical doubts about the historicity, chronology, and order of many of the Gospel traditions. In English scholarship, this has seldom been the case. If one compares Rudolf Bultmann's *History of the Synoptic Tradition* with Vincent Taylor's *The Formation of the Gospel Tradition,* this difference in perspective and in the conclusions drawn becomes immediately obvious. In the preface to his work, Taylor has written: "If in the hands of Professor Bultmann Form-Criticism has taken a skeptical direction, this is not the necessary trend of the method; on the contrary, where its limitations are recognized, Form-Criticism seems to me to furnish constructive suggestions which in many ways confirm the historical trustworthiness of the Gospel tradition" (vi). This more cautious assessment of form criticism is admirably reflected in the following statements by T. W. Manson.

After thirty years it is possible at least to attempt a rough appraisal of Form-Criticism; and it may perhaps be suggested that it has by now done about all that it could do, and more than it ought. Strictly speaking the term "form-criticism" should be reserved for the study of the various units of narrative and teaching, which go to make up the Gospels, in respect of their form, and that alone. It is concerned with the structure of these units; and it is certainly interesting to learn that there are a number of anecdotes in Mark, Matthew, and Luke, in which a brief statement of time and place leads up to a short conversation between Jesus and someone else, which is terminated by a dogmatic pronouncement from our Lord. It is interesting but not epoch-making. So far as structure goes, similar stories can be found in Boswell's *Life of Samuel Johnson* and elsewhere. We can list these stories in the Gospels. We can label them, and other units, when we are agreed about the terminology of the science. But a paragraph of Mark is not a penny the better or the worse as historical evidence for being labelled "apophthegm" or "pronouncement story" or "paradigm." In fact if Form-Criticism had been confined to this descriptive activity, it would probably have made little stir. We should have taken it as we take the forms of Hebrew poetry or the forms of musical composition. But Form-Criticism got mixed up with . . . the *doctrine* of the *Sitz im Leben.* . . .

The *Sitz im Leben* introduces a new set of considerations, which again have little or nothing to do with Form-Criticism in the strict sense of the word. It is undoubtedly a good thing that the Gospels should be studied in the context—so far as we can know it—of the interests, problems, and practical needs of the people who first used them. No doubt the stories and sayings were useful to missionary preachers of the first century. No doubt they gave guidance to the early communities on questions of faith and conduct. But we shall be travelling much too far and far too fast if we infer from that that they were created by the community to serve these ends or to meet these needs. In most cases it is equally possible, and a good deal more likely, that the tasks, problems, and needs of the first-century Church affected the selection, and in some cases the interpretation, of what went into the Gospels out of a much larger mass of available material. But even that may not be the whole truth of the matter. It is at least conceivable that one of the chief motives for preserving the stories at all, and for selecting those that were embodied in the Gospels, was just plain admiration and love for their hero. It is conceivable that he was no less interesting, *for his own sake,* to people in the first century than he is to historians in the twentieth ("The Life of Jesus," 212-14).

A second characteristic of this approach is its high regard for the transmission process through which the traditions of Jesus were passed on in the church. The stress falls on the reliability of the transmission process rather than the creativity of the church in using the materials to meet new life situations. The function of the church was the preservation not the creation of tradition. This approach argues that the intention in the collection and transmission of the tradition was always to hand on what Jesus himself taught, and to bring this home to the hearers or readers. Dodd has written the following about the Synoptic Gospels and their reflection of the "corporate memory" which handed down the traditions:

When all allowance has been made for . . . limiting factors—the chances of oral transmission, the effect of translation, the interest of teachers in making the sayings "contemporary," and simple human fallibility—it remains that the first three gospels offer a body of sayings on the whole so consistent, so coherent, and withal so distinctive in manner, style content, that no reasonable critic should doubt, whatever reservations he may have about individual sayings, that we find reflected here the thought of a single, unique teacher (*The Founder of Christianity,* 21-22).

The question, how far this or that story may be taken as an accurate account of what happened on this or that occasion is one upon which judgments will vary. Some, as they stand, may be found more credible than others. One or the other may be felt to be not in character. But taken together, these stories, told from many different points of view, converge to give a distinct impression of a real person in action upon a recognizable scene (36).

A third interest evidenced in this approach is reflected in the stress laid on the historical references contained in the kerygma. The biblical materials are recognized as serving a preaching or kerygmatic concern but within this concern lies a devotion to the facts of the historical Jesus. C. H. Dodd stressed, in his influential study *The Apostolic Preaching and its Developments,* that there was an "immense range of variety in the interpretation that is given to the *kerygma*" but argued "that in all such interpretation the essential elements of the original *kerygma* are steadily kept in view" (74). The implications of the consistency of the kergymatic portrayal of Jesus have been drawn by T. W. Manson.

The nerve of the argument is that when we examine the early Christian convictions, which may be supposed to have shaped or even created the story of Jesus, we find a single and consistent story of Jesus in brief. We have abstracts of the propaganda speeches of the earliest Christians in Acts; and when we compare these with similar passages in the Pauline Epistles, we find a singular unanimity. It is natural to infer that such close agreement between men as different as Peter and Paul is the result neither of accident nor of design; that their claims for Jesus Christ tally because they are founded on facts. Whatever may be said about this or that detail in the Gospels, there was a total impression made by Jesus on those who came nearest to him and knew him best; and it is that total impression that is embodied in the *kerygma* ("The Life of Jesus," 215-16).

A fourth characteristic of this approach is a great respect for the Marcan outline and order of the life of Jesus. Although

Wrede, Schmidt, and German form critics in general were suspicious of the order and structure of the Gospel of Mark, this suspicion has not been characteristic of British scholarship. Dodd wrote of Mark that "he appears to have reproduced what came down to him with comparatively little attempt to write it up in his own way. . . . In Mark, within a very broad general scheme, there is a certain freedom and looseness of arrangement, and in his rather rough and informal style we seem often to overhear the tones of the living voice telling a story. We are probably near to the 'original eyewitnesses and servants of the gospel' " (*The Founder of Christianity*, 24). T. W. Manson is more emphatic about the value of the Gospel of Mark even when only speaking of the teachings of Jesus which are very slim in the Gospel. "We have in Mark only an outline and we have to apply to the other sources for fuller information at almost every point. But—and this is the crux of the matter—it is an outline which we can trust: and if we wish to frame a comprehensive picture of the teaching as a whole, as it developed during the course of the ministry, it is this Marcan outline which we must make the foundation" (*The Teaching of Jesus*, 26-27).

An emphasis on the realized aspects of eschatology as opposed to a futuristic interpretation has been a fifth characteristic. Dodd was the prime and most significant spokesman for "realized eschatology."

From . . . many . . . passages it is surely clear that, for the New Testament writers in general, the *eschaton* has entered history; the hidden rule of God has been revealed; the Age to Come has come. The Gospel of primitive Christianity is a Gospel of realized eschatology (*The Apostolic Preaching*, 85).

While, however, the New Testament affirms with full seriousness that the great divine event has happened, there remains a residue of eschatology which is not exhausted in the "realized eschatology" of the Gospel, namely, the element of sheer finality. . . . Thus the idea of a second coming of Christ appears along with the emphatic assertion that His coming in history satisfies all the conditions of the eschatological event, *except* that of absolute finality (93).

This school of interpreters claims that the stress on the realized character of the kingdom represents not only the interpretation of the early church—it goes back in origin to Jesus who saw in his own life and work the coming of the kingdom.

A final characteristic of this group of scholars is their willingness to utilize the Gospel of John as a source for the historical Jesus. Such a use of the Gospel nowhere approaches the utilization made of it by such scholars as David Smith and Ethelbert Stauffer. Much of Dodd's research during his last years focused on the Fourth Gospel and the traditions lying behind it. In commenting on the usage of the Fourth Gospel in discussing the historical Jesus, Dodd has written:

The "set pieces" of the Fourth Gospel, composed with great art, are comparable with the Greek philosophical dialogue. Yet dispersed among these elaborate literary compositions, or even embedded in them, there are sayings which stand out because they have the familiar ring. Some indeed are recognizably identical with sayings reported in the other gospels, though the wording may differ because the writer has his own linguistic habits, and sometimes he gives what seems to be a different translation of the same Aramaic original. In addition, on a closer examination of the dialogues and discourses it often turns out that the writer is only spelling out, in his own idiom of thought, what is already implicit in sayings reported in the other gospels. All this encourages the belief that the writer drew from the same general reservoir of tradition. That reservoir, we may be sure, contained more than has come through in our written gospels. There are sayings of Jesus recorded only in the Fourth Gospel which seem to bring into relief aspects of his teachings slenderly represented, if at all, in the others, and these may be of importance to complete the picture. It would be unwise to neglect them, though to make use of them in a strictly historical investigation calls for some critical tact *(The Founder of Christianity*, 22-23).

The two representative examples of an interpretation of Jesus as the messianic suffering servant which we will now examine are by T. W. Manson and John W. Bowman. At points, these scholars' arguments will be augmented by statements of others who share a similar perspective.

Integral to this presentation of Jesus is the fundamental conviction that Jesus understood himself as the Jewish messiah, but that he understood his role and function in this capacity in terms radically different from those of contemporary Judaism.

The typical Jewish belief in the messiah centered on a victorious political leader who would serve as the agent for the fulfilment of God's plan and the establishment of God's kingdom. Jesus' ministry did not conform to this widely expected pattern. Nonetheless, Jesus was the messiah who in a creative fashion understood his role by interpreting and combining several concepts borrowed from the Old Testament. This creative interpretation which understood and redefined messiahship in terms of a suffering and dying messiah was the characteristic interpretation of the early church, but it had its origin in the depths of Jesus' own spirit. The pattern of Jesus' life is to be understood, at least partially, as his refusal to fit the pattern of the typical Jewish messianic expectations.

The central violent contradiction between the primitive Christian *kerygma* and the Jewish Messianic hope is that which sets the crucified Messiah of Christian experience over against the triumphant hero of Jewish fancy. Now it is easy to see that the notion of a crucified Messiah is a stumbling-block to the Jews (I Cor. i. 23): to complete the picture we have also to realise that the Jewish hope of a successful Messiah was equally a stumbling-block to Jesus. It is from this point of view of the fundamental contradiction between the Jewish Messianic hope and Jesus' convictions concerning his own Ministry that the Gospel story becomes, in its main lines, an intelligible piece of history (T. W. Manson, *The Servant-Messiah*, 36). . . .

The whole Ministry—the teaching of Jesus, his acts, and finally the Cross, are a standing denial of the current beliefs and hopes (50).

Jesus' understanding of his life and ministry seems to have bypassed the typical Jewish concepts of his day and to have been based on a fresh understanding of the Old Testament prophets. "Jesus simply bypassed all contemporary Jewish groups, going back to the prophetic Scriptures for what stimulus he required, and . . . set before himself a reconstructed image of Messiahship, one of a highly spiritual and moral type, universalistic and so nonracial in character" (Bowman, *Which Jesus?*, 144).

The dominant pattern in Jesus' understanding of his ministry resulted from his combination of the messianic office with that of the figure of the suffering servant depicted in several passages in the book of Isaiah. In these passages, the servant is described as "one who has been given and has accepted a calling from God, and devoted himself body and soul to his service, bearing witness to the truth of God, enduring many sufferings, and in the end laying down his life for the sake of others" (Dodd, *The Founder of Christianity*, 103-4). It was Jesus and he alone, so it is argued, who was responsible for the creative fusion of these two concepts which had prior to his time remained separate and isolated.

The traditions of the baptism of Jesus give expression to this view of messiahship which it became Jesus' intention to fulfil.

The evangelists are united in their testimony that from this moment [his baptism] the Holy Spirit of prophecy came upon Jesus in a unique way and that that Spirit remained with him to direct and teach throughout his ministry. Moreover, the voice of his Father spoke to him saying, "Thou art my Son, the Beloved one; with Thee I am well pleased." It is probable, as Mk implies, that none but Jesus heard the voice speaking to him out of heaven. For it is characteristic of the voices of scripture that they are heard only by those prepared to receive them (cf. Jn 12:27-30; Ac. 22:7-9). And yet this voice, though spoken only to Jesus himself, is clearly indicated as being an objective one; it is the voice of the eternal Father speaking to his eternal Son. It quotes, moreover, from two passages of scripture—Ps. 2:7 and Isa. 42:1. The former of these is from a coronation psalm, wherein is narrated the coronation of the reigning messiah by the Lord God himself. In the psalm the words "Thou art my Son" form the first part of the coronation formula which serves to constitute the reigning king of Israel or Judah as the Lord's current viceroy. Equally, in the latter quotation is to be found the ordination formula of the Suffering Servant of Yahweh pronounced by the Lord himself. As used of Jesus, accordingly, these combined formulae serve at once to declare him Messiah and Suffering Servant of the Lord (Bowman, "The Life and Teaching of Jesus," 734-35).

The temptations of Jesus are to be understood as Jesus' repudiation of various other forms which his messiahship might have taken. T. W. Manson has written "that what Jesus rejects in the Temptations are methods of 'bringing in' the kingdom of God: (a) the economic . . .; (b) the game of political intrigue backed by military force; (c) propaganda which would eventually create an artificial nimbus for the national leader. All three were familiar phenomena in the life of the time" (*The Servant-Messiah*, 56-57). In other words, if the baptism "may be regarded as the announcement of God's choice and appointment of Jesus as Messiah, the [temptations] may equally be regarded as our Lord's deliberate choice of God as the sole object of his loyalty, trust and obedience, that is, as his King. In all his work the Father is to be the paramount chief and the paramount interest: everything that he does is to be done for God, with God, and under God. He is to be in the most complete sense the Servant of the Lord, the perfect subject of a perfect King" (*The Teaching of Jesus*, 197).

This unique understanding of his ministry in terms of a suffering-servant messiah meant that Jesus' ministry was to possess a certain character—a character which did not overtly encounter his audience with a claim to messiahship. Thus there was, in a certain sense, a messianic secret which goes back to the historical life of Jesus.

Jesus at no time would have been found "in character" had he stepped out into the marketplace or the Temple and shouted out: "Look at me! I am the Messiah, the Son of Man, the Suffering Servant," or any like title for himself. Rather, by word and deed, everything he ever said and did simply added up to what these words may mean. Of this he was always cognizant; so as he went about as Mediator of the Kingdom of God to men, he did not have to be continually stating his case; he had merely to go on *being* these things, thereby challenging all his contemporaries in one way or another to *see* them for themselves and to make the *believing response* they were calculated to inspire (Bowman, *Which Jesus?*, 139-40).

The miracles or mighty works of Jesus were an integral part of his public ministry. They were the means by which he carried out the implications of his preaching "in the form of philanthropic work calculated to ameliorate man's distresses at every level of his life" (Bowman, "The Life and Teaching of Jesus," 737). Jesus' miracles were not performed to startle his audience or to produce wonder and awe in his power.

It is true that Jesus would perform no *sign* of an unmistakably supernatural kind such as his enemies constantly demanded of him (Mk 8:11f.) To have complied with such a request would have been quite out of character on the part of Jesus who by all accounts never set out merely to prove anything about his person or mission. It was characteristic of him rather that he looked for that spiritual insight in men with which they could very well pass their own judgments (737).

The mighty works of Jesus were therefore not performed primarily to produce faith, they were basically the natural expression of his person. They were performed for humanitarian reasons to meet the temporal needs of man. "In a very real sense, therefore, Jesus' miracles were 'memorial signs' for those who possessed the spiritual insight to discern in them the sovereignty of God at work in the midst of his people; they were, so to speak, 'acted parables,' demonstrating the presence of the kingdom of God as having arrived in and through Jesus." Some of the so-called nature miracles are to be understood, as they now appear in the text, as the result of a mistranslation of some Greek idiom (walking on the seashore not the sea), as miracles of divine providence (the stilling of the storm), or as acted parables (the feeding of the multitudes) (737).

In his ministry of words—teaching and preaching—"Jesus assumes the role of the Gospel Herald who declares that the epoch referred to in the writing of the prophet [Isaiah] has now arrived; Jesus' contemporaries stand upon the very threshold of the Kingdom's inauguration" (Bowman, "The Life and Teaching of Jesus," 739). Thus Jesus' words and works supplemented each other and pointed to the nearness and arrival of the kingdom. Jesus' message of the kingdom was eschatologically oriented. The word "kingdom" is an abstract word meaning sovereignty or lordship. In the preaching of Jesus, references to the kingdom of God as near at hand meant "for Jesus that God's lordship is about to be realised in some sense in human experience."

Before Peter's confession at Caesarea Philippi, Jesus spoke of the Kingdom of God as *something that was about to come* and . . . after the confession his message was "The Kingdom has now come. Come in." . . . Accordingly, the Kingdom will have come, in Jesus' meaning of the term, with the confession of Peter. For to acknowledge God's Messiah (his viceroy) will be the same as to acknowledge God's lordship itself. When a man does this, then the Kingdom has come in his experience. . . . The Kingdom was, therefore, in the teaching of Jesus, in the first instance an individual experience of God's lordship over the life of the disciple who acknowledged the same. But there can be no doubt that Jesus also had in view a group, the prophetic remnant composed of his little band of disciples, in whose corporate experience of fellowship with one another and with Jesus as their Lord and Master the Kingdom was realised. . . . Finally, Jesus also no doubt looked forward to the final consummation of the Kingdom of God at the end of history and on more than one occasion expressed himself after this fashion (Mk 8:38, 13, 14:62) (739).

Thus the kingdom of God was proclaimed in the preaching of Jesus as God's lordship, as near at hand, as realized in a man or group's submission to this lordship, and as something to be consummated at the end of history.

The call of an intimate circle of followers was an important and deliberate activity of Jesus.

His aim was to constitute a community worthy of the name of a people of God, a divine commonwealth, through individual response to God coming in his kingdom. ... Those who accept his kingdom "like a child" enter in, and so by act of God himself, which is especially exhibited in the forgiveness of sins, his people is formed within the old Israel, ready to emerge in due time (Dodd, *The Founder of Christianity*, 90-91).

For Bowman, Jesus' call of twelve disciples is a special, symbolic, and actual move to create a new Israel, a new people of God. Behind such action lies the biblical concept of a faithful group—a remnant—within the community as a whole, which was loyal and submissive to God. In Jesus' function as the suffering-servant messiah, he embodied within himself the true remnant. With the selection of twelve, Jesus began to build up a new assembly of God's people, starting from the Twelve as a remnant to form the new people of God, what in later times was termed the church. Bowman argues however that the decisive move of Jesus to create a new remnant only occurred after Jesus was rejected by his own people when he preached in the synagogue in Nazareth (Luke 4:16-30). "Jesus' appointment of the Twelve is somehow to be related to his rejection from the assembly of his people." After this event, "Jesus never again darkens the door of a synagogue" (*Which Jesus?*, 146). *"It would seem that Jesus considered the Nazareth incident as a definite symbol of his 'extirpation' from the congregation of the Old Israel."*

Taken together, these data seem to tell us that as Jesus was in the course of being ejected from among the people of God, he was at the same time taking steps to raise up a new Israel—a "remnant" of the old. The old congregation had condemned itself in judging its Messiah as unworthy to have a place within its ranks. So he turned to the task of gathering a new and worthier congregation about his own person as its center and obvious leader (Bowman, *The Intention of Jesus*, 217).

In preparing the disciples as the remnant of a new people of God, Jesus gave special instruction and training to the twelve. Thus the emphasis in the Gospels on Jesus' special private instruction to his disciples reflects a true historical element in the ministry of Jesus. "The culmination of this period of activity comes as Jesus turns his feet toward Caesarea Philippi at the foot of Mount Hermon with a view to a quiet time of retreat with his disciples away from the multitudes" (Bowman, "The Life and Teaching of Jesus, 740). This withdrawal of Jesus from the crowds and the subsequent events at Caesarea Philippi mark the watershed of the ministry of Jesus dividing it into two distinct phases. At Caesarea, Peter acknowledged Jesus as the messiah, and Jesus' instruction of his disciples became more serious and pointed.

It is here that we have the great turning point in the Ministry marked by Peter's recognition of Jesus as the expected Messiah. And here the clash between the two messianic ideals is manifest. What does Peter mean when he says, "You are the Messiah?" And how does Jesus receive the statement? Mark's answer to the latter question is that Jesus forbade the disciples to speak to anyone about himself. The context requires us to add the words "as Messiah." As for the former question the answer is given almost immediately in Mark, when Peter indignantly repudiates the idea that the messianic destiny can be anything but glory and success. Jesus is equally uncompromising in maintaining that the task of the Son of Man is of another kind and that its glory and success will be very different from the gaudy triumphs on which the hearts of Peter and the other disciples are set. With that the calling of the disciples begins all over again. The terms of discipleship are made terribly plain: he who swears fealty to me makes his compact with scorn and derision, defeat and death. From this point onwards three themes are closely linked in Mark's narrative: the relentless claims of Jesus on his disciples, the stubborn hopes and ambitions of the disciples themselves, and the repeated predictions of the Passion of the Son of Man (Manson, *The Servant-Messiah*, 71-72).

In the Caesarea episode, Jesus is said to have told the disciples that the Son of man must suffer many things, be rejected by the elders, chief priests, and scribes, be killed, and after three days rise again (Mark 8:31). The third important title—in addition to messiah and suffering servant—here enters the picture. How does this particular strand of interpretation understand the term "Son of man" and Jesus' employment of that title in his self-understanding?

T. W. Manson has written the following concerning the interpretation of the title Son of man in the Gospels:

"Son of Man" in the Gospels is the final term in a series of conceptions, all of which are found in the Old Testament. These are: the Remnant (Isaiah), the Servant of Jehovah [Yahweh] (II Isaiah), the "I" of the Psalms, and the Son of Man (Daniel). . . . It is the idea of the Remnant which is the essential feature about each of these: . . . Son of Man in the Gospels is another embodiment of the Remnant idea. In other words, the Son of Man is, like the Servant of Jehovah, an ideal figure and stands for the manifestation of the Kingdom of God on earth in a people wholly devoted to their heavenly King . . . [Jesus'] mission is to create the Son of Man, the Kingdom of the saints of the Most High, to realise in Israel the ideal contained in the term. This task is attempted in two ways: first by public appeal to the people through the medium of parable and sermon and by the mission of the disciples: then, when this appeal produced no adequate response, by the consolidation of his own band of followers. Finally, when it becomes apparent that not even the disciples are ready to rise to the demands of the ideal, he stands alone, embodying in his own person the perfect human response to the regal claims of God (*The Teaching of Jesus*, 227-28).

Thus the Son of man title reflects, according to Manson, a collective or corporate meaning which refers to the obedient saints of God—the true remnant—and an individual meaning, the ideal obedient Israelite which Jesus used in understanding himself and his ministry.

Sometime shortly after the Caesarea Philippi episode, Jesus left Galilee for the south and ultimately Jerusalem. Why did Jesus go up to Jerusalem? In discussing this issue, Manson has written:

The question has often enough been asked already, and we have a good many answers to choose from. The older lives of Jesus, written from the standpoint of dogmatic orthodoxy, were ready with an answer in terms of orthodox dogmatics [that is, Jesus went up to die]. More rationalising studies tended to make the death of Jesus a regrettable incident like the death of Socrates. Jesus goes up to Jerusalem to give a course of lecture-sermons on the Fatherhood of God and the Brotherhood of Man, and then becomes the victim of an unfortunate miscarriage of justice. Thoroughgoing eschatology tends to make the Cross an unsuccessful gamble, something like what happens when a chess-player sacrifices his queen in the hope of forcing a mate, and it does not come off (*The Servant-Messiah*, 75-76).

We must ask, not, Why did Jesus go up to Jerusalem?, but rather, Is "going up to Jerusalem" an adequate description of what Jesus did when he left Galilee for the last time? I venture to think that it is not. No doubt Jerusalem is the ultimate goal of the journey; but I think it would be more in keeping with what we know about the mind of Jesus, and also truer to the facts, to say that Jesus left Galilee to continue in the south, that is in Judaea and Peraea, the same kind of Ministry that he had begun in the north (77).

Jesus' Jerusalem ministry was carried out, according to Bowman, with a spirit of assurance and with Jesus totally in command of the situation.

This spirit of assurance never leaves him to the end. Everything happens as he wills that it shall happen and at the time which he has determined for it. And yet, throughout all this confident activity, Jesus in act and word exhibits a gracious redemptive purpose. It is with this purpose that he successively challenges the nation and its ruling classes, the city of Jerusalem and its multitudes, to exhibit faith in himself as the moral and spiritual leader whom God has appointed for them. Amid this week's rapidly shifting scenes, one gains the impression that Jesus sees his ministry drawing to a focus. His "hour" has at last arrived. And he will see it through in masterful fashion ("The Life and Teaching of Jesus," 742).

Jesus' assurance of his messiahship and his understanding of the form of that messiahship brought him into the final conflict with Israel and Rome.

Jesus: The Messianic Suffering Servant

Every day it becomes clearer to the Messiah Jesus, if to nobody else, that the kingdom of God does not come, cannot come, by defeating the kingdoms of the world at their own game; that the Messiah is not, and cannot be, the latest, loudest, and most successful of a long line of international gangsters; that Israel is not to be, and rightly understood cannot be, just another and a greater Rome. But neither Israel nor Rome can see that. Jewish hopes and Roman suspicions are concentrated on the same object, an object far removed from the thoughts of Jesus (Manson, *The Servant-Messiah,* 76).

Except for the crucifixion, the two dominating events in Jesus' ministry in Jerusalem are the triumphal entry and the cleansing of the temple. In entering the city, according to well-laid plans, Jesus was "consciously fulfilling the prophecy of Zech. 9:9 with a view to challenging the capital city to see in him God's true Messiah. But neither the city nor Jesus' own disciples discern his purpose and they give him merely the reception accorded to the usual pilgrim band coming up to Jerusalem from the ends of the earth to worship at the feast [of Passover]" (Bowman, "The Life and Teaching of Jesus," 743). Jesus' cleansing of the temple was directed against the trading and selling, in themselves legitimate, which took place in the court of the Gentiles. Jesus' objections to this practice were "(a) that it offended against the principle of universalism at the heart of all true religion, and (b) that the type of control involved was debasing the practices of religion to a materialistic level" (Bowman, "The Life and Teaching of Jesus," 743).

This challenge to the Jewish leaders and the assumption that he made exalted claims for himself eventually led to his arrest and crucifixion. The trial—or preliminary hearing—before the Sanhedrin and the trial before Pilate focused on Jesus as a threat to peace and stability—that is on the issue of his messiahship. Condemned by both, Jesus was crucified.

[Pilate] was not greatly impressed by the case. His private opinion seems to have been that the whole affair arose out of the malice and ill-will of the Jewish authorities, and that he

was being used for their purposes. There his judgement was
sound. He also came to the conclusion, after seeing Jesus
and questioning him, that he was harmless. . . . There was a
case of sorts; and even if Jesus was practically harmless alive,
he would be quite harmless dead. So sentence was passed
and execution followed without delay. By sunset on Friday it
was over; and Jesus, with all the hopes and fears he had
aroused, was buried in the rock tomb.

And most of the people who had been concerned doubtless
went to bed that night with fairly easy consciences. Pilate
had earned another day's salary as Procurator of Judaea; and
his province was quiet and peaceful—at any rate on the
surface. The Temple authorities could feel that they had
made things secure against untimely reforming zeal—for the
time being at least. Patriotic Jews could tell themselves that it
had been a mistake ever to imagine that Jesus was the kind of
leader they were looking for—and in that they were not
mistaken. Devout Jews could reflect that such an end as that
which had overtaken Jesus was hardly to be wondered at,
after the way in which he had flouted the scribes and even
criticised the provisions of the Law itself. We might almost
say that Jesus was crucified with the best intentions; and
that those who sent him to the Cross believed that they were
doing their plain duty by the Empire or the Temple or the
Law or the hope of Israel. Doubtless many, perhaps most, of
them did so believe. . . . In Pilate, Caiaphas, and the rest the
lesser loyalties united against the kingdom of God incarnate
in Jesus the Messiah; and so Jesus went to the Cross—and
made it his everlasting throne (Manson, *The Servant-
Messiah*, 87-88).

But the story does not end here for the disciples
encountered the risen Lord. The stories of the resurrection
appearances and the empty tomb are difficult, if not
impossible to harmonize, but they all point to the essential
truth: *"Christians do not inherit their task from Christ, they
share it with him. We are not the successors of Jesus, but his
companions"* (*The Servant-Messiah*, 98).

8. JESUS: THE POLITICAL REVOLUTIONARY

> The iconolaters have never for a moment conceived Jesus as a real person, who meant what he said, as a fact, as a force like electricity, only needing the invention of suitable political machinery to be applied to the affairs of mankind with revolutionary effect. Thus it is not disbelief that is dangerous in our society; it is belief. The moment it strikes you (as it may any day) that Jesus is not the lifeless, harmless image he has hitherto been to you, but a rallying centre for revolutionary influence, which all established States and Churches fight, you must look to yourselves, for you have brought the image to life, and the mob may not be able to stand that horror. —George Bernard Shaw, *Androcles and the Lion* (preface)

Throughout the course of research on the historical Jesus, the view that Jesus was a revolutionary who sought the overthrow of the Jewish-Roman establishment of his day has been frequently considered and occasionally expounded. Recently the thesis has been proposed anew and has attracted academic and popular concern—both support and repudiation.

Reimarus was the first to propose that Jesus' ministry was a call to political revolt. In discussing Jesus' sending out of the disciples to announce that the kingdom of heaven was at hand Reimarus wrote:

He knew that if the people believed his messengers, they would look for a worldly king, and would attach themselves to him with the conviction that he was this king; because, unless they received further and better instruction, they could have no other conception of the kingdom of heaven or kingdom of God, or of any faith in the same, than that which they had learned according to the popular meaning of the words, and to the prevailing impression of them. . . . But Jesus did not convey to them any better idea of himself. . . .

151

Jesus then must have been well aware that by such a plain announcement of the kingdom of heaven, he would only awaken the Jews to the hope of a worldly Messiah; consequently, this must have been his object in so awakening them. . . . In sending such missionaries, he could have had no other object than to rouse the Jews in all parts of Judea, who had so long been groaning under the Roman yoke, and so long been preparing for the hoped-for deliverance, and to induce them to flock to Jerusalem.

With this intention the rest of the acts agree. ("Concerning the Intention of Jesus and His Teaching," 136-38).

Jesus and John the Baptist had actually arranged the course of their ministry and their preaching toward the end of political revolt: "Neither John nor Jesus could have had any other object than that of awakening the people to a speedy arrival of the long-hoped-for deliverer, and of making them eager for his coming" (141). When the Jews sought to make Jesus king, "Jesus slipped away from them and escaped to a mountain. It is remarkable that he did not seize this opportunity of reproving the people, of assuring them that they were mistaken, and that he had come for a very different purpose. This would have been most necessary if Jesus really had had another object in view, and wished the people to think so" (142). Jesus refused on that occasion to be made king, not because he opposed the idea but because the setting and timing were not correct.

It was not his intention to allow himself to be made a king in a desert place, and by a common rabble, such as then surrounded him. Neither the time nor the place suited him. His thoughts were bent upon a grand entry into the city of Jerusalem, at the Passover, a time when all Israelites throughout Judea would be assembled there, and when it would be conducted in a festive manner, and when, by the united voices of the populace he would be proclaimed King of the Jews (142-43).

Jesus chose his hour, laid his plans, and rode into Jerusalem on an ass to appear as the king spoken of in Zechariah 9:9. The crowds welcomed him enthusiastically, and the town was thrown into a state of excitement. "This extraordinary public procession, which was not only tolerated by Jesus, but had been diligently encouraged by him, could not have been aimed at anything but a worldly kingdom. He wished that all the people of Israel who were there gathered together should unanimously proclaim him king" (146). Jesus failed to receive the support of the nation; only the common rabble accepted him. His scheme crumbled and Jesus lost courage.

He ordered some swords to be procured to defend himself with in case of attack, but was uneasy, lest even one of his own disciples should divulge his place of retreat. He began to quiver and quake when he saw that his adventure might cost him his life. Judas betrayed his hiding-place, and pointed out his person. . . . He ended his life with the words, *"Eli Eli, lama sabachthani? My God, my God, why hast thou forsaken me?"* [Matt 27:46]—a confession which can hardly be otherwise interpreted than that God had not helped him to carry out his intention and attain his object as he had hoped he would have done. It was then clearly not the intention or the object of Jesus to suffer and to die, but to build up a worldly kingdom, and to deliver the Israelites from bondage. It was in this that God had forsaken him, it was in this that his hopes had been frustrated (150).

This possible political-revolutionary factor in the career of Jesus has been stressed by a wide spectrum of scholars. Julius Wellhausen has written that Jesus sought to free his people "from the yoke of hierocracy and nomocracy. For this purpose he perhaps did not act merely as a teacher but also as an agitator, and inwardly laid claim for himself to messianic authority to rule, or at least give the appearance of doing so. During the cleansing of the temple he did not hesitate to use violence; his disciples had weapons and tried to fight when they were taken by surprise" (*Einleitung in die drei ersten Evangelien*, 83). The idea of Jesus as a social revolutionist was especially attractive to socialist interpreters of Jesus at the turn of the century. The socialist Karl Kautsky wrote in 1908: "The assumption that the execution of Jesus was due to the fact that he was a rebel is ... not only the sole assumption which can make the indications in the Gospel clear, but it is also completely in accordance with the character of the epoch and of the locality" (*Foundations of Christianity,* 369).

The first full treatment of the subject of Jesus as a political revolutionary was the two volume work of Robert Eisler published in 1929–30 with a Greek title which can be translated "Jesus, a King not Reigning." Eisler's theory was founded upon references in ancient Jewish and Christian sources, including the New Testament, and upon some materials found in the Slavonic, or Old Russian, version of the history of the Jewish war written by Josephus. The passage in Josephus which contributed greatly to Eisler's theory contains the following account of a wonder-worker whom scholars almost unanimously see as Jesus although most do not consider the text to be from Josephus.

At that time there appeared a man, if it is permissible to call him a man. His nature and form were human, but his appearance was something more than that of a man; notwithstanding his works were divine. He worked miracles wonderful and mighty. Therefore it is impossible for me to call him a man; but again, if I look at the nature which he shared with all, I will not call him an angel. And everything whatsoever he wrought through an invisible power, he wrought by word and command. Some said of him, "Our first lawgiver is risen from the dead and hath performed many healings and arts," while others thought that he was sent from God. Howbeit in many things he disobeyed the Law and kept not the Sabbath according to our fathers' customs. Yet, on the other hand, he did nothing shameful; nor did he do anything with aid of hands, but by word alone did he provide everything.

And many of the multitude followed after him and harkened to his teaching; and many souls were in commotion, thinking that thereby the Jewish tribes might free themselves from Roman hands. Now it was his custom in general to sojourn over against the city upon the Mount of Olives; and there, too, he bestowed his healings upon the people.

And there assembled unto him of ministers one hundred

and fifty, and a multitude of the people. Now when they saw his power, that he accomplished whatsoever he would by a word, and when they had made known to him their will, that he should enter into the city and cut down the Roman troops and Pilate and rule over us, he disdained us not.

And when thereafter knowledge of it came to the Jewish leaders, they assembled together with the high-priest and spake: "We are powerless and too weak to withstand the Romans. Seeing, moreover, that the bow is bent, we will go and communicate to Pilate what we have heard, and we shall be clear of trouble, lest he hear it from others, and we be robbed of our substance and ourselves slaughtered and our children scattered." And they went and communicated it to Pilate. And he sent and had many of the multitude slain. And he had that Wonder-worker brought up, and after instituting an inquiry concerning him, he pronounced judgment: "He is a benefactor, not a malefactor, nor a rebel, nor covetous of kingship." And he let him go; for he had healed his dying wife.

And he went to his wonted place and did his wonted works. And when more people again assembled round him, he glorified himself through his actions more than all. The teachers of the Law were overcome with envy, and gave thirty talents to Pilate, in order that he should put him to death. And he took it and gave them liberty to execute their will themselves. And they laid hands on him and crucified him contrary to the law of their fathers (*The Jewish War,* between II., 174-75).

Using this passage and certain New Testament references, Eisler argued that Jesus was reluctantly persuaded by his followers to participate in armed insurrection against the Romans. Eisler placed Jesus squarely within the camp of patriotic Jewish resistance to Roman rule in Palestine. In the cleansing-of-the-temple episode, Jesus led an armed revolt against the Romans, seized the temple, was expelled by the Romans, taken captive, and executed for insurrection.

The theory of Eisler was revived in popular form by the American Jewish writer Joel Carmichael in 1962 in a volume entitled *The Death of Jesus.* Carmichael summarizes his presentation of Jesus in the following terms:

Jesus was the Herald of the Kingdom of God, and he tried to take it by storm. In the strangely blurred and mutilated recollections of his career we can dimly discern the outlines of a visionary who was also a man of action and who attempted to set in motion the machinery of God's will.

He was squarely in the tradition of the Jewish religious patriots, tortured by the crushing weight of the Roman Empire, who arose in Palestine and assaulted the Roman power and its vassals.

We see his enterprise frustrated and himself undone; his followers scattered and his movement, doubtless, drowned in blood. He ended like many others in Israel—in agony and death, a prey to the powers of this world (203).

The most recent thorough attempt to portray Jesus as a political revolutionary is the work by S. G. F. Brandon entitled *Jesus and the Zealots: A Study of the Political Factor in Primitive Christianity*. Brandon begins his investigation with the following statement: "Ironic though it be, the most certain thing known about Jesus of Nazareth is that he was crucified by the Romans as a rebel against their government in Judaea" (1). In order to understand and explain this fact and the character of the historical Jesus which it implies, Brandon examines the revolutionary and political relations between the Romans and the Jews during the years between A.D. 6-73, the Zealots and their philosophy which lay behind many of the altercations with Rome, how the death of Jesus came to be explained in a manner that played down its true character and presented him as a pacifist, and the evidence which might suggest that Jesus was a patriotic rebel against Roman authority.

Brandon dates the origin of the Zealot party in Judaism to the revolt led by Judas the Galilean at the time of the census undertaken by the Roman legate in Syria, P. Sulpicius Quirinius, in A.D. 6 when Archelaus, a son of Herod the Great, was deposed and Judaea placed under direct Roman control. This census was the "cause of the first act of rebellion against their heathen masters and the founding of a party, the Zealots, who were destined some sixty years later to lead their people into the fatal war of independence against Rome" (26). Judas the Galilean was the son of a certain Ezekias, a "brigand chief," who had operated in Galilee during the early governorship of Herod over that area. Herod had executed Ezekias and suppressed his followers (about 47 B.C.), an act for which he was summoned before the Sanhedrin for an explanation. Brandon suggests that this need to make an official explanation implied that Ezekias had a great significance for the Jews who had mourned his death. Judas had his first altercation with the Romans during the unrest which followed the death of Herod in 4 B.C. At that time, "Judas broke into the Herodian palace at Sepphoris in Galilee and seized the property and arms stored there. His exploits caused him to be greatly feared; he is also reported to have aspired to royalty." The uprisings at the time, of which that led by Judas was only one among many, were suppressed by Varus, the Roman governor of Syria, and two legions of troops. "The punishment inflicted on the captured rebels was savage: two thousand of them were crucified" (29).

At the time of the census in A.D. 6, according to Josephus, "Judas incited his countrymen to revolt, upbraiding them as cowards for consenting to pay tribute to Rome and tolerating mortal masters, after having God for their Lord" (*The Jewish War,* II, 367). Josephus then points out that Judas founded a sect of his own in association with Saddok, a Pharisee. Of this "philosophical" sect, Josephus wrote: "Its sectaries associated themselves in general with the doctrine of the Pharisees; but they had an invincible love of liberty, for they held God to be their only lord and master. They showed an indifference toward the fortunes of their parents and friends, in their resolve to call no man master" (*Antiquities*, XVIII, 23). Josephus sought to blame such brigand groups for the war against Rome which led to the destruction of Jerusalem. Since Josephus wrote his history of the war "to commemorate the victories of his imperial patrons" (35) and to argue that the revolt did not reflect the true sympathies of the Jewish people, he played down, according to Brandon, the true attitude of the Zealots and the real support they had among the people. In spite of these desires, "client of the Roman Caesars he was, Josephus could not wholly suppress recognition of the religious motives that had inspired Zealotism" (36-37).

Josephus does not use the name Zealot with regard to Judas' movement although he later traces the Sicarii, who got their name from the Roman *sica* used in assassinations, to the followers of Judas. Brandon explains this lack of the term in the following way:

In the light of this evidence, various and fragmentary though it is, the reason for Josephus' apparent embarrassment over the name "Zealot" becomes clear. The name was an honourable one, proudly assumed by those who, following the example of Phinehas [Num. 25:6-13], uncompromisingly sought to maintain Israel's absolute conformity to the Torah and its complete loyalty to Yahweh as its sovereign Lord. . . . In writing of recent Jewish affairs for his Roman readers, it was obviously more politic for him to represent the Zealots as criminals, who misled the Jewish people into making their fatal challenge to Roman power, than as patriots who sacrificed themselves for their ideal of Israel as a theocracy under Yahweh (46-47).

In light of the theocratic ideal in Judaism and the apocalyptic expectation current at the time, Brandon argues that the Zealot beliefs may have been more than just patriotic fanaticism. "It is, therefore, a necessary inference that Judas and Saddok, when they called upon their people to withstand the Roman demand, also believed that the kingdom of God was at hand. Even Josephus admits that they expected God's succour, and it is likely that, no less vividly than Jesus, they might have envisaged the intervention of twelve legions of angels" (51). Brandon considers it probable that the "Zealots were animated by hopes which passed beyond the freeing of Israel from its servitude to Rome to some concept of world-mastery" (60). For Brandon, "Zealotism was essentially a popular movement, embodying both the religious and social aspirations and resentments of the 'people of the land' " (68). "Zealotism must be recognised as a true and inherently noble expression of Jewish religious faith, and one that was sanctioned and inspired by the example of many revered figures of Israel's heroic past" (63-64).

The offspring of Judas continued to lead uprisings against the Romans. Two of his sons, Jacob and Simon, were crucified by the procurator Tiberius Alexander (c. A.D. 46–48). In the summer of A.D. 66, Menahem, a son of Judas, seized the fortress at Masada. He later marched to Jerusalem "as a king" but was assassinated by the followers of the priest Eleazar. Masada was under the control of another Eleazar, a descendant of Judas, until the Jews holding the massive mountainous fortress chose to commit suicide rather than surrender to the Romans in A.D. 73.

In discussing the Zealots, Brandon sought to demonstrate that the movement was in existence as a powerful force among the Jews throughout the time of the life and career of Jesus. In summarizing the discussion of this political movement, he writes:

The Zealots stood in true succession to the Yahwist prophets of old. They were, like Phinehas, zealous for the God of Israel. Their ideal was the ancient prophetic one of Israel as the Elect People of Yahweh. In their zeal to maintain that ideal they could be cruelly uncompromising and fanatical; but no more so than many of the revered heroes of their sacred tradition. Their tragedy was that, unlike the Maccabees before them in their struggle with the ramshackle empire of the Seleucids, in Rome they had themselves to contend with the greatest power of the ancient world, and, for all their courage and zeal, that power was invincible to them. But, if they could not win, they knew how to suffer for their faith.
. . . The cross was the symbol of Zealot sacrifice before it was transformed into the sign of Christian salvation (145).

In a chapter entitled "Israel's Cause Against Rome, A.D. 6-73" (65-145), Brandon surveys the numerous encounters between the Roman authority in Palestine and the Jews. At times these altercations involved the majority of the Jews, as when the emperor Gaius ordered that a statue of Zeus be set up in the temple at Jerusalem, and at other times, they only involved small groups, often Zealot-led, intent on overthrowing Roman rule.

In seeking to establish a relationship between early Christians and these Jewish rebellions, Brandon argues that during the period from the death of Jesus until the fall of Jerusalem Jewish Christians retained a firm relationship to Judaism and shared the Zealot ideal. Brandon concludes, on the basis of the book of Acts and later texts which discuss early Jewish Christianity, that Jewish Christians held beliefs greatly different from that of Gentile Christians. Gentile Christianity, inaugurated by Stephen and given expression by Paul, tended to break with Judaism and go its separate way. In describing this Jewish Christianity, Brandon writes:

We have discerned a community of Jews, who, recognising in Jesus the Messiah of Israel, surmounted the shock of his death at the hands of the Romans. Convinced that God had raised him from death, these disciples' faith in his Messiahship was intensified, taking the form of an urgent expectation that he would soon return, with supernatural power, to fulfil his Messianic task of "restoring the kingdom to Israel." In anticipation of that glorious event, they believed that it was their vocation to prepare their fellow-Jews by presenting Jesus to them as the Messiah, by urging them to repent of those sins which had caused him to die a martyr's death to Roman cruelty and Jewish obduracy, and by exhorting them to be worthy of divine redemption. When faced with the unexpected and unwelcomed fact of Gentile adherents to their movement, they required their confirmation to certain Jewish laws, even seeking to have them circumcised as a guarantee against Paul's antinomianism. Thus they continued as zealous Jews, distinguished from their compatriots only by their expectation that Jesus would soon return to earth as the Messiah. Their movement was given both dynastic continuity and effective leadership by James, the brother of Jesus, and on his death, if later tradition is to be trusted, the succession passed to another relative, Symeon [a cousin of Jesus]. The reputation of the movement seems to have stood high in Jewish religious circles, and it attracted the allegiance of both priests and Pharisees, and its members merited the description "zealots of the Torah" [Acts 21:20] (190).

Jesus: The Political Revolutionary

Brandon argues that these Jewish Christians supported and fought in the great Jewish revolt against the Romans. "Indeed, from all our knowledge of them, it would seem that their attitude towards the Romans would scarcely have differed from that of the Zealots" (199). According to Brandon, the Gospel of Matthew was produced by Jewish Christians in Alexandria in Egypt who shared the same faith as those of the mother church in Jerusalem, although written after the pacificist character of Jesus had been developed following the wars with Rome.

Brandon, of course, recognizes that the four Gospels argue that Jesus was innocent of the charge of sedition for which he was crucified by the Romans. "What makes the Christian accounts of the crucifixion specially notable, as records of historical fact, is that they represent Jesus as being innocent of the charge on which he was condemned. Although they vary in some details, the four Gospel accounts agree in showing that Jesus was falsely accused of sedition by the Jewish authorities, and that these authorities forced the Roman governor, Pontius Pilate, against his better judgment, to condemn and execute him" (1-2). Confronting this fact, Brandon tackles the question of the origin of this apology of innocence, that is, the origin of the oldest Gospel account.

Brandon traces the origin of the idea of Jesus' innocence of the charge of sedition to the writer of the Gospel of Mark, a Gospel which he designates an *Apologia ad Christanos Romanos*. The fact that Mark represents the first written Gospel and was thus a radical innovative development in Christianity demands explanation, according to Brandon. His explanation centers around the idea that Mark was written shortly after the fall of Jerusalem in A.D. 70 as an apology for Gentile readers in Rome where anti-Jewish sentiment was rampant. His general conclusions are:

Faced by the need to explain the Roman execution of Jesus, the author of Mark replaced the original Jewish Christian story of the martyr's death, at the hands of the heathen Romans and their Jewish collaborators, by that of the long-intentioned murder of the Son of God by the Jewish leaders, supported by their people. Seeking to remove any suggestion that Jesus had been implicated in the Jewish freedom movement, Mark presents him as serenely insulated from contemporary political interests and concerns, except that he is shown as endorsing the payment of tribute to Rome. . . .

This abstraction of Jesus from the political life of his time meant also the representing of him as essentially detached from his racial origins and heritage (280).

Brandon draws upon various arguments to support these conclusions. Accepting the ancient tradition which associated the Gospel of Mark with Rome as well as modern scholarly dating of the book to the period A.D. 60-75, Brandon argues that the most likely time for writing was just after the fall of Jerusalem, an event which not only provided the occasion but also the impetus for the work. "In the year 71 popular interest in Jewish affairs was powerfully stimulated in Rome by the magnificent triumph with which the new emperor Vespasian and his son Titus celebrated their conquest of rebel Judaea" (225). Spoils from the victory, including items taken from the temple, and Jewish captives were presented before the Romans in the triumphant processions. Coins were struck showing Judaea humiliated and bearing the inscription *Judaea Capta*. It was a time when interest in and hostility toward Jewish revolutionary activity were widespread. Certainly it was no time to preach Jesus as a Jewish messiah condemned to death by the Romans as a freedom fighter. "A most pressing need, then, existed in the Christian community in Rome at this time for an explanation of Pilate's condemnation and execution of Jesus as a revolutionary against Rome's superiority over Judaea" (247).

A portrayal of Jesus that would separate him from Jewish revolutionary elements and present Jesus as acceptable to Romans in the anti-Jewish atmosphere of the time was achieved by Mark through a number of means. He showed Jesus as one who supported the Jewish payment of tribute to Rome. Mark 12:13-17 would have been so read by a Roman audience. Mark shows Jesus as a predictor of the destruction of the Jewish temple (Mark 13:1-4). The rending of the temple veil (Mark 15:38) signified the obsolescence of Judaism and the temple in the light of Jesus' death. Jesus is depicted not as a Jewish messiah but as the Son of God, in the sense expounded in Paul's version of Christianity, a factor unrecognized by anyone in the Gospel narratives except for the Gentile Roman soldier at the cross (Mark 15:39). Jesus is shown being opposed by his family, misunderstood by his Jewish disciples, and persecuted by the Jewish leaders. In turn, the rejected Jesus is pictured as rejecting his fellow Jews. Mark thus contains a repudiation of the Jews, a defamation of the family of Jesus, and a derogatory presentation of the apostles. Jesus was, in other words, not really a Jew, certainly no freedom fighter for those who misunderstood and abused him. "Jesus, though born a Jew, was never properly appreciated by Jews and . . . implicitly repudiated his racial relationship with the Jews" (265). "Jesus is represented as setting aside any claim that his Jewish nationality might have had on him" (273).

Mark fails to point out that Simon, one of Jesus' disciples, was a Zealot by simply not translating the Aramaic word Cananaean which means "the Zealot." In not providing a translation, Mark broke with his typical pattern of explaining Aramaic terms with their Greek equivalents. The trial of Jesus is presented by Mark in such a way as totally to blame the Jews. The crucifixion was only the culmination of their attitude toward him. The Barabbas episode in which the Jews chose release for Barabbas and crucifixion for Jesus is considered unhistorical by Brandon for two reasons. There is no other attestation to this practice in Jewish or Latin sources in spite of the fact that Josephus was intent on pointing out all privileges granted to Jews by the Romans and such a practice would have hampered effective government in so seething a country as Judaea. In his depiction of Pilate, Mark covers over the actual course of the trial. Pilate is pictured by Mark as a man uncertain of Jesus' guilt but who is forced by the Jewish leaders into pronouncing sentence. Pilate is said to have perceived that it was the envy of the priests which made them push their charges against Jesus. Mark suggests (Mark 15:14) that Pilate privately recognized the innocence of Jesus but does not have the procurator publicly declare such an awkward position. In addition to presenting Jesus' death as an act resultant upon the hatred of the Jewish leaders, Mark ignored the disturbances in Palestine caused by Pilate's rule. Pilate is presented in Mark's Gospel as an indecisive man, but Brandon argues that what we know of him from other sources depict him as a decisive individual prone to over- rather than under-react.

When the other Gospels were produced some ten to fifteen years later with their portraits of Jesus, several changes were made in the traditions. "Their authors utilised traditions not included in Mark; they were not immediately involved with the consequences of the Jewish War and so were not obliged to be so circumspect as the Markan writer; and they elaborated the Markan portrait of Jesus into that of the pacific Christ [who taught acceptance of injury at the hands of others], which became the established tradition of Christianity" (284-85). These developments produced two results: Jesus is presented in several respects as even more unconcerned with actual political realities than in the Gospel of Mark. At the same time, some elements in the Christian tradition which suggest Jesus' political involvement are not so repressed as in Mark. In regard to Matthew's version of the trial, for example, the First Gospel introduces Pilate's wife as testifying to Jesus' innocence and Pilate symbolically washes his hands to disavow any responsibility for the death. The Jews are consequently made even more to blame for Jesus' death: "His blood be on us and on our children" (Matthew 27:24-5). When Jesus is arrested in Gethsemane, Jesus tells his disciple to put away his sword, since those who take to the sword will perish by the sword (Matthew 26:52). Whereas Mark only mentions the temptations of Jesus in the wilderness, Matthew and Luke use these to show that Jesus clearly renounced any claim to "an earthly kingdom and its acquisition by force of arms" (310).

After these lengthy preliminary considerations, Brandon

turns to the New Testament evidence which suggests that Jesus was intentionally put to death by the Romans because Pilate was convinced that he was politically dangerous and that a "bond of common sympathy surely united Jesus and his followers with those who sought to maintain the ideals of Judas of Galilee" (358).

The presence of a Zealot among Jesus' intimate band of disciples suggests, to Brandon, "that Jesus deliberately chose a professed Zealot for an Apostle, which, in turn, indicates that the profession of Zealot principles and aims was not incompatible with intimate participation in the mission of Jesus" (355). The events narrated about Jesus' Jerusalem ministry in the Synoptic Gospels suggest to Brandon the clearest association of Jesus with Zealot and revolutionary principles. In his cleansing of the temple, Jesus was conducting an attack on the trading system of the temple. The selling of sacrificial animals and the money exchange in the temple were controlled by the priestly and aristocratic magnates who directed and profited from its operations. "The organisation and maintenance of the Temple and its cultus were an immense undertaking, involving enormous economic resources and the employment of a great body of officials and servants, control of which was lucrative and conferred great power and influence" (331). "This attack on the Temple trading system constituted, therefore, a most radical challenge to the authority of the sacerdotal aristocracy, and it was a truly revolutionary act, for the high priest held his office and authority from the Romans, and was thus an essential factor of the Roman government in Judaea. To challenge the rule of the high priest was thus, in effect, to challenge the Roman rule" (332). The Gospels depict Jesus making the attack alone, but Brandon considers this highly unlikely since the company of traders, the temple police, and the Roman troops in the fortress of Antonia overlooking the temple precincts could have easily subdued one man. Brandon suggests that the attack "was achieved by the aid of an excited crowd of his supporters and was attended by violence and pillage" (333). This would explain why no action was taken against him for fear of the multitude (Mark 11:18). Perhaps Jesus may also have uttered some threat against the temple since this charge was brought against him in his trial. "By attacking the system which the sacerdotal aristocracy authorised and from which it drew a considerable revenue, and by making some pronouncement of his intention to destroy the present ordering of the temple and replace it by another more pure and holy, Jesus anticipated what the Zealots achieved in A.D. 66" (335).

The cleansing of the temple, according to Brandon, "coincided with an insurrection in the city, in which Zealots appear to have been involved" (339) (Mark 15:6-7) although the relationship between the two events is uncertain. "In the end, it would seem that the movement of Jews and that of the Zealots converged in revolutionary action in Jerusalem" (356). For Brandon, Jesus' attack on the temple may have been only of symbolic character, although he raises the question as to whether or not Jesus and his supporters may not have intended to seize the rest of the temple with its treasury and thus gain control of the greatest source of sacerdotal power. At any rate, Jesus seems to have seen the ranks of the temple and Sanhedrin hierarchy as the major impediment to a reformed people, deserving of God's salvation. "Clearly, while they ruled Israel for Caesar and to their own advantage, the nation could never be made ready for God's kingdom" (338). The sacerdotal aristocracy saw Jesus' attack on the temple "as a declaration of war against them by Jesus," and they moved to seize him (339).

The events surrounding the Last Supper and the arrest in the garden of Gethsemane suggest Jesus' revolutionary associations. The movement of Jesus and his disciples to the garden late at night points to a prearranged meeting "since Judas Iscariot knew of it and was able to inform the Jewish leaders in time to allow their organisation of an arresting force." Brandon suggests that Mark 14:27-8 "may preserve some memory of Jesus' intention of withdrawing to the desert places of Galilee after the failure of his coup in Jerusalem, thus following the Zealot pattern" (340). At the Last Supper,

Jesus checked on the armament of his followers (Luke 22:35-8), and Brandon considers it unlikely that the disciples were only lightly armed. "With how many swords the disciples were armed is immaterial; it is scarcely likely that it was only two" (341). Whether Jesus intended to resist arrest or whether "he had realised that the tide of events was turning against him, and that he was hesitating whether to give up and withdraw to Galilee" cannot be determined. Resistance was offered, but the Gospels speak of only one incident. "They may well be right: except for one of their number who reacted quickly, the disciples may have been confounded by a sudden and determined assault, and Jesus, realising that resistance was hopeless, surrendered himself. The possibility must be allowed, however, in view of the apologetical concern of the Gospel writers, which we have noted, that the resistance was of a more serious nature, even though it proved ineffective" (342).

Is it possible to determine Jesus' attitude toward Roman power which lay behind the sacerdotal aristocracy whom Jesus attacked in the cleansing of the temple? Brandon believes that it is and that several factors provide the clue. The first of these is Jesus' preaching of the kingdom of God. According to Brandon: "Jesus looked forward to the achievement of an apocalyptic situation that necessarily involved the elimination of the Roman government in Judaea" (344). The proclamation of the kingdom's nearness and the belief that Jesus himself was playing a crucial role in preparing for its advent show that Jesus must have known that conflict with the Romans was inevitable. Secondly, Jesus' statement to his disciples that any who would follow him must take up his cross (Mark 8:34) shows that Jesus saw his mission embroiling himself and his followers with the Romans, since crucifixion was the Roman punishment for extreme Jewish patriots.

Brandon argues further that Jesus' reply about tribute money (Mark 12:13-17) was originally stated as a protest against paying tribute to the Romans. "It was, indeed, a saying of which any Zealot would have approved, because . . .

for the Zealot there was no doubt that God owned the land of Israel, not Caesar" (347). Only when the passage is looked at from a Roman perspective does it support the payment of tribute to the Romans.

Luke's specification of the priestly charges against Jesus before Pilate (Luke 23:2,5) notes three accusations: (1) perverting the nation, (2) forbidding payment of tribute to Caesar, and (3) claiming to be a messianic king. Brandon considers these to be the legitimate charges brought against Jesus, charges anchored in the actions and teachings of Jesus, actions and teachings of a dynamic leader not a visionary swept along by forces he unleashed but could no longer control.

Jesus himself may not have been a member of the Zealot movement, but his revolutionary teachings and actions placed him firmly in the philosophy of political and religious revolution which characterized his day. He differed from the Zealots only in the fact that he was more immediately concerned to attack the Jewish sacerdotal aristocracy, and thus the Romans indirectly, than to engage the Romans openly.

The following is Brandon's summary of the course of Jesus' life and his espousal of revolutionary thought which led to his crucifixion by the Romans for sedition:

Believing that the kingdom of God was at hand, Jesus sought to prepare his fellow-Jews morally and spiritually for membership of this kingdom, whose advent would achieve Israel's destiny as the Elect People of God. Two great obstacles stood in the way of the fulfilment of his mission: the Jewish sacerdotal aristocracy and the Roman government. Jesus seems to have been more concerned with the former, probably because its members were Jews and the traditional leaders of Israel. Consequently, he saw their mode of life and abuse of power as constituting a scandalous contradiction of his ideal of a holy people, ready and prepared for the coming of God's kingdom. Their power, therefore, had to be challenged, and perhaps broken. How long Jesus took in coming to this conclusion is not clear; but our sources point to his finally making a decision to go to Jerusalem at the

Jesus: The Political Revolutionary

Passover, for action that he believed would be fateful. He carefully planned an entry into the city, which was designed to demonstrate his Messianic role. This challenging action was quickly followed by his attack on the Temple trading system. The Gospels do not permit us to know whether this "Cleansing of the Temple" was intended to be the prelude to further action against the hierarchy, although this would seem to be its logical implication. So far as our evidence shows, the "Cleansing of the Temple" was not followed by measures designed to prevent the traffic from restarting; yet it appears that the Jewish leaders did not then feel strong enough to arrest Jesus publicly. The operation in the Temple apparently took place about the same time as an insurrection elsewhere in the city, which the Romans suppressed. This rising was undoubtedly instigated by the Zealots, and it is difficult to believe that it was quite unconnected with Jesus' action in the Temple, although the Gospels mention no connection. The Gospel record gives the impression that the action which Jesus had initiated by coming to Jerusalem proved in some way abortive, and that, by the time of the Passover, Jesus had to take precautions against a surprise attack by the Jewish authorities.

What plans Jesus had, when he was arrested, are unknown. The fact that he was taken by night, after his rendezvous had been betrayed to the Jewish leaders by Judas, suggests that he had no intention of surrendering himself voluntarily, as a kind of sacrificial victim, to his enemies. The latter, whose authority had been gravely challenged by him, proceeded, as we have seen, in a manner that is intelligible in terms of their responsibility to the Roman government for Jewish affairs. After his arrest, they examined him to obtain all possible information about his intentions, and probably the identity and strength of his followers, preparatory to delivering him to Pilate as guilty of subversive views and actions. That Pilate sentenced him to death for sedition was the logical sequel to the case submitted by the Jewish authorities—that he also ordered him to be crucified between two . . . , who were probably Zealots, suggests that he connected Jesus with the insurrection that had coincided with Jesus' activities in Jerusalem (350-51).

169

9. JESUS: THE BLACK MESSIAH

For nearly 500 years the illusion that Jesus was white dominated the world only because white Europeans dominated the world. Now, with the emergence of the nationalist movements of the world's colored majority, the historic truth is finally beginning to emerge—that Jesus was the non-white leader of non-white people struggling for national liberation against the rule of a white nation, Rome. —Albert B. Cleage, Jr., *The Black Messiah* (p. 3)

In recent years, black consciousness has come to expression if not to realization and fulfillment in the United States and throughout much of the world. In the 1950s and 1960s, the movement toward full civil rights for blacks reached a new plateau. In the wake of the civil rights movement, black power was born and, in the shadow of black power, a renascent black theology has grown.

Black theology has been defined by the National Committee of Black Churchmen in the following terms:

For us, Black Theology is the theology of black liberation. It seeks to plumb the black condition in the light of God's revelation in Jesus Christ, so that the black community can see that the gospel is commensurate with the achievement of black humanity. Black Theology is a theology of "blackness." It is the affirmation of black humanity that emancipates black people from white racism thus providing authentic freedom for both white and black people. It affirms the humanity of white people in that it says "No" to the encroachment of white oppression. The message of liberation is the revelation of God as revealed in the incarnation of Jesus Christ. Freedom IS the gospel. Jesus is the Liberator!

Jesus: The Black Messiah

The development of a black theology and a black interpretation of Jesus may be viewed from three different perspectives. On the one hand, black theology arose because "white theology is severely limited in its interpretation of the Christian faith in so far as the non-white peoples of the world are concerned" (Bishop Joseph A. Johnson, Jr., "Jesus: The Liberator," 87). Johnson expounds on the limitations of traditional or white theology in the following manner:

The interpretation of Christian Theology and of Jesus expounded by white American theologians is severely limited. This is due to the simple reason that these white scholars have never been lowered into the murky depth of the black experience of reality. They never conceived the black Jesus walking the dark streets of the ghettos of the north and the sharecropper's farms in the deep south without a job, busted, and emasculated. These white theologians could never hear the voice of Jesus speaking in the dialect of blacks from the southern farms, or in the idiom of the blacks of the ghetto. This severe limitation of the white theologians' inability to articulate the full meaning of the Christian faith has given rise to the development of Black Theology (88).

A second perspective which precipitated the rise of black theology has been the association of traditional Christianity with oppression of the blacks. Again Bishop Johnson gives expression to this factor:

The tragedy of the interpretations of Jesus by white American theologians during the last three hundred years is that Jesus has been too often identified with the oppressive structures and forces of the prevailing society. His teachings have been used to justify wars, exploitation of the poor and oppressed peoples of the world. In His name the most vicious form of racism has been condoned and advocated. In a more tragic sense this Jesus of the white church establishment has been white, straight haired, blue eyed, Anglo-Saxon, that is, presented in the image of the oppressor. This "whiteness" has prevailed to the extent that the black, brown, or red peoples of the world, who have accepted Jesus as Lord and Savior, were denied full Christian fellowship in His church and were not accepted as brothers for whom Jesus died (86-87). . . . White theology has not been able to re-shape the

171

life of the white church so as to cleanse it of its racism and to liberate it from the iron claws of the white racist establishment of this nation. White theology has presented the blacks a religion of contentment in the state of life in which they find themselves. Such an interpretation of the Christian faith avoided questions about personal dignity, collective power, freedom, equality and self-determination. The white church establishment presented to the black people a religion carefully tailored to fit the purposes of the white oppressors, corrupted in language, interpretation and application by the conscious and unconscious racism of white Christians from the first plantation missionary down to Billy Graham.

The white Christ of the white church establishment is the enemy of the black man (90).

The two previously noted perspectives on black theology have possessed a negative connotation. Black theology is however a theology with a positive orientation or, as expressed by James H. Cone, a "theology whose sole purpose is to apply the freeing power of the gospel to black people under white oppression" (*Black Theology and Black Power,* 31). It is a "theology whose sole purpose is to emancipate the gospel from its 'whiteness' so that blacks may be capable of making an honest self-affirmation through Jesus Christ" (32). "The task of Black Theology . . . is *to analyze the black man's condition in the light of God's revelation in Jesus Christ with the purpose of creating a new understanding of black dignity among black people, and providing the necessary soul in that people, to destroy white racism*" (117).

The double focus on black theology has been expressed by Gayraud S. Wilmore in the following terms:

Black theology expresses both affirmation and negation. It affirms the real possibility of freedom and manhood for Black people, and it negates every power that seeks to demean and rob Black people for the determination of their own destiny. Black theology's contribution to the universal knowledge of God does not lie in its being only the reverse side of traditional Christian theology—white theology in Black vesture. ... Rather, in its illumination of the religious meaning of Black liberation, Black theology breaks with the determinative norms of white theology and unveils the deepest meaning of human freedom for all men (*Black Religion and Black Radicalism,* 297).

Jesus—his life and teachings—occupies an important position in practically all expressions of black theology. "Black Theology . . . takes seriously the historical Jesus. We want to know who Jesus *was* because we believe that that is the only way to assess who he *is.* If we have no historical information about the character and behavior of that particular Galilean in the first century, then it is impossible to determine the mode of his existence now. Without some continuity between the historical Jesus and the kerygmatic Christ, the Christian gospel becomes nothing but the subjective reflections of the early Christian community" (James Cone, *A Black Theology of Liberation,* 201).

Black theologians, in stressing the importance of the figure of Jesus for black theology, have come to speak of a black Jesus or a black messiah. What does such a concept mean and what understanding of the historical Jesus does it imply?

For Albert Cleage, the idea of Jesus as the black messiah means exactly what it says: "Jesus was a revolutionary black leader, a Zealot, seeking to lead a Black Nation to freedom" (*The Black Messiah,* 4). Cleage argues that the traditional form of Christianity and its understanding of Jesus is a radical distortion of Jesus and his message. In a sermon to his congregation, the Shrine of the Black Madonna in Detroit, he expresses this idea in the following way:

I would say to you, you are Christian, and the things you believe are the teachings of a Black Messiah named Jesus, and the things you do are the will of a black God called Jehovah; and almost everything you have heard about Christianity is essentially a lie.

You have been misled. Christianity for you has been misinterpreted. That which you believe to be Christianity, the theology and philosophy of history which you reject, is not Christianity. The Christianity which we see in the world today was not shaped by Jesus. It was put together by the Apostle Paul who never saw Jesus, and given form and shape during the Middle Ages when most of the hymns were written, the hymns which for the most part enunciate white supremacy. "Fairest Lord Jesus." Most of the famous religious pictures that you see were painted between the fourteenth and the seventeenth centuries by white artists. When Dutch artists painted religious pictures, everything looks just like it all happened in Holland. When French artists painted religious pictures, the biblical characters look French.

But we didn't realize this when we looked at our Sunday School literature as children. When we turned the pages and always saw a white Jesus, when we saw pictures of a white God pointing down at creation, we didn't realize that these were not statements of fact but statements by white men depicting what they wanted to believe was true. I say, what they wanted to believe was true, because essentially they knew that white men did not create Christianity. They borrowed it, more bluntly, they stole it. In fact, of all the peoples on earth, the one people who have never created a religion worthy of the name religion are white people.

All religions stem from black people. Think of them for a moment. The Muslim religion, the Buddhist religion, the Jewish religion, the Christian religion, they all come from parts of the world dominated by non-white peoples (37-38).

In claiming that Jesus was nonwhite, Cleage argues that the Jewish nation from which Jesus came was nonwhite. "The intermingling of the races in Africa and the Mediterranean area is an established fact. The Nation Israel was a mixture of Chaldeans, Egyptians, Midianites, Ethiopians, Kushites, Babylonians and other dark peoples, all of whom were already mixed with the black people of Central Africa" (3).

Abraham was a Chaldean—probably nonwhite—and Abraham, Moses, and other Israelites married Egyptians. Thus Israel was closely related to Africans. Upon their entry into Canaan, the Hebrews intermarried with the local population and again in captivity, the Israelites mixed with the people of Babylonia, which was a nonwhite nation. "Israel was a mixed-blood, non-white nation. What usually confuses you is the fact that the Jews you see today in America are white. Most of them are the descendants of white Europeans and Asiatics who were converted to Judaism about one thousand years ago. The Jews were scattered all over the world. In Europe and Russia, they converted white people to Judaism. The Jews who stayed in that part of the world where black people are predominant, remained black" (41).

Jesus came to the Black Nation Israel. We are not talking now about "God the Father." We are concerned here with the actual blood line. Jesus was born to Mary, a Jew of the tribe of Judah, a non-white people; black people in the same sense that the Arabs were black people, in the same sense that the Egyptians were black people. Jesus was a Black Messiah born to a black woman.

The pictures of the Black Madonna which are all over the world did not all turn black through some mysterious accident. Portraits of the Black Madonna are historic, and today in many countries they are afraid to take the ancient pictures of the Black Madonna out of storage so that people can see them. . . . But the Black Madonna is an historic fact, and Jesus as a Black Messiah is an historic fact (42).

Jesus' ministry was directed to the nation of Israel and stood in the line of the Hebrew prophets who sought to build God's kingdom out of the nation Israel. Jesus' preaching of the kingdom was not otherworldly, but totally this-worldly. "Jesus talked of the kingdom of God on earth" (44). During his career, Jesus sought to build Israel into a nation again. He however had to counter the despair of the people which saw no hope for the future.

Each individual was trying to secure his own little individual benefits from his relationship with the Roman oppressor, some little favor, some little special privilege. The Black Nation of Israel had degenerated into total corruption and hopelessness. Black people no longer believed in themselves and black people no longer loved each other. Their lives were molded by what they thought they could get out of the Romans. They loved their oppressors and hated their brothers because their oppressors had power and their brothers were powerless (60). . . .

So no real Nation existed when Jesus began his ministry.

He walked from village to village, preaching, teaching, healing, performing miracles, anything to get a group of people together so that he might give him his simple message. "It is necessary that you turn your back upon individualism and join with your brothers to again build a Black Nation of which we can be proud." Jesus called men to a real decision. In all probability his disciples were already committed to the revolutionary struggle as Zealots before they saw Jesus, but when they heard him, they accepted his leadership and followed him (61). . . .

With the death of John the Baptist, Jesus moved into unquestioned leadership of Israel's revolutionary forces, making inevitable the combined opposition of the white oppressor, Rome, and those black collaborators who feared that revolution might destroy their privileged positions. There were the revolutionary Zealots on one side and the collaborating Scribes and Pharisees on the other, but most of the people hesitated to make a decision and refused to support either side (62). . . .

Jesus didn't spend his life waiting to be crucified. A lot of people seem to have the impression that Jesus walked around with his hands folded, waiting for his enemies to nail him to a cross. That's a lie. He was fighting and twisting and turning all of his life, trying to teach and organize, even while he knew that his enemies were working day and night to destroy him and his influence with the people. When Jesus finally came before Pilate and the people screamed "crucify him, crucify him," this was the result of the campaign of vilification that had been carried on against him by the priests, the Scribes, the Pharisees, and the people in power who were afraid that their power would be lost if a Black Nation came into being. There were the friends who said that he was insane, or he wouldn't be risking himself, and there were the enemies who said that he was evil and in league with the devil. These were the people who killed Jesus. Not the white Gentiles, but his own black people (67).

Jesus did not preach an individualistic ethic; he spent his days fighting against an individualistic form of religion. Jesus sought to root out individualism and stressed the importance of the people as a group, as a nation, seeking to lead the people as a whole from oppression and suffering through revolutionary action. Neither was Jesus a preacher of universal love.

Jesus didn't spend all of his time walking around talking about love. He was trying to bring the Nation together. When he said, "Go the second mile, turn the other cheek," he meant inside the Black Nation. When he said, "Don't come to the altar and try to pray unless you've made peace with your brother," he was talking about inside the Nation. When a Gentile woman came to Jesus and said, "My little girl is on the verge of death. Do something for her," he said, "I don't know you. You're not in the Nation. I came to Israel." She fell on her knees and said, "At least give me the crumbs from the table." And he looked at her and said, "You have a lot of faith," and he healed the little girl. But he didn't come to the Gentiles (98). . . .

Christian people have for so many years misunderstood the teachings of Jesus. Turn the other cheek, go the second mile; if a man takes your coat, give him your cloak as well—these are the internal ethics of a people who are struggling to become a Nation. Jesus meant that you should turn the other cheek to your black brother and to your black sister. For Jesus, the whole idea of brotherhood and love had to do with brotherhood and love within the Nation Israel. He was calling black people from a sense of identification with their white oppressor, and telling them that they must turn their backs on a world in which they were relegated to a second-class position. They must accept the fact that their power lay in their unity, in their willingness to forgive each other and to work and fight and struggle together (215).

For Cleage, the significant aspect of Jesus' ministry was his life and teachings—his efforts to insure the salvation and growth of a nation—and not his submissive acceptance of suffering, the cross, and death. The activities of Jesus in Jerusalem were not undertaken to die and thus to fulfill prophecy. His activity in the capital city was undertaken to insure some success for his movement, to rescue the nation from oppression, and to create a new nation.

When he went into Jerusalem, he didn't just go in to meet with Pontius Pilate and Herod and let them make speeches. He went in to confront an enemy. That's the difference. He went in to do battle against an enemy. The first night he got out of sight as quickly as possible. The next day he came back into the city and went to the Temple. The Temple was the center of the corruption that was destroying the Nation. The priests, Scribes, and the Pharisees controlled the power there. But it wasn't real power. It was Uncle Tom power. They depended upon Rome for their very existence, but Rome let them carry on their little rackets. . . . Everything in the Temple had been reduced to a racket, and the rackets were operated by Jews with the connivance of Rome (78-79). . . .

Jesus went through the whole of Holy Week fighting to salvage what he could of his Movement, leaving people something that they could pass on when he was killed. Every day of this climactic week before his crucifixion he tried to do what he could to see that his teachings about the Nation were understood. On Wednesday he went to Bethany with his friends. He made almost a whole day's journey to sit down alone with the people who were to be the nucleus of the Nation. He sat down in the home of Mary and Martha with others who were committed to the revolution, and talked to them all day and far into the night. You remember the woman who came bringing the expensive ointment. "She anoints me for my burial," he said. But he was trying to tell them the things they were to remember.

Then, on Thursday, he went back for the Passover meal with his disciples. He knew that if anything was to be preserved after his death it all depended upon the understanding of these twelve men. They had heard him. They knew his message. If they couldn't carry it on, it was done, it was lost and his work was finished. So on Thursday he sat down with the twelve and talked to them. He tried to get them to understand that the Nation can come into being only when we are willing to sacrifice and be humble (81).

The importance of the resurrection is not to be found in the resurrection of the physical Jesus; the significance of the resurrection lies in the rebirth of the nation. One must read the stories of the resurrection and realize that these were written many years after the death of Jesus when its true significance had been clouded by later interpretations.

So the Resurrection that we celebrate is not the Resurrection of the physical body of Jesus, but the Resurrection of the Black Nation which he started, the Resurrection of his ideas and his teachings. The immortality which Jesus has lies in the fact that two thousand years later we remember, and two thousand years later we are trying to do the same thing he tried to do with the Black Nation in Palestine. Today, in the midst of corruption, we are drawing people one by one, two by two, into the Black Nation. This task and the faith that it can be done, this is the Resurrection (99). . . .

Jesus undertook the Resurrection of the Nation. This is why the Disciples were not greatly concerned when the women went to the tomb and found that Jesus was not there. They were not primarily concerned with the Resurrection of Jesus as an individual. Jesus had taught that a Black Nation was to come into being out of a people who had ceased to believe in the possibilities of a new Nation and his Disciples had begun to catch a glimpse of this kind of Resurrection (93).

The distortion of the true life and message of Jesus, the black messiah, was primarily the work of the apostle Paul.

During this early period when people were trying to determine the meaning of the life and death of Jesus, the Apostle Paul came on the scene with an entirely new interpretation. He had never seen Jesus in the flesh, but his interpretation dominated the early Church and greatly influenced the Gospels when they were written. So in the Book of Galatians and in the Acts of the Apostles, you have a whole lot of arguing going on between the Disciples and the Apostle Paul. Paul was out in the field moving from city to city, organizing churches. He was a great organizer in the modern sense. He did whatever was necessary to put an organization together. The Disciples and the followers of Jesus back in Jerusalem said, "This man is not organizing the right kind of churches. He has forgotten the things that were important to Jesus." But Paul wrote letters and they wrote nothing. Why were the followers of Jesus critical of the Apostle Paul? Because the Apostle Paul was leaning over backward to convert the Gentiles. "Apostle to the Gentiles" meant Apostle to the white people. Paul was taking the religion of a Black Nation to white people who had no background in religion. But to make it acceptable to them he had to change it (88-89). . . .

The Apostle Paul was a Jew. He went to the Gentiles with a religion about a Black Messiah and immediately he began to change it so that they would be able to accept it. Greece and Rome were heathen nations. They conceived of God in primitive terms as someone who went around throwing thunderbolts at his enemies. . . . So when the Apostle Paul tried to take the religion of Jesus to them, he distorted the Black Messiah to make him fit their primitive conceptions. To understand what paganism did to Jesus, compare the Gospel of Mark with the Gospel of John. That is because the Gospel of John has taken on the pagan, heathen philosophy of the Gentiles and tried to weave it into the life of Jesus. The historic Jesus is completely lost (89).

For some black theologians, the concept of Jesus as the black messiah does not carry the historical implications found in Cleage, implications about the history and nature of ancient Israel out of which Christ came. For example, James Cone can write: "But some whites will ask, Does Black Theology believe that Christ was *really* black? It seems to me that the *literal* color of Jesus is irrelevant, as are the different shades of blackness in America. . . . But as it happens, *he was not white* in any sense of the word, literally or theologically. Therefore, the Reverend Cleage is not too far wrong when he describes Jesus as a black Jew; and he is certainly on solid grounds when he describes him as the Black Messiah" (*A Black Theology of Liberation,* 218). In a somewhat similar vein, J. Deotis Roberts declares: "I do not take the figure of a black Messiah in a literal historical sense. It is rather a symbol or a myth with profound meaning for black people" (*Liberation and Reconciliation,* 130). From these quotes, it appears that Cone stands closer to Cleage than Roberts.

For Cone and Roberts, and for other black theologians, the concept of Jesus as the black messiah is an interpretative concept or symbol which serves both a negative and positive function. On the one hand, it is the means for the repudiation of the traditional portrait and interpretation of Jesus within white Christendom or what has been called "whiteanity." The white messiah of western Christianity has been one in whose name whites have subjected and oppressed the nonwhites of the world. Such a Christ appears as the enemy not the friend and liberator of the oppressed.

The task of explicating the existence of Christ for black people is not easy since we live in a white society that uses

Christianity as an instrument of oppression. The white conservatives and liberals alike present images of a white Christ that are completely alien to the liberation of the black community. Their Christ is a mild, easy-going white American who can afford to mouth the luxuries of "love," "mercy," "long-suffering," and other white irrelevancies, because he has a multi-billion-dollar military force to protect him from the encroachments of the ghetto and the "communist conspiracy." But black existence is existence in a hostile world without the protection of the law. If Christ is to have any meaning for us, he must leave the security of the suburbs by joining black people in their condition. What need have we for a white Christ when we are not white but black? If Christ is white and not black, he is an oppressor, and we must kill him. The appearance of Black Theology means that the black community is now ready to do something about the white Christ, so that he cannot get in the way of our revolution (Cone, *A Black Theology of Liberation,* 198-99).

On the other hand, the idea of Jesus as the black messiah is a means for understanding the central thrust of the life and ministry of the historical Jesus and the means for making Jesus relevant to the struggles of blacks in today's world. For black theologians, a central feature of the historical Jesus was his identity as an oppressed and his identity with the oppressed.

Taking seriously the New Testament Jesus, Black Theology believes that the historical kernel is the manifestation of Jesus as the Oppressed One whose earthly existence was bound up with the oppressed of the land. . . . To understand the historical Jesus without seeing his identification with the poor as decisive is to misunderstand him and thus distort his historical person. And a proper theological analysis of Jesus' historical identification with the helpless is indispensible for our interpretation of the gospel today (202-3).

The stage of his ministry was the streets. His congregation consisted of those who were written off by the established church and state. He ministered to those who needed him, "the nobodies of the world," the sick, the blind, the lame and the demon possessed. He invaded the chambers of sickness and death and hallowed these with the healing words of

health and life. He invaded the minds of the demon
possessed and in those dark chambers of night he brought
light, sanity and order. Jesus ministered to men in their
sorrow, sin and degradation and offered them hope and light
and courage and strength. He offered comfort to the poor
who did not fit into the structure of the world. Jesus
comforted the mourner and offered hope to the humble. He
had a message for the men and women who had been pushed
to the limits of human existence and on these he pronounced
his blessedness.

The people who received help from Jesus are throughout
the Gospels on the fringe of society—men who because of
fate, guilt and prejudices were considered marked men
(Johnson, "Jesus: the Liberator," 95-96).

The black Jesus is understood as the liberator, as the one
who came to bring redemption from oppression, as the
revolutionary political messiah whose goal in living was
human freedom. "Jesus' proclamation of the kingdom is an
announcement of God's decision about oppressed man. 'The
time is fulfilled, and the kingdom of God is at hand,' that is,
slavery is about to end, since the reign of God displaces all
false authorities" (Cone, *A Black Theology of Liberation*,
207). "Jesus is the Oppressed One whose work is that of
liberating humanity from inhumanity. Through him the
oppressed are set free to be what they are" (209).

The black messiah is the means for making Jesus relevant
to the total struggles of today's blacks.

The Black Christ is he who threatens the structure of evil as
seen in white society, rebelling against it, thereby becoming
the embodiment of what the black community knows that it
must become. Because he has become black as we are, we
now know what black empowerment is. It is black people
determining the way they are going to behave in the world
(216). . . .

In our language today, the oppressed are the people of the
black ghettos, the Indian reservations, the Spanish *barrios,*
and other places where whiteness has created misery. To
participate in God's salvation is to cooperate with the Black
Christ as he liberates his people from bondage. Salvation
then primarily has to do with earthly reality and the injustice

inflicted on those who are helpless and poor. To see the
salvation of God is to see these people rise up against their
oppressors, demanding that justice become a reality now and
not tomorrow. . . . The new day is the presence of the Black
Christ as expressed in the liberation of the black community
(226-27).

The black Christ liberates and the universal Christ
reconciles. The Jesus of the disinherited set us free. The
Jesus who breaks through the color line reconciles all men.
But all persons must be confronted by Jesus and take
seriously his personal claims on their lives and their people
before he can become Lord of all. We cannot fully know
Jesus in the role of reconciler until we know him in his role as
liberator. The way to a knowledge of Christ as reconciler
passes through his "liberator role." *Jesus means freedom!*
(Roberts, *A Black Political Theology,* 138).

10. JESUS: THE MESSIANIC SCHEMER

> The destined road for Jesus led to torture at Jerusalem on a Roman cross, to be followed by resurrection. But these things had to come about in the manner predicted by the Scriptures and after preliminaries entailing the most careful scheming and plotting to produce them. Moves and situations had to be anticipated, rulers and associates had to perform their functions without realizing that they were being used. A conspiracy had to be organized of which the victim was himself the deliberate secret instigator. It was a nightmarish conception and undertaking, the outcome of the frightening logic of a sick mind, or of a genius. And it worked out.
> —Hugh J. Schonfield, *The Passover Plot* (p. 125)

As a young Jewish college student, Hugh J. Schonfield says he read numerous Jewish and Christian interpretations of Jesus and felt they were partly right and partly wrong. For him, "there was a mystery which called for further explanation" (2). His explanation of that mystery has now been presented in his best-selling book, *The Passover Plot*.

Like many other scholars in the course of the study of the historical Jesus, Schonfield feels that, as the New Testament tells the story, something is missing. A major piece of the puzzle must still be put into its proper place in order to understand the full plot which made up the life of Jesus. Schonfield is not here concerned merely with the fact that the early church overlaid the historical Jesus with its "pagan assessment of his worth in terms of deity" (3). Nor with the traditional portraiture which is so "baffling in its apparent contradiction of the terms of our earthly existence" (2). Nor is he merely referring to the fact that the Gospel writers produced their works with "meager resources of documentation and living recollection. This was because of the Jewish

184

revolt against Rome in A.D. 66 which resulted in the devastation of Palestine and Jerusalem and largely extinguished access to fuller information." This latter problem, like the former ones, can be overcome for, in attempting to understand Jesus, "actually we are better placed now than they were. When the Gospels were composed, legend, special pleading, the new environment of Christianity after the war, and a changed view of the nature of Jesus, gave them a flavour of which we have to be fully conscious when we enlist their essential aid in the quest of the historical Jesus" (6).

The missing element which allows a true understanding of Jesus' career is the recognition that "awareness of being the Messiah meant everything to Jesus" and that "in affirmation of that office, that peculiar and incredibly difficult function, he directed his life, anticipated his execution, and envisaged his resurrection." In other words, the plot of Jesus' life was the plot given to it by Jesus who planned and controlled not only its major contours but contrived to bring to pass those details around which the Christian faith would be built. The "plot" is thus the element "which strikes the keynote of the whole extraordinary undertaking to which Jesus committed himself."

This book reveals him as a master of his destiny, expecting events to conform to the requirements of prophetic intimations, contriving those events when necessary, contending with friends and foes to ensure that the predictions would be fulfilled. Such strength of will founded on faith, such concentration of purpose, such astuteness in planning, such psychological insight as we find him displaying, marks him out as a dominant and dynamic personality, with a capacity for action which matched the greatness of his vision. He could be tender and compassionate, but he was no milk-and-water Messiah. He accepted that authority had been conferred upon him by God, and he exercised it with profound effect, whether favourable or unfavourable, on those who came in contact with him (7).

For Schonfield, the overriding factor in the life of Jesus was his belief that he was the Jewish messiah. This was also the fundamental element in the faith of the early church: "Christianity . . . did not begin as a new religion but as a movement of monotheistic Jews who held Jesus to be their God-sent king and deliverer. Here, in a sentence, is what it is imperative to know about the origins of Christianity" (12).

But behind the man Jesus and the faith of the early church lies an idea upon which they both were founded. "It is often said that Christianity is founded upon a person. That is true. But it is only part of the historical truth. What, so to speak, was the person founded upon? The answer is that he was founded upon an idea, a strange idea current among the Jews of his time, an idea alien to Western thought which many non-Jewish theologians still find very inconvenient, the idea of Messianism" (12).

In order to understand the idea behind the man, Schonfield argues, it is absolutely necessary to realize that Jesus accepted a current interpretation of the messiah and acted on the basis of this interpretation without attempting any reinterpretation of the concept.

We have no right to say that while Jesus accepted the designation of Messiah he did so in a sense quite different from any expectations entertained in his time. It would be unthinkable for him to do this, firstly because being the Messiah meant answering to certain prophetic requirements which for him were divinely inspired, and secondly because he would consciously have been depriving his people of any possibility of acknowledging him: he would be inviting them to reject him as a false Messiah (13).

What elements made up this messianism which Jesus inherited and applied to himself? In the first place, it did not involve any "paganised doctrine of the incarnation of the Godhead with which for Christians it has become intermingled" (13). The messianism of the time in no way identified the messiah with God—a blasphemous concept threatening to Jewish monotheism—so that "Jesus as much as any other Jew would have regarded as blasphemous the manner in which he is depicted, for instance, in the Fourth Gospel" (14). The messianism that was rampant in the days of Jesus focused upon the "establishment of the Kingdom of God on earth, for which the prerequisite was a righteous Israel, or at least a righteous remnant of Israel" (19). The fulfilment of prophetic predictions, such as those in the book of Daniel, led people to believe they were living in the last days just before the end. Various groups, like the Pharisees and Essenes, were aiming at the perfection of the community and the satisfaction of daily life.

Strange imaginings had gripped the Jewish people at this time, the time Jesus came into the world, fed by those who interpreted the Scriptures to them. According to many preachers, the eleventh hour had come, the Last Times had begun, the Kingdom of God was at hand. The world was on the eve of Wrath and Judgment. The Messiah would appear (26).

Jesus was thus born into an environment ablaze with messianic fervor. But how was the messiah conceived? What would be his character? The expected messiah was not understood in terms of a militant warrior. "In fact in references to the Messiah up to the time of Jesus the conception of a Warrior Messiah does not appear" (27). Only among the Palestinian peasantry and the oppressed was any such warrior messiah expected. The general view of the expected messiah saw him as just, holy, the perfect Israelite, the messiah of righteousness, living in close communion with God and obedient to his will. Among the Galilean sectarian groups of which Jesus had some knowledge, there existed an "ancient Israelitish type of religion" (31) in whose thought the righteous king figure had been combined with the idea of the suffering just one; and the conception of the messiah had been infused with the concept of son of man. So all the material lay at hand for Jesus to appear as the messiah.

The right understanding of Jesus commences with the realisation that he identified himself with the fulfilment of the Messianic Hope. Only on this basis do the traditions about him become wholly intelligible. He was no charlatan, wilfully and deliberately misleading his people, well knowing that his posing as the Messiah was fraudulent. There is not the slightest suspicion of pretence on his part. On the contrary, no one could be more sure of his vocation than was Jesus, and not even the threat of imminent death by the horrible torture of crucifixion could make him deny his messiahship. We have to accept the absolute sincerity of Jesus (33).

How did Jesus come to believe himself the messiah? Schonfield suggests that this must have come to him in his tender years of childhood. It was not something given in a miracle of birth, for "there was nothing peculiar about the birth of Jesus. He was not God incarnate and no Virgin Mother bore him" (42). "He was as completely human as every baby" (44). He may have sensed his messiahship because of some parental hopes associated with a first born child, or due to some external circumstance, or a chance laudatory remark about his future, or perhaps from hearing of the Galilean struggles and hopes. It was, nonetheless, during his early years that Jesus came to his understanding of himself as the messiah, since "the major features of what he had to do were clear to Jesus before he went to be baptised by John" (46).

Of Jesus' youthful years and their impact upon Jesus, Schonfield writes:

So the picture we can form of the young Jesus is of a quiet, dutiful, watchful individual, with an inner life of his own and a deep-seated faith. He had a bright intelligence and was by no means aloof from his surroundings, yet was prone to detach himself from them. He was not at all uncommunicative when it came to finding out what he wished to know; but he was rather a strange boy and something of a puzzle to his parents, not readily drawing attention to himself, and inwardly busy with tremendous imaginings which it was impossible for him to reveal. What some of his cherished thoughts were about we may hazard a confident guess: they were about the world, about God's dealings with Israel, and about the deliverer who had been promised to his people (48).

The form which Jesus understood his messiahship must take was the result of a number of factors. Most dominant of all was his insight into and understanding of the messianic interpretation of the scriptures. On the basis of such texts or oracles and some instruction and insight borrowed from the Galilean sectarians, Jesus developed his understanding of what must befall the messiah. "A prophetic blueprint of the Days of the Messiah was the outcome of his investigations. The Scriptures thus disclosed to him the character of his mission, how his message would be received, his fate, and his subsequent appearance in glory as king and judge of the nations " (59).

Jesus seems also to have possessed what might be called a "father fixation" (53), perhaps developed because of the unexpected early death of his father Joseph. His understanding of his special sonship to God was no doubt influenced by this factor. He may also have obtained from the communities of the sectarian saints some "elements of the healing art cultivated and practised" (57) by them. Also, Jesus was an astute observer of life.

While he would often seek solitude, he did not lock himself away in a private world of his own. He became a keen student of life and human character. Very little escaped his penetrating notice. The man we meet in the Gospels is one who knows the countryside of Galilee intimately, its flowers and trees, fields and orchards, the activities of the people in work and worship, in their social, spiritual, political and economic affairs. The things he teaches and the realistic tales he tells to illustrate his teaching, are proof of how much he has absorbed. Such a store of information could only have been the outcome of prolonged and acute observation. There had been nothing somnambulistic in his walks abroad. He had deemed it to be vital to his equipment that he should have firsthand knowledge of the ways of the world (55).

Jesus' recognition and realization of himself as the messiah must have presented Jesus with great personal struggles; it was not easy for Jesus to own himself as the man his people awaited. Such a recognition was not an act of megalomania, for Jesus saw himself as servant.

Jesus came forth as the messiah to put "into operation a

programme which was the outcome of his prior messianic investigations. . . . His visualisation of the role of the Messiah was highly theatrical," and the messianic predictions had "acquired the form of a drama."

He played out the part like an actor with careful timing and appreciation of what every act called for. His calculated moves, his symbolic actions such as the forty days in the wilderness and the choice of twelve apostles, his staging of the triumphal entry into Jerusalem and the Last Supper, all testify to his dramatic consciousness, as do many of his gestures and declamations. Only one who possessed such a consciousness could have conceived, contrived, and carried out the Passover Plot so masterfully and so superbly. But the portrayal of the Messiah's tragedy, and the anticipation of the happy ending, was utter sincere. This was reality not make-believe.

For Jesus it was of the essence of his faith that God in his mysterious ways had made choice of him, a descendant of David, as the means of fulfilling those purposes which from age to age the Lord had inspired his messengers to proclaim. It was a knowledge which he could not communicate to anyone, could not even hint at before his call came. He could only prepare himself, and wait (61).

With the appearance of John the Baptist, Jesus' "trying years of waiting were over" (65). Elijah had appeared as the prophetic oracles had predicted. Jesus went to be baptized by John—to undergo his anointment—confident that he would undergo a great experience and receive the gift of the Spirit.

Never had Jesus witnessed such a scene or listened to such words. Truly here was a prophet who spoke with the voice of God, spoke in language that united with all he had thought and believed! He stepped into the chill stream, and the hairy hand of John was upon him, sending him down, down into the depths. Jesus prayed. Slowly he rose up out of the water; and then he had the experience. Tradition says that he heard a Voice from heaven, and that the Spirit of God descended upon him like a dove, or in the likeness of a dove, and entered into him, thus signifying that he was the Messiah (68).

Jesus: The Messianic Schemer

With a faithfulness to unalterable divine decrees, Jesus began his ministry in Galilee. His messiahship however had to be kept secret, for its acknowledgement would have been disastrous. Since the messiah was the legitimate king, the Romans would have pounced upon him with the charge of sedition. So in the beginning, Jesus gave the impression of being a "harmless religious enthusiast" (74). In his call to repentance, his teachings, and his miracles, Jesus was "walking on a knife-edge" (75). He had to guard against any overenthusiasm by his followers and prevent his ministry from being cut short like that of John. So Jesus spoke of himself as the Son of man, a term which gave him external anonymity, since it was a term whose messianic connotations were understood only by the communities of the saints which posed no threat to him. Jesus had thus to secure for himself safety and freedom of movement. The inner circle of the disciples, who were patriotic and possessed by a simple faith, was physically strong and personally loyal. They made up a useful bodyguard and possessed boats which Jesus could use to avoid the multitudes or to flee from hostile sentiments.

The multitudes who were attracted to Jesus, primarily because of his miraculous cures, presented a problem to Jesus.

The essential problem which Jesus had to overcome was the difficulty created by the crowds which everywhere surrounded him and besought his help, and made it hard for him to extend quickly enough the areas in which he could hope to deliver his message personally. What with teaching and healing, and people struggling frantically to reach him, to touch even the sacred fringe of his robe as he passed, by the end of most days he was utterly exhausted. At one time by the lake to gain freedom to speak he used a boat moored off-shore as his pulpit. He even crossed to the other side for a brief respite. But the people ran round the coast to meet him as he landed, or followed in other boats. He could not get away (78).

To overcome this problem and to make the most of the valuable time available, Jesus sent out his twelve disciples on a preaching mission. But the disciples, who only reported success in demon subjection, and Jesus experienced this first phase of his career as a failure. He knew from prophecy that his message would not be received, but he still hoped for a miracle. His preaching had fallen on deaf eyes, and Jesus was moved and hurt by his failure. His feelings expressed themselves in some bitter and scathing words.

At the same time, some aspects of Jesus' preaching and some of his actions antagonized the Pharisees who devoted their days to attempts to produce a faithful people. These opponents set out, not to have Jesus killed, but put out of operation, silenced so that his influence would be checked.

The execution of John the Baptist triggered the second phase of Jesus' ministry—a phase in which he secretly taught his disciples his true identity. At Caesarea Philippi, Peter made it known to Jesus that his true identity had been revealed to his disciples. Jesus then began to teach his disciples of his forthcoming suffering in terms of the Old Testament oracles, almost like a testimony book, which spoke of the rejection, suffering, and execution of the messiah. Such oracles Jesus had extracted from the scriptures, interpreted them, and integrated them so that in one figure were woven together what have originally been distinct messianic personalities—the prophet like Moses, the suffering just one, the son of David, and the apocalyptic Son of man. "With the help of the Oracles Jesus had deduced that he was required to suffer ignominiously at the hands of the rulers at Jerusalem." The reaction of his disciples to his disclosures, however, made it plain to Jesus that "he could not take them fully into his confidence" (91). The disciples could participate in but they could not share in the knowledge about the greatest plot of all.

Jesus had now to prepare for the most difficult and dangerous part of his present mission, which demanded the utmost caution, and the most careful organisation and timing. He could not look to his disciples to assist him directly in the arrangements for his coming ordeal. He could not even trust them not to work against him if he told them too much; and they might easily ruin everything which he had to contrive. They were devoted to him, and loyal in their own way, but of limited intelligence, simple Galileans for the most part, who would not be at all at home in the sophisticated atmosphere of Jerusalem. What Jesus had need of now for the furtherance of his designs were dependable friends in Judea (92).

For Jesus' activity in Jerusalem and what transpired during the passion week, the Gospel of John provides the clues. Only the Fourth Gospel tells us of Nicodemus, Lazarus of Bethany, and the unnamed, beloved Judaean disciple. The Fourth Gospel is correct when it suggests a three-month ministry in Jerusalem extending from the Feast of Tabernacles (October) until the Feast of Dedication (January) with a period of withdrawal followed by the events of the final week.

Jerusalem at the time was caught up in a struggle between Pilate and the chief priests. The latter were openly friendly to Pilate while at the same time scheming to get him discredited so that the Emperor Tiberius would recall him. The priests had to make every effort to prevent any anti-Roman outbursts, for this would have played into Pilate's hands. The priests were distraught over Pilate's actions, for he had laid impious hands on the sacred treasury of the temple to build a water conduit to Jerusalem. By coming to Jerusalem, Jesus was adding a further complication to the top-level struggle already in progress.

Jesus' plans had to be well laid and executed to perfection, for he was now in critical Judea where a false move could have wrecked everything. In his preaching in the temple, Jesus was attaining two immediate objectives: "He was proclaiming his message where it would have the maximum effect, in the centre of Jewish worship, and he was bringing himself prominently to the attention both of rulers and people" (102). He taught not in the streets but in the temple where he could avoid undue risk, and he had available the family and home of Lazarus into which he could withdraw, rest, not be taken easily by surprise, and plan methodically his great final undertaking. For his confidants, Jesus chose two close Judaean disciples, Lazarus and the young unnamed priest—the disciple whom Jesus loved—whom Schonfield calls John. The latter was most important, for he had contact with secret disciples and the Sanhedrin and could be used in carrying messages and keeping Jesus informed of the plans and actions of the Council. In working out his plans, Jesus had his eye on one other man—Judas Iscariot.

By the time Jesus left Jerusalem in January his business there was very nearly finished and the stage set for the drama to be enacted at the Passover some three months later. There was every reason why he should choose this festival in particular as the season of his revelation and of his suffering. Its symbolism and associations were altogether appropriate and in keeping with the prophecies (104). . . .
Thus it was settled that at the coming Passover Jesus would reveal himself publicly to Israel as the Messiah. His hour, so long awaited, would have come (105).

Jesus withdrew from Jerusalem following the Feast of Dedication and crossed into Transjordan. His withdrawal was temporarily interrupted by news that Lazarus was seriously ill. Jesus returned to Bethany, and although what happened there can no longer be accurately ascertained, it gave rise to the report that Jesus had performed a major miracle. The Sanhedrin—the Council—heard this report and suspected that Jesus was now making his move to lead an uprising. In a specially convened session, the Sanhedrin reached the decision that Jesus must now be liquidated. Friends on the Council, among whom was Nicodemus, speedily provided an intelligence report to Jesus informing him of the results of the meeting. Jesus quickly withdrew again, ultimately making his way to Galilee where he would stay until he returned to Jerusalem for Passover accompanied by a substantial body of Galileans.

Jesus proclaimed publicly his messiahship upon his triumphal entry—a well-laid plan carried out through the aid of Lazarus, who arranged for the ass upon which Jesus could ride as the predicted king. "Jesus came to Jerusalem as a king in the most open manner" (114). He was acclaimed by the crowd as Son of David. Jesus' well laid plans had assured that the Sanhedrin could not intervene. Accompanied by his Galilean and some Judaean supporters, Jesus' popularity meant that the Sanhedrin would be treated as Roman lackeys if they took action. At the same time, the Sanhedrin could not ignore the matter; otherwise they were open to the charge of aiding and abetting treason and would thus incur Rome's disfavor. "This Jesus, in his mad folly, had placed them between the devil and the deep blue sea" (116).

With Jesus' triumphant entry into Jerusalem, "the die was cast, and now there could be no turning back. Jesus had boldly and publicly committed himself in the way he had planned. . . . By so doing he had made himself guilty of treason against Caesar. . . . The action of Jesus had been intentional and deliberate, and he was fully aware that there could be only one outcome, his arrest and execution" (114).

The events which preceded the crucifixion were all played according to the plan masterminded by Jesus and executed with special help unknown to his twelve disciples. Jesus' anointment in Bethany was carried out by private arrangement with Mary, sister of Lazarus, in order to trigger Judas' betrayal as well as to point toward Jesus' death.

Judas knew that Jesus expected to be betrayed. He had been saying so again and again, and once more now he had spoken about his death. We may believe, however, that not until this moment had Judas thought of himself as the betrayer. It was the worth of the ointment and Jesus talking about his burial which put it into his head. Suddenly like an inspiration it came to him that money was to be made by doing what Jesus plainly wanted. It seemed as if in a subtle way Jesus was telling him this, inviting him to profit by doing his will. The tempter came in the guise of his Master (129).

Judas went to the Council to lay plans for the betrayal. Both he and the Council were unknowing participants in the greatest drama of Jesus' ministry. "The Council might imagine they were exercising their own free will in determining to destroy Jesus, and Judas Iscariot might believe the same in betraying him; but in fact the comprehensive engineer of the Passover Plot was Jesus himself. Their responses were governed by his ability to assess their reactions when he applied appropriate stimuli. Thus it was that the Scriptures would be fulfilled" (130-31).

The Last Supper was observed in the Jerusalem home of the beloved disciple who was the eye-witness source behind the Fourth Gospel. Arrangements were made and executed, all without the knowledge of the Twelve. There were fourteen at the supper that night, Jesus, the Twelve, and the beloved disciple.

Jesus' trial was based on his political pretensions, not on theological grounds. As always, Jesus' actions and especially his silence while on trial were to fulfill the prophetic oracles—"he was dumb like a sheep before his shearers" (Isaiah 53:7).

Just as he had always planned ahead so Jesus had calculated about his death and resurrection.

The plans of Jesus were laid with remarkable care for timing. He had singled out a particular Passover as the season when he would suffer, and had taken every precaution to ensure that he would not be arrested beforehand. During the first half of Passion Week, keeping himself in the public eye by conducting his activities in the Temple, he had aggravated the ecclesiastical authorities to the pitch that they were determined to destroy him as soon as it should be feasible without risk of a tumult; but he was careful not to help them by staying in the city after dark. Not until Wednesday evening did Jesus apply the pressure that decided Judas to go to the Council with an offer to betray him, and by his secret arrangements he saw to it that the arrest would not take place until Thursday evening after he had partaken of the Last Supper in Jerusalem with his disciples. All this suggests that he intended that his crucifixion should be on Friday, which would be the eve of the Sabbath. Calculating that it would require some hours on Friday morning for the Council to obtain his condemnation by Pilate, which could not be withheld as the charge was treason against the emperor, and knowing that in accordance with custom he would not be left on the cross over the Sabbath, but would be taken down well before sunset when the Sabbath commenced, Jesus could roughly reckon that he would experience crucifixion for not much more than three or four hours, whereas normally the agonies of the crucified lasted for as many days (153-54).

Jesus was convinced that he must suffer but not die on the cross, since the messiah would survive his terrible ordeal. Thus he laid plans to insure that this was the case. One cannot follow the Gospel accounts on what happened here, since their authors worked with such scanty material and were influenced by various legends and misunderstood stories, some from the writings of Josephus. For the success of the rescue from the cross, Jesus had to have a drug administered to him to create the impression of death, and he had to arrange for a speedy delivery of his body to his secret disciples. At the signal words, "I am thirsty," Jesus was passed the drug and lapsed quickly into unconsciousness. Swiftly, Joseph of Arimathea, a secret disciple, carried out the prearranged plans and asked Pilate for the body. Pilate, checking with the centurion in charge and thinking that death had occurred, turned over what he thought was the corpse of Jesus.

As Schonfield reconstructs the subsequent events, Jesus was taken to the tomb of Joseph, an act witnessed by the women. In the course of the night, he was brought out of the tomb by the persons involved in the scheme. For a time, he regained consciousness and commissioned one of the secret followers to carry a message to his disciples. Jesus died later, that night from his wounds, especially the unplanned soldier's spearthrust in his side. Instead of returning the body to the original tomb where the burial clothes had been left, his body was "quickly yet reverently interred" elsewhere (165). The women coming to the garden discovered the empty tomb and saw a man, probably the same person who had passed the drugged drink to Jesus at the time of the crucifixion. John the priest and Peter came to the tomb, saw the burial clothes, and John was convinced of the resurrection. Although John had participated in part of the plot, Jesus had dealt singly and individually with his Judaean followers who were in a position to aid his plans, and had not brought everyone in on the whole plot. John thus knew nothing of the crucifixion phase of the plot. Mary Magdalene encountered the man in the garden who tried to pass along the final message of Jesus, but was mistaken for Jesus. The man who appeared to the two on the road to Emmaus and to the disciples in Galilee was the same man who appeared in all the resurrection stories. He was anxious to deliver to the disciples the message which Jesus had given him as he lay dying. His message was that the messiah had risen in accordance with the scriptures. "Finally he was able to discharge his obligation" (172).

In proclaiming the resurrection, there was no deliberate untruth perpetuated by the disciples. On the basis of the evidence, they had reached the inescapable conclusion. Jesus too had acted in faith to fulfil the scriptures.

Neither had there been any fraud on the part of Jesus himself. He had schemed in faith for his physical recovery, and what he expected had been frustrated by circumstances quite beyond his control. Yet when he sank into sleep his faith was unimpaired, and by an extraordinary series of contributory events, partly resulting from his own planning, it proved to have been justified. In a manner he had not forseen resurrection had come to him. And surely this was for the best, since there would have been no future for a Messiah who returned temporarily to this troubled world possibly crippled in mind and body.

By his planning beyond the cross and the tomb, by his implicit confidence in the coming of the Kingdom of God over which he was deputed to reign, Jesus had won through to victory. The messianic programme was saved from the grave of all dead hopes to become a guiding light and inspiration to men. Wherever mankind strives to bring in the rule of justice, righteousness and peace, there the deathless presence of Jesus the Messiah is with them. Wherever a people of God is found labouring in the cause of human brotherhood, love and compassion, there the King of the Jews is enthroned. No other will ever come to be what he was and do what he did. The special conditions which produced him at a peculiar and pregnant moment in history are never likely to occur again. But doubtless there will be other moments having their own strange features, and other men through whom the vision will speak at an appointed time. Meanwhile we have not exhausted the potentialities of the vision of Jesus (173-74).

11. JESUS: THE FOUNDER OF A SECRET SOCIETY

All this history is merely plausible, and plausibility is not proof. Things probably happened thus, though they may have happened otherwise. History, however, is by definition the search for the *most probable* explanations of preserved phenomena. When several explanations are possible, the historian must always choose the most probable one. But the truth is that improbable things sometimes happen. Therefore truth is necessarily stranger than history. —Morton Smith, *The Secret Gospel* (p. 148)

Quite early in the history of the church, secret and closed groups sprung up within Christianity claiming to possess a superior knowledge (gnosis) and a truer understanding of Christianity than that available to the church at large. These gnostic groups had many similarities to the mystery religions which were widespread in the Greco-Roman world at the time of the church's earliest days. Persons were especially initiated into the mystery community. Initiation rituals generally involved purifications of various types, instruction in the secrets and mysteries of the group, and various rites. Generally a myth about the founder or the god concerned with the group formed an important element in their belief system. Initiation and community rituals generally involved some form of union with the deity and promised the worshiper personal salvation and beatitude. Members were generally sworn to secrecy about the community's beliefs and practices.

The Dead Sea Scrolls community, which will be discussed in the next chapter, was in a way a mystery community. It possessed its special beliefs, unique interpretation of Old Testament scriptures, and ritual practices. Initiates were taught the beliefs and secrets of the community and advanced into full membership by stages. Members were sworn to secrecy not to divulge the innermost beliefs upon penalty of death.

The existence of gnostics in early Christianity is evidenced by Paul's refutation of some of their beliefs. The Johannine epistles polemicize against Christians with gnostic characteristics among which were a denial of the full humanity of Jesus. Numerous church fathers combated heretical teachers and movements in early Christianity which claimed to possess a secret, esoteric form of Christianity traced back to an origin in the life and teachings of Jesus or to special revelations granted by the risen Christ.

In the 1940s, a number of manuscripts belonging to a gnostic form of Christianity were discovered at Nag Hammadi in Egypt. The community to which these belonged may go back in time to the beginning of the second century A.D. Some of these documents were gospels in form. The most famous of these is the so-called Gospel of Thomas which contains approximately 112 sayings attributed to Jesus. Many of these sayings are similar and some identical to sayings of Jesus contained in the canonical Gospels. Others are quite different and present a gnostic interpretation of Jesus stressing salvation through knowledge. The opening lines of the Gospel of Thomas read: "These are the secret words which Jesus the Living spoke and which Didymus Judas Thomas wrote. And He said: He who will find the interpretation of these words will not taste death." This introduction stresses the idea of secret sayings communicated by Jesus, that is, sayings which were not for the whole of the church but for the special few. The sayings are traced back to the disciple Thomas and thus claim an apostolic origin. Possession of a proper understanding of the sayings carried with it the promise of salvation over death.

Throughout church history, groups have claimed that Jesus taught in two different forms, one openly for the multitudes and one in esoteric and secret fashion for the special elect. In modern times, the Rosicrucians, whose movement dates from the seventeenth century, are a secret brotherhood whose philosophy is partially based on secret teachings traced back to Jesus.

The theory that Jesus was the founder of a closed secret society has been recently proposed by Morton Smith in his popular work *The Secret Gospel: The Discovery and Interpretation of the Secret Gospel According to Mark* and his scholarly volume *Clement of Alexandria and a Secret Gospel of Mark*. Smith's theory is based on a passage from a secret gospel of Mark which he discovered in 1958 in the library of the Mar Saba monastery. The monastery, founded in the fifth century, is located in the mountainous desert region about twelve miles southeast of Jerusalem. Mar Saba is, in addition to St. Katherine in the Sinai, one of the great desert monasteries of the Orthodox Church.

Smith discovered a copy of a letter of Clement of Alexandria while photographing manuscripts in the Mar Saba library. The letter had been copied into the back of an edition of the letters of St. Ignatius of Antioch published in Amsterdam in 1646. The material in the letter was previously unknown, although Smith has shown, with reasonable probability, that the seventy-two line fragment is a copy of an authentic letter written between A.D. 175 and 200. Clement was an important leader in the Alexandrian church where he headed the Catechetical School until he was forced out of Egypt during the persecution of the church by the Roman emperor Septimius Severus about A.D. 202.

The heading of the document states that it is from the letters of Clement and was addressed to someone named Theodore. The letter commends Theodore for opposing the Carpocratians, a gnostic sect during the second century. Carpocrates worked in Alexandria sometime during the first half of the second century. According to the church father Irenaeus, Carpocrates "believed that Jesus was the son of Joseph and was brought up in Judaism, realized the inadequacy of the Jewish law, turned to higher truths, and so received a supernatural power by which he was enabled to rise above the angels who had created this world, purging himself of his worldly passions as he went, and ascend to the supreme god" (*The Secret Gospel,* 134). He seems to have believed that a similar contempt for the human law would allow men to experience a similar possession of power. They would then dominate the angelic powers and utilize these powers in the performance of miracles. He seems also to have taught that one must commit all possible sins in order to satisfy the spiritual rulers of this world and thus be freed for the heavenly world. Thus Carpocrates advocated a libertine approach to life, arguing that man was saved by faith alone. Reincarnation of the soul was apparently also taught by him. Carpocrates and his followers appealed to secret teachings of Jesus contained in their sectarian writings. Smith sums up the main evidence about the Carpocratians: "From Irenaeus' arguments against them it appears that they had considerable fame as miracle workers, denied the resurrection of the body, and practiced (or were accused of) extreme libertinism, especially in sexual relations." Their basic emphasis seemed to have stressed "gift of the spirit, ascent to God, freedom from the law, and magical powers" (135).

In the letter, Clement opposed the Carpocratian teaching and spoke of the sect's abandonment of the way of the commandments for a life of carnal and bodily sins. Clement points out that they pride themselves in knowledge but denies that they possess the truth.

The letter then proceeds to discuss the claims of the Carpocratians "about the divinely inspired Gospel according to Mark." Clement discusses the origin of Mark's Gospel by saying that Mark wrote an account of the Lord's doing while Peter was staying in Rome. However, Mark did not write down everything but omitted many of the secret things. After Peter's death, according to the letter, Mark came to Alexandria bringing along his own and Peter's notes. In Alexandria, "he composed a more spiritual Gospel for the use of those who were being perfected." This was done by supplementing his former work in such a way as to aid in the progress toward gnosis. In spite of producing this spiritual gospel, Mark still did not divulge some of the secret things nor write down the hierophantic teachings of the Lord—that is, the teachings dealing with the secret mysteries. Mark's spiritual gospel, according to the letter, was preserved and guarded in Alexandria where it was read only to those who were being initiated into the great mysteries. Carpocrates secured a copy of this secret gospel by deceiving an elder in the Alexandrian church. He then, according to this letter, perverted the secret gospel with his own admixture of doctrine and shameless lies.

Clement then seeks to inform Theodore, who had written to him, about the content of this secret gospel over against the falsified version of the Carpocratians. He quotes a passage from this secret Gospel saying that it occurs after what is now Mark 10:34. The passage from the *Secret Gospel* is as follows:

And they come into Bethany, and a certain woman, whose brother had died, was there. And, coming, she prostrated herself before Jesus and says to him: "Son of David, have mercy on me." But the disciples rebuked her. And Jesus, being angered, went off with her into the garden where the tomb was, and straightway a great cry was heard from the tomb. And going near Jesus rolled away the stone from the door of the tomb. And straightway, going in where the youth was, he stretched forth his hand and raised him, seizing his hand. But the youth, looking upon him, loved him and began to beseech him that he might be with him. And going out of the tomb they came into the house of the youth, for he was rich. And after six days Jesus told him what to do and in the evening the youth comes to him, wearing a linen cloth over [his] naked [body]. And he remained with him that night, for Jesus taught him the mystery of the kingdom of God. And thence, arising, he returned to the other side of the Jordan (16-17).

After translating the text, Smith spent several years comparing the vocabulary and style of the entire letter with the known writings of Clement and comparing the quote from the *Secret Gospel of Mark* with the canonical Mark. In addition, other scholars were consulted on the date of the letter and its possible authenticity as well as the relationship of the Markan text to our Gospel of Mark. Some of Smith's conclusions were (1) that the story of the resurrection of the youth lies behind John's account of the resurrection of Lazarus, which romanticized and legendized the earlier material; (2) that the latter halves of the Gospels of Mark and John run parallel if the secret text is inserted into our present form of Mark; (3) that John and Mark may have been dependent in these parallel sections on an early Aramaic tradition; (4) that the youth in the story in the secret gospel is the same as the youth in the story of Mark 10:17-22; (5) that the secret text must be understood in relationship to a baptismal initiation; (6) and that the text represents an authentic early tradition which points toward an interpretation of Jesus as the founder of a secret society.

Smith proceeded to see if the evidence drawn from the New Testament and material contemporary with the early church allow for such an interpretation and understanding of Jesus. In the account of the secret gospel, Jesus is said to have taught the youth the mystery of the kingdom of God. Smith points to the fact that Mark 4:11-12 has Jesus say to his disciples: "To you has been given the secret of the kingdom of God, but for those outside everything is in parables, so that they may indeed see but not perceive, and may indeed hear but not understand; lest they should turn again, and be forgiven." This passage distinguishes between Jesus' public preaching in parables and his revelation of the secret of the kingdom to his intimate group of disciples. Smith, in noting parallels to the secret gospel tradition elsewhere in Mark, refers to the story of Jesus' planned movement into Jerusalem and his communal meal alone with his intimate circle (Mark 14:12-26) after which there follows the story of the events in Gethsemane (Mark 14:27-52). In this latter material, Jesus placed three of his disciples as guards. In the story of the arrest, reference is made to the fact that a "young man followed him, with nothing but a linen cloth about his body; and they seized him, but he left the linen cloth and ran away naked." Smith argues that if one reads Mark 14:51-52 in light of the secret gospel text, then Jesus was here inducting the young man into the secret society. "The business in hand was a baptism; the youth wore the required costume. The time—night— agrees with the story in the secret gospel; the place—beside a stream in a lonely garden—is suitable. The preceding secrecy has obvious prudential explanations." Thus in reading Mark and the secret gospel passage, Smith could conclude: "Jesus had a 'mystery of the kingdom of God,' a baptismal rite, which he administered to some, at least, of his disciples. It was nocturnal, secret, and Mark thought it required six days' preparation" (81).

In attempting to ascertain more explictly what the secret of the kingdom really was, Smith notes that secret cults and mystery groups who gave their mysteries to the new members at the time of initiation were widespread at the time of Jesus. By comparing John the Baptist with Jesus, Smith feels that one can ascertain Jesus' special relationship to the kingdom. What could and did Jesus offer his disciples and followers that John could not? John was a prophet preaching repentance and warning that the end was near at hand. He also proclaimed that his hearers could prepare for the coming judgment by undergoing a baptism for the remission of sins. This baptism was the unique factor that made John more than a prophet and distinguished his movement from all others. John not only announced the kingdom, he purified men for entrance into the coming kingdom. With Jesus, the kingdom was present. On the basis of his analysis of Mark and the secret gospel, Smith concludes that Jesus introduced a baptismal rite in which persons were inducted into the kingdom. Smith points to John 3:22 and suggests that the Aramaic of John 4:2 may have read—Jesus himself baptized no one except his disciples—to support the idea of Jesus' baptismal rite. Smith notes that Jesus himself was baptized and that the early church appears on the scene as a baptizing community. All of which supports the argument that Jesus baptized into the kingdom just as the early Christians baptized into the church. Thus Smith concludes: Jesus "could admit his followers to the kingdom of God, and he could do it in some special way, so that they were not there merely by anticipation, nor by virtue of belief and obedience, nor by some other figure of speech, but were really, actually, in" (94). "Jesus probably admitted his chosen followers to the kingdom by some sort of baptism. *This was the mystery of the kingdom—the mystery rite by which the kingdom was entered*" (96).

Smith argues that if one compares baptism as practiced by John the Baptist and baptism as practiced and understood by Paul, then one can determine how Jesus understood baptism. Smith assumes, unlike many scholars, that the theology of Paul is based directly on the theology of Jesus; so Paul could in no way be considered the creator of Christianity. Since only a few years separate John from Paul and since Paul, even though he was a creative thinker, was dependent upon the tradition passed along to him, such a comparison could allow one to determine the elements which came from Jesus.

The Baptist stood on one side of Jesus; on the other stood Paul. Jesus might be defined as the middle term between them—and a short middle term, at that. According to all reports, his ministry began soon after his baptism and lasted, at most, about three years. Paul's conversion, according to his own account in Galatians, must have occurred within four or five years of the Crucifixion, perhaps less. So not more than eight years, and probably less, separated Paul from the Baptist. Why not, then, compare the Baptist with Paul, determine the differences, and try to see how many of these could be traced back to Jesus? (74).

For Paul (see Romans 6:3-9; I Corinthians 12:12-13; Galatians 3:26-29; Colossians 2:9-3:4), according to Smith, the following are characteristic of his practice of baptism: "1. Paul's baptism was first of all a ritual for union with Jesus. . . . 2. The union in Paul's baptism was affected by the spirit. . . . 3. The closest parallels to Paul's baptism are found in magical material. . . . 4. Paul's baptism was connected with ascent into the heavens. . . . 5. Finally, Paul's baptism freed the recipient from the law" (101). Do these elements go back to Jesus?

Smith argues that since Jesus introduced the communion ritual in which union with Christ was achieved through eating his body and drinking his blood, it is entirely possible that Jesus introduced also the ritual baptism of union with himself. Since the Spirit is so closely associated with Jesus in the Gospels, for example, it descends upon him at his baptism, it seems probable that the work of the Spirit in baptism goes back to Jesus. Since the marvelous and miraculous power of Jesus in the Gospels—his exorcisms, cures, etc.—show his magical power, so the element of magical ritual probably goes back to him as well. The idea of ascent into heaven—the kingdom of God par excellence—probably also goes back to Jesus. The experience of the heavenly world, shared in by Jesus and his disciples, is probably most clearly reflected in the transfiguration story. Smith claims that the idea of the experience of translation to the heavenly world was not unknown at the time. Even Paul claims to have been carried into the third heaven (II Corinthians 12:2). Statements of Jesus about knowing the truth which could set one free and that the law and prophets were until John but from then on the kingdom of God is proclaimed suggest that Jesus too conceived of entrance into the kingdom as freedom from the law. Smith summarizes his arguments as follows:

Thus from the differences between Paul's baptism and that of the Baptist, and from the scattered indications in the canonical Gospels and the secret Gospel of Mark, we can put together a picture of Jesus' baptism, "the mystery of the kingdom of God." It was a water baptism administered by Jesus to chosen disciples, singly and by night. The costume, for the disciple, was a linen cloth worn over the naked body. This cloth was probably removed for the baptism proper, the immersion in water, which was now reduced to a preparatory purification. After that, by unknown ceremonies, the disciple was possessed by Jesus' spirit and so united with Jesus. One with him, he participated by hallucination in Jesus' ascent into the heavens, he entered the kingdom of God, and was thereby set free from the laws ordained for and in the lower world. Freedom from the law may have resulted in completion of the spiritual union by physical union [homosexual practices]. This certainly occurred in many forms of gnostic Christianity; how early it began there is no telling (113-14).

The theory of Jesus as the founder of a secret society, a society oriented toward admission to the kingdom and union with Jesus, suggests a number of elements in the life of Jesus. Jesus' followers must have been divided into various circles already during his lifetime. Smith suggests three circles: an inner circle to whom he had given the secret and whom he had baptized, one or more outer circles such as his less intimate followers, his family, and acquaintances to whom the secret was not revealed, and the circle of those outside, that is those hostile and indifferent to Jesus.

Jesus' teaching to these groups would have been quite different. If one examines the New Testament, Jesus' teaching on the law, for example, seems to reflect contradictory statements. On the one hand, he proclaims a freedom from the law (Luke 16:16; Matthew 11:12-13; Mark 2:22; Luke 5:36; Mark 2:28; Matthew 11:18-19; Mark 2:15-16; Matthew 11:29-30; John 1:17-18; Luke 10:22; John 8:31-32), but on the other hand, Jesus preached that the law is still binding (Matthew 5:17-20 and elsewhere). Smith explains this phenomenon in the following way: "the legalistic material represents Jesus' teaching for 'those outside.' For them he held that the law was still binding and he interpreted it as did the other legal teachers of his time; about one point he would have a more lenient opinion, about another, a stricter one—such variation appears in the rulings of almost all ancient rabbis. But he himself was free of the law, and so were those who had been baptized with his spirit. The contradictions of the present Gospels probably result from a gradual seepage of secret material into texts originally meant for outsiders . . . it was probably from Jesus' secret teaching and practice that Paul derived, through the intermediation of Jesus' immediate followers, his notion that

baptism freed the baptized from the requirements of the law"
(112-13).

The resurrection visions "are best understandable as
consequences of Jesus' baptismal practice, reflections of the
visions he suggested to the young men he initiated" (116).
Spirit possession and ecstatic experience, characteristic of
early Christianity, go back to the individual possession
experienced in Jesus' baptism. Jesus seems to have had a
special attraction to and hold over schizophrenic types—
"persons whose suppressed impulses had broken through
their rational control and expressed themselves in violent and
destructive actions explained as the work of 'demons'";
"women who had been cured of evil spirits (Luke 8:2)"; and
disciples whose willingness totally to abandon ordinary life to
follow Jesus reveals an instability in character (116-17).
Jesus' society as a group freed from the law explains the fact
that Jesus was a "figure notorious for his libertine teaching
and practice. He broke the Sabbath, he neglected the purity
rules, he refused to fast, made friends with publicans and
sinners, and was known as 'a gluttonous man and a
winebibber.' He not only taught his disciples that the law had
come to an end with the Baptist, and that the least in the
kingdom was greater than the Baptist, but he also administered a baptism of his own—'the mystery of the kingdom of
God'—by which he enabled some of his disciples, united with
himself, to enter the kingdom and to enjoy his own freedom
from the law" (130).

The divisions within the early and developing church can
thus be traced back to Jesus himself.

Therefore, in our picture of pre-Pauline Christianity,
alongside the legalistic interpretation of the religion we must
set the libertine. The legalistic interpretation went back to
the (mainly Pharisaic?) converts of the Jerusalem church,
and appealed to the tradition of Jesus' exoteric teaching. The
libertine interpretation went back to Jesus himself and
preserved and developed elements of his esoteric teaching. It
was dominant in the Jerusalem church in the earliest days,
but it lost its hold as the small group of Jesus' original,

initiated disciples was outnumbered by the new converts under the leadership of Jesus' brother, James, and it went underground when Peter, the leader of the original disciples, was driven out of the city by the persecution under Herod Agrippa I. This libertine tradition, its strength, its diffusion, its unanimity, and its evident age, is explicable only by our understanding of Jesus' teaching about the mystery of the kingdom. This is strong evidence that the understanding is correct (131).

Thus, the secret gnostic sects—like the Carpocratians— were the true heirs of Jesus' secret teachings—although they infused these teachings were diverse materials drawn from other sources—and were the true continuation of Jesus' secret society.

12. JESUS: THE QUMRAN ESSENE

If . . . we look at Jesus in the perspective supplied by the scrolls, we can trace a new continuity and, at last, get some sense of the drama that culminated in Christianity. We can see how the movement represented by the Essenes stood up for perhaps two centuries to the coercion of the Greeks and the Romans, and how it resisted not merely the methods of Rome but also the Roman ideals. We can guess how, about a half century before its refuge was burned together with the Temple of the Jewish God, this movement had inspired a leader who was to transcend both Judaism and Essenism, and whose followers would found a church that was to outlive the Roman Empire and ultimately be identified with Rome herself.—Edmund Wilson, *The Scrolls from the Dead Sea* (p. 97)

In late 1947 and early 1948, the scholarly world became acquainted with the story of the discovery of the now famous Dead Sea (or Qumran) Scrolls. Sometime earlier, probably in the spring of 1947, a young Arab bedouin of the Ta'amireh tribe, Muhammad the Wolf, had accidentally discovered seven ancient scrolls in a cave near where the Wadi Qumran flows into the Dead Sea. It was several months before the true antiquity and nature of the scrolls were determined. When their true character became known, the scrolls were declared by W. F. Albright to be the "greatest manuscript discovery of modern times" which could "revolutionize our approach to the beginnings of Christiantiy."

Since 1947, ten other caves in the Qumran area and a dozen or so caves elsewhere in the near vicinity have yielded manuscripts or manuscript fragments. Most of these scrolls have been dated to a period extending from the fourth century B.C. to the second century A.D. In addition, archaeologists have explored, often trying unsuccessfully to beat the bedouin to finds, and excavated dozens of caves and ruins along the western bank of the Dead Sea.

Our concern here is with only those scrolls from the Qumran area. The hundreds of manuscripts, almost all in very fragmentary form, have not yet been fully published. However, it is possible to give a general description of the Qumran materials by dividing them into four categories. Some of the manuscripts are copies of Old Testament biblical books. Fragments of every Old Testament book, except for Esther, have been found. Some of these provide scholars with copies of parts of the Old Testament a thousand years older than the texts from which our Old Testament translations are made. A second group of manuscripts are Old Testament texts with running commentary. Passages are quoted and an exegesis and interpretation are given relating the text to events and factors later than the text. Sometimes these commentaries do not follow the order of a particular book but are collections of texts from various books accompanied by exegetical interpretation. A third group of manuscripts are copies of books which did not make it into the Old Testament canon but which have been known in various translations from ancient times. A fourth class of manuscripts are writings unique to the community and previously unknown. These texts present the fullest expression of the beliefs of those who produced the documents.

The quantity of documentary material recovered from the Qumran caves is enormous. What is also historically intriguing is the fact that several ancient writers made references to scrolls being found in the area in antiquity—as early as the fourth and as late as the ninth century of the present era.

Ruins located in the vicinity of the caves were excavated in the early fifties. These ruins seemed to have been the center for a rather large community. Dining halls, kitchens, storage rooms, pantries, and a kiln were unearthed. In addition, the complex was supplied by an aquaduct which brought water into a network of large cisterns and smaller "baths." A cemetery in the area contains over a thousand graves and the skeletal remains of men, women, and children have been found in those graves, all with individual burials, which have been opened. The ruins of the community do not seem to reflect any living quarters in the buildings themselves. Apparently those who used the building complex lived elsewhere, perhaps some in the caves and in tents in the vicinity. No manuscript remains in any form were found in the ruins of the buildings although some writing paraphernalia—ink wells and perhaps writing desks—were recovered.

On the basis of the archaeological evidence and through attempts to date the scrolls, the majority of scholars now assign the existence of the community and the writing of the scrolls, which are related to the community, to a period roughly from the middle of the second century B.C. to the time of the first Jewish revolt which began in A.D. 66 and lasted until A.D. 73. Dating of the scrolls, however, is still a highly controversial issue. Some scholars assume that the scrolls and the ruins were at most only accidentally related; others date the scrolls either earlier or later, some consider them medieval in origin, if not fraudulent. The existence of the community and the scrolls at the time of Jesus' life, in spite of continuing controversy, is apparently a safe assumption.

From the scrolls we can know something of the community, its origin, beliefs, character, and history. The community was organized and led into the desert by a person called the Teacher of Righteousness. This teacher provided the community with many of its beliefs and its method of interpreting scripture in light of later events and especially in light of the community's particular history and beliefs. The Teacher of Righteousness was persecuted and perhaps put to death by a character called the Wicked Priest.

The community called itself by numerous designations— the many, the elect, the sons of light, the new covenant. Its members were composed of priests, levites, laymen, and possibly proselytes. Entrance into the community was made through several stages apparently extending over two or three years. Initiation into the community was a special affair. Members were sworn to secrecy about the important beliefs and actions of the community. Rules by which the community was governed were drawn up and display a strict loyalty to the law and rather severe penalties for infractions of the law of Moses and the special rules of the community.

The community believed itself to be the chosen people living in the end of days. Even the Jews outside the community were considered apostate. The community followed a calendar different from that used in the Jerusalem temple. The community, at least according to one document, was living in anticipation of the coming of a great prophet and two messiahs—one from the priestly house of Aaron and the other a political messiah from the house of David. The priestly messiah was to take precedence over the political messiah. The community celebrated a ritual meal of bread and wine interpreted in light of the great banquet to be eaten with the coming messiah(s). Ritual purification baths were part of the ordinary routine. The community was ruled over by persons who held administrative and/or teaching functions. There also seems to have been a special council of twelve or fifteen members. Some of the documents suggest that there was community ownership of property. Reading and study of the scriptures played an important role in the community's life.

The community believed that mankind was divided into two groups—the children of light (or the good spirit) and the children of darkness (or the evil spirit). Before the final consummation of God's purpose, there was to be a forty-year war between the two groups in which the elect would triumph.

After the discovery and study of the scrolls, many scholars began to compare the beliefs and the community with a Jewish sect known as the Essenes who are mentioned and described by the Jewish writers Josephus and Philo and the Roman historian Pliny. The persons who wrote the texts never refer to themselves as Essenes. Nonetheless, most scholars identify the two.

The parallels and similarities between the life and faith of the Qumran community and the early church immediately led to comparisons and in some cases to identification of the two. The church was compared to the community itself and Jesus to the Teacher of Righteousness. In 1950, the imminent French scholar A. Dupont-Sommer wrote:

Everything in the Jewish New Covenant heralds and prepares the way for the Christian New Covenant. The Galilean Master, as He is presented to us in the writings of the New Testament, appears in many respects as an astonishing reincarnation of the Master of Justice [Teacher of Righteousness]. Like the latter He preached pentitence, poverty, humility, love of one's neighbor, chastity. Like him, He prescribed the observance of the Law of Moses, the whole Law, but the Law finished and perfected, thanks to His own revelations. Like him He was the Elect and the Messiah of God, the Messiah redeemer of the world. Like him, He was the object of the hostility of the priests, the party of the Sadducees. Like him He was condemned and put to death. Like him He pronounced judgment on Jerusalem, which was taken and destroyed by the Romans for having put Him to death. Like him, at the end of time, He will be the supreme judge. Like him He founded a Church whose adherents fervently awaited His glorious return. In the Christian Church, just as in the Essene Church, the essential rite is the sacred meal, whose ministers are the priests. Here and there at the head of each community there is the overseer, the "bishop." And the ideal of both churches is essentially that of unity, communion in love—even going so far as the sharing of common property.

All these similarities—and here I only touch upon the subject—together, constitute a very impressive whole. The question at once arises, to which of the two sects, the Jewish or the Christian, does the priority belong? Which of the two was able to influence the other? The reply leaves no room for doubt. The Master of Justice died about 65-63 B.C.; Jesus the Nazarene died about A.D. 30. In every case in which the resemblance compels or invites us to think of a borrowing, this was on the part of Christianity. But on the other hand, the appearance of faith in Jesus—the foundation of the New Church—can scarcely be explained without the real historic activity of a new Prophet, a new Messiah, who rekindled the flame and concentrated on himself the adoration of men (*The Dead Sea Scrolls,* 99-100).

Jesus: The Qumran Essene

Some scholars initially argued that the texts clearly identified the Teacher of Righteousness with the messiah, spoke of his death by crucifixion, and proclaimed his return at the end of history. These judgments have not held up against further study, thus they have been either abandoned or considerably modified.

Are the life and teachings of Jesus to be understood against the background of the Qumran community? Many scholars would answer with an emphatic affirmative. Two books which received wide circulation were published early in the 1950s claiming that the Qumran community contributed significantly to the origin of Christianity. The first of these was by the internationally renowned critic Edmund Wilson. His work on the scrolls was originally published in the *New Yorker* magazine (May, 1955). Wilson's article brought the issue of the scrolls to the attention of a wide audience. Wilson accused Christian scholars of deliberately boycotting the scrolls because of fear of what they would find there. He spoke of a "certain nervousness, a reluctance to take hold of the subject and to place it in historical perspective" which characterized those who "have taken Christian orders or been trained in the rabbinical tradition" and were thus "inhibited in dealing with such questions . . . by their various religious commitments" (*The Scrolls from the Dead Sea*, 98). Wilson assigned a great significance to the scrolls for the possible light they would shed on Christianity as the following quote illustrates:

The spirit of the Essene brotherhood, even before its expulsion from its sunken base, had already thus made itself free to range through the whole ancient world, touching souls with that Gospel of purity and light to which the brotherhood had consecrated itself, and teaching the contempt of those eagles which they had noted—with evident astonishment—that the army of their enemy worshipped. The monastery, this structure of stone that endures, between the bitter waters and precipitous cliffs, with its oven and its inkwells, its mill and its cesspool, its constellation of sacred fonts and the unadorned graves of its dead, is perhaps, more than Bethlehem or Nazareth, the cradle of Christianity (97-98).

The second volume published on the scrolls arguing for a close connection between Qumran and Christianity was *The Meaning of the Dead Sea Scrolls* by A. Powell Davies. Davies' book does not make the type of claims asserted by Wilson. It was written from the perspective of a liberal theologian who could argue "that God can work through natural events in a gradual social evolution just as well as in some other way. Indeed, this is the way that he does work. A religion is not one whit the less because it has no supernatural origin, no miracles and not too much uniqueness. What we need is not the victory of one religion over other religions but the recognition of the noble and the good in all religions" (131). For Davies, the scrolls seemed to represent one more element in the scholarly recognition that Christianity probably didn't originate in the way it is commonly explained.

When theological scholars say, as they have recently been saying, that the discovery of the Scrolls has brought them no information that obliges them to revise their view of Christian beginning—or at least not extensively—it can be *for them* the truth. But they should go on to tell the laity in what sense it is the truth. What they mean, if they would express it more informatively, is *that they have known for a long time that the traditional view of Christian origins is not supported by history so much as theology.* Unlike the layman, they are familiar with New Testament historical problems to which it has never been possible to find historical solutions. Dogmatic solutions are another matter. But what the layman thinks he is dealing with in trying to grasp the meaning of the Scrolls is not theology but history, not dogma but fact.

Theological scholars have long been aware, for instance, of the impossibility of knowing, historically, where Jesus was born, or when, or by what means the portrait of him in the first three Gospels (the Synoptics) can be reconciled with the quite different portrait of him in the Gospel of John. This is only the beginning of the matter. Theological scholars know (again as the layman usually does not) something of the extensive debt of Christianity to Pagan religion during the first centuries of its development in the Mediterranean area.

Jesus: The Qumran Essene

Theological scholars have known for some time that there were important resemblances between Essenic organization and that of the early Christian churches and have had reason to suspect that the two may have been organically connected (84).

The Lost Years of Jesus by C. F. Potter, published in 1958, sought to associate closely not only the early church and the Essene movement but also Jesus and the Teacher of Righteousness. The title to his book implies an association of Jesus with the Qumran community prior to his public appearance.

Hundreds of . . . evidences of the Essene origin of the ideas, beliefs, and teachings of Jesus, John the Baptist, John the Disciple, Paul, and the other New Testament writers have been noted by scholars working on the Scrolls. . . .
And now that the proven Mother of Christianity is known to have been the prior community of the New Covenant commonly called the Essenes, the momentous question challenging the conscience of all Christendom is whether the child will have the grace, courage, and honesty to acknowledge and honor its own mother! (13)

Potter, like Wilson and Davies, accused scholars of not leveling with the church about the true nature of the Dead Sea Scrolls and the similarity between many of their teachings and those of early Christianity.

To date, the theologians have had time enough to tell their communicants the epochal significance of the finding of the Essene library, but their utterances have been—especially in America—singularly hesitant, reluctant, and incomplete. Some distort the meaning of the Scrolls for their own purposes. Others are waiting a generation or two before making up their minds! (13)

Potter assigned great significance to the fact that the Qumran community predated Christianity. Since this was the case, then similarity in thought, theology, and expression would point to dependence of Christianity upon the scrolls and not vice versa.

A century or more before the Christian New Testament was written, the Qumran Essenes were familiar with the ideas, proverbs, prayers, beatitudes, blessings, and even the beautiful sentences in Jesus' Sermon on the Mount, which he was quoting from Essene Scrolls, as he and his audience knew, though we may not. Even the preaching of the Gospel, the Good News, or, as the now current theological phrase has it, the "kerygma" of Kingdom Come, was evidently out of Qumran by John the Baptist, as well as the baptism wherewith he baptized Jesus "to fulfill all righteousness," a key Essenian phrase. And the very name of the Christian Bible, the New Testament, came from those monks of Qumran, who never called themselves Essenes, but the "Sons of Zadok" (King David's high priest), or, significantly, the Community of the New Covenant. And "New Covenant" was a better word to translate the Aramaic word which Christianity later translated as "New Testament" (12-13).

Those books of the Old Testament—Isaiah, Deuteronomy, and Psalms—which were most popular at Qumran are also the books most popular in the early church, assuming that New Testament quotations are an indication of popularity. For Potter, the book of Enoch which was quoted directly in the New Testament (Jude 14) was a link associating the early church with Qumran. Fragments of Enoch were found among the scrolls and Potter concludes that the similarities in ideas and vocabulary between passages in Enoch, and other apocryphal books, point to this literature as the missing link between the Old Testament and early Christianity. "Old Enoch is on his way back home now, after long exile, and should soon take his rightful place back in our Bible. For, if the Qumran community was the mother of Christianity, Enoch was the father" (101).

If a number of copies of Enoch were in the Qumran community library, and if Jesus spent part of the so-called "silent years" as a member, or associate member, or even only as a resident student, that might explain why he and his disciples were so well acquainted with the Enochan literature that we find not merely the same ideas and doctrines in the New Testament, but even the same phrases and sentences (52).

Jesus: The Qumran Essene

In their view of the last days and the coming of the messiah, Potter notices many similarities between Christianity and the Qumran community.

In a very real sense, since the word Christian means Messianist (the Greek word Christos being the exact equivalent of the Hebrew word Messiah, meaning the anointed one), and since the Essenes were very much concerned with the coming of Judgment Day and the Messiah, they were Messianists; and, to use the Greek form of the word, they were Christians before Jesus Christ was born. The fact that later generations of the followers of Jesus filled the words "Christ" and "Christian" and "Christianity" with complicated theological meanings, adding more and more doctrines for several centuries, until being a "Christian" meant believing a complex system of dogmas that the Jewish Jesus never heard of, does not alter the fact that when his disciples were first called Christians at Antioch in Syria, they were Christians much like the Essenes were, or any pious Jew who was waiting in earnest expectation of the Messiah (129).

Jesus must be understood as having contact of some sort with the Qumran Essene community prior to his public ministry. It was during this contact that the content of Jesus' preaching was developed. "Indeed, the opinion that Jesus either lived for several years in the Qumran Community which produced the Scrolls or at least visited it often is gaining ground among unprejudiced students" (139). Thus the scrolls provide the clue for understanding Jesus and his origin.

Now the scientists, in the light of the Qumran discoveries, can get much closer to that remarkable young man who emerged from "the wilderness" to give to the world his synthesis of the wisdom, faith and hopes of several cultures he had studied in the remarkable community and its wonderful library by the shore of the Salty Sea (83).

What the laymen suspected when the scrolls were first published—that they challenged the uniqueness of Jesus—and what scholars generally refused to admit may be correct.

What the laymen suspect regarding the cave finds is true. The dogmas and doctrines, the theological twists and turns, the tampering with texts to corroborate newly invented creedal statements, all these additions of later centuries to the simple ethical humanitarian faith of Jesus the Teacher of Righteousness are revealed by these older Scroll manuscripts to have been like the tawdry tinsel and bright-colored finery with which ignorant peasants adorn the statues of their gods.

For Jesus the Galilean, baptized by John the Baptist into the great fellowship of the pacifistic, socialistic, cooperative Essenes of the New Covenant, later evidently carried out in its principles into the wide world, improving those principles in some respects, but preaching them best by living up to them to the limit, even to death on the Roman cross (155).

13. JESUS: THE SEXUAL BEING

> To speak of Jesus as being truly human is also to speak of him as a sexual being. Whatever ways he may have chosen to express or to re-channel his sexuality (and about this we know nothing), it is clear that when his sinlessness is mentioned we do not, or should not, take this to imply a-sexuality. Alas, however, much Christian thinking has done just this; in consequence we have the anaemic, lifeless, almost effeminate Christ of the Victorian stained-glass windows and of some popular portraits. Had Jesus been married, the exercise of sexuality within that relationship would not have constituted sin; were he not of the marrying kind, his homosexual tendency would not have constituted sin. To think otherwise is to denigrate God's creation, to succumb to a Manichean view of nature, and to deny the goodness of the sexuality with which God has endowed his human (and other) creatures.—Norman Pittenger, *Christology Reconsidered* (p. 61)

A dominant concern behind the quest of the historical Jesus has been a desire to rediscover him as a human being. This desire to understand Jesus as truly human has raised the question of Jesus' sexuality. If Jesus was a man like every other man, did he undergo normal sexual development, pass through puberty, and experience sexual drive and desires? If so, how did Jesus react to and channel these sexual drives and passions?

Some recent study of Jesus, perhaps influenced by the so-called "sexual revolution" which has brought the matter of sex into open discussion, has argued that no serious search for the real Jesus can avoid dealing with the question of Jesus' sexuality.

The question of Jesus' sexuality is of course not an issue which the church has never discussed. At the same time, the matter has never been a dominant concern of church theology and has been discussed primarily within the context of theories expounding sexual ethics for Christians, and particularly for Christian clerics.

The New Testament is silent on the question of Jesus' sexuality. It contains no reference or discussion of the matter although several sayings of Jesus are related to the question of man's sexuality.

The writers of the New Testament and the early church fathers combated any theory that suggested Jesus was not fully human. Quite early, some Christians expounded the belief that Jesus was not fully human, that he was totally divine and only appeared to be human. He was more like an angel who masqueraded as a man but without undergoing hunger, thirst, suffering, or death. This theory that Jesus was not human was called "Docetism" from a Greek word meaning "to appear." The letters of I and II John denounced and proclaimed as unorthodox any belief that denied the humanity of Jesus. "Many deceivers have gone out into the world, men who will not acknowledge the coming of Jesus Christ in the flesh; such a one is the deceiver and the antichrist" (II John 7). "By this you know the Spirit of God: every spirit that confesses that Jesus Christ has come in the flesh is of God" (I John 4:2). At the same time, the church proclaimed that Jesus had undergone the gamut of human temptations: "We have not a high priest who is unable to sympathize with our weakness, but one who in every respect has been tempted as we are, yet without sinning" (Hebrews 4:15). Nonetheless, in discussing the humanity and temptations of Jesus, the New Testament does not so much as allude to the question of his sexuality.

Quite early, in the mainstream of the Christian tradition, theologians argued that Jesus' life was one of complete celibacy, that Jesus took a disparaging attitude toward sexuality in general, and that these two attitudes should be characteristic of Christians and especially of the priesthood. Several sayings of Jesus contained in the Gospels were used to support such theories. These are the sayings most frequently used in expounding such a view:

You have heard that it was said, "You shall not commit adultery." But I say to you that every one who looks at a woman lustfully has already committed adultery with her (Matthew 5:27-28).

If any one comes to me and does not hate his own father and mother and wife and children and brothers and sisters, yea, and even his own life, he cannot be my disciple (Luke 14:26).

There are eunuchs who have been so from birth, and there are eunuchs who have been made eunuchs by men, and there are eunuchs who have made themselves eunuchs for the sake of the kingdom of heaven. He who is able to receive this, let him receive it (Matthew 19:12).

Jesus said to the Sadducees, "The sons of this age marry and are given in marriage; but those who are accounted worthy to attain to that age and to the resurrection from the dead neither marry nor are given in marriage, for they cannot die any more, because they are equal to angels and are sons of God, being sons of the resurrection" (Luke 20:34-36).

Exegesis of these passages combined with theological speculation led to the theory that virginity, celibacy, and sexual abstinence were superior to married life and that in marriage sex should be engaged in only with the object of procreation. Sexual drives thus came to be understood as sinful. The epitome of this argument was reached with Saint Augustine who argued that sinful nature was transmitted through sex, and since Jesus was sinless and born of a virgin he possessed no sexual drives or passions. Jesus was fully human but being born in a manner that bypassed sexual activity, Jesus possessed no real sexuality.

This theory of sexual ethics which stressed the superiority of virginity and celibacy was challenged at the time of the Protestant Reformation. Such a challenge opened the way for the discussion of Jesus' sexuality although the topic does not seem to have occupied much concern among the reformers. Luther, for example, suggested in one of his discussions that Jesus probably had sexual relations with Mary Magdalene and perhaps other women (*Tabletalk*, number 1472). The comment by Luther however was recorded without any reference to the context of his statement or to exactly what he meant or implied by such a statement. Since Luther no where else in his writings takes up this theme, one should not take the statement as representative of his interpretation of Jesus. Luther was prone to make rather earthy off-the-cuff comments which often didn't represent his sober thought on a subject. At any rate, the statement does suggest that he had given some thought to the question of Jesus' sexuality.

Some of the early Mormon theologians like Orson Hyde and Brigham Young, according to a secondary source in the case of the latter, not only argued that Jesus was a man of normal sexual impulses but also that he was a polygamist having been married to Mary Magdalene as well as to Mary and Martha, the sisters of Lazarus. The marriage feast in Cana of Galilee at which Jesus turned the water into wine (John 2:1-11) was understood by some of the early Mormons as one of Jesus' own weddings.

Until quite recently, few modern interpreters of Jesus had given consideration to the question of his sexuality. It has occasionally been hinted at as, for example, in the following quote from John Erskine:

It has been suggested . . . that during these eighteen silent years he was moved by the hopes and ambitions proper to manhood—love, marriage, parenthood—and that in equal measure he suffered disappointment or bereavement. There is no basis in fact for these theories . . . yet just because man's normal emotional life is near to us all, it does not seem improbable that he did fall in love and have some experience of parenthood. Here I try to choose my words carefully, not to start unworthy thoughts or to seem to invent for the Saviour any acquaintance with cheap romance. But reading his words carefully as I have done all my life, I long ago had the impression that he understood women very well indeed, with the special understanding of a man who has been hurt by one of them. In the development of his character there was, I am inclined to believe, over against the blessed influence of Mary, another influence far less happy. I think he early met someone who charmed but who was unworthy, someone he idealized, and by whom he was cruelly disillusioned. . . .

Though we have no specific details about his early manhood, yet the accounts of the public ministry contain facts which may throw light on the unrecorded years. The Gospels indicate that Jesus had an extraordinary fondness for children, and a special understanding of the relation between father and son. . . . Whether, as some people would like to believe, he ever married and had a son is an irrelevant question. What is pertinent is his capacity for love and his genius for parenthood. The father of the Prodigal Son is not a portrait of Joseph, but the record of human yearning for a child. Whether these emotions in Jesus ever attached themselves to particular objects, the story does not say, but his character renders it for me utterly impossible that his youth and manhood could have been unmoved by warm, human emotions. . . . If he really took our nature upon him and was human, then he had our equipment of sex. . . . I interpret the history of the unknown years as a period, not of indecision, but of a wrestling with the human loves which might have held him back from a love universal and divine. Perhaps the conflict was never entirely ended until the hours on Calvary (*The Human Life of Jesus*, 27-28).

Poets and novelists have, on occasion, dealt with the questions of Jesus' sexuality and his confrontation with sexual temptations. In his poem, *Judas*, Ronald Duncan depicts an imaginary encounter between Jesus and a prostitute:

Remembering the brothel we'd passed outside the city
Where an old whore had lifted her skirts in the doorway
And challenged Jesus to prove He was a man
And how He had surprised us by going up to the woman
And had drawn the sore from her lips, the years
    from her eyes
    and,—it was this that shocked Peter—
How He had then kissed her, and pulled her hair
    in a tease as she repeated her challenge
Not realising that He had proved much more.

Two novelists—D. H. Lawrence and Nikos Kazantzakis —have made the issue of Jesus' sexuality a central theme of two of their works. In his short story, *The Man Who Died*, Lawrence depicted the true meaning of Jesus' resurrection, with some punning with holy phraseology, as his awakening and surrendering to sexual desire which he had previously suppressed and denied. In *The Last Temptation of Christ,* Kazantzakis portrays Jesus as tempted constantly through his life by sexual passion, especially with regard to Mary Magdalene. Kazantzakis' Jesus is depicted as a man locked in a fight between spiritual vocation and carnal love who in the end repudiated domestic love for vocational service. Although in Kazantzakis' work Jesus does not give in to sexual desire, he is portrayed as one who was fully sexual, tempted as all men.

During the 1960s, the sexual revolution and human sexuality were topics of widespread discussion. Simultaneously, a renewed interest in the sexuality of Jesus developed. This discussion of the sexuality of Jesus was not simply a reflex to the social trend with its general interest in sexuality. It was also reflective of a genuine desire to recover a more human figure behind the Christ of faith and the reconstructed pictures of the historical Jesus. Professor Tom Driver expressed the issues in the following manner:

Exegesis might go on forever proving that sex is not necessarily sin. Ethics might echo the tune. But if The Man for Men was conceived to be without sexuality—was never, unlike the saints, even tempted by sex—then all would labor in vain who strove to prove that the Christian God looks favorably upon the sexual life of humanity. Hunger Jesus knew, and thirst. Death He endured. Pride, sloth, envy, desire for power, idolatry—all came close to Him and were overcome in favor of the virtues of which they are the perversions. But where do we find Jesus taking our sexuality upon Him? Human love, yes. Love extended liberally even to those who, in a sexual way, have "loved much." But never, so far as we are told, a man stirred in himself by that desire which for the rest of us is part of our created nature.

To put it bluntly, a sexless Jesus can hardly be conceived to be fully human. As long as Jesus is somehow above masculinity or femininity, the drift toward a Docetic Christ is inevitable. I do not know why this has not been more often observed. Lacking such a pervasively human element, the humanity of Christ tends to become a mere affirmation, a matter of pure dogma. Jesus is then man in principle but not in fact. If to this is added the belief that He was conceived in the womb of a virgin, His separation from our sexuality becomes complete. "Veiled in flesh," He is not flesh. He has the appearance of humanity but not its limiting substance, however much might be said in the abstract about "finitude." It is an inherent part of my finitude, and yours, that our lives are shaped in many decisive ways by our sexual histories ("Sexuality and Jesus," 239). . . . The traditional view of the Gospel's silence about sexuality in Jesus himself must be abandoned and a new interpretation put on the facts. . . . If we take it that the Gospels do not intend to present a Docetic Christ, if this may be true even of the Fourth Gospel, which in any case speaks most about Jesus' love for particular individuals, then the absence of all comment in them about Jesus' sexuality cannot be taken to imply that he had no sexual feelings. That would land us back into the traditional view, according to which the Christ redeems us *from* sexuality, it being the part of our nature He did not share. If the Christian, who is a member of the Body of Christ, is to grow up into a psychologically healthy and morally right sexual life, then the God-Man cannot be totally apart from the sexual realm ("Sexuality and Jesus," 243).

Those who place some emphasis on the sexuality of Jesus generally take one of four alternatives in offering suggestions as to how Jesus dealt with his sexual drives. One alternative suggests that Jesus was a fully sexual being with normal sexual passions but who controlled these so that they were never given overt expression. This alternative would be the most widely accepted current view. A second alternative would be to argue that Jesus gave expression to his sexuality in heterosexual relations outside marriage. *Jesus Christ Superstar* certainly raises this issue with regard to Jesus and Mary Magdalene but leaves the matter as an open question. In this regard, Timothy Rice who wrote the lyrics for *Superstar* has denied that the work intends to make any theological statement about Jesus beyond "seeing Jesus as a man, so He can be better understood by today's young people, who'd rather listen to rock than go to church. . . . It merely tells the old story in new terms. In no respects does it clash with fundamental Christian teachings. No intelligent churchman would take *Superstar* as anything more than an entertainment. It's ridiculous to give it theological importance it doesn't deserve. The only importance is its commercial success" ("'Superstar' Gospel Is Shekels," 12). Nonetheless, any discussion which aims at "seeing Jesus as a man" involves a theological perspective. In the opera, it is only Mary Magdalene who treats Jesus with total respect, and she is shown caressing and kissing him, but a bit bewildered by not knowing how to love him. All to the consternation of Judas. At the same time, Jesus is made to say that Mary was the only one who tried to give him what he needed here and now. Jesus is certainly not pictured as either sexless or homosexual. Neither is he depicted beyond sexuality.

A third alternative is the suggestion that Jesus' sexuality was basically homosexual rather than heterosexual in orientation. (See the discussion of Morton Smith's presentation in chapter eleven.) Without discussing whether Jesus even gave overt expression to his sexuality, Canon Hugh Montefiore, vicar of Great St. Mary's in Cambridge, England, has offered the suggestion that Jesus was homosexually inclined.

My concern to show Christ's complete identification with mankind . . . raises for me a question about our Lord's celibacy. I raise it with reference to those thirty "Hidden Years" at Nazareth, when it seems that as yet he did not know either his vocation to be Messiah or his status as Son of God. Why did he not marry? After all he was fully a man. Of course there is no evidence, and we can only speculate, and speculation must be done with reverence. But having raised the question we must look it in the face—why did he not marry? Could the answer be that Jesus was not by nature the marrying sort? I want to make it crystal clear that when I suggest this possible answer, no question of Jesus being less than perfect was or is involved or implied. It is of course important not to confuse temptation with sin. Jesus was tempted as we all are in every possible way; yet without sin (*For God's Sake,* 182).

In elaboration of this proposal, Montefiore has stated, in an effort to be "serious and relevant," the following: "Women were his friends, but it is men he is said to have loved. The homosexual explanation is one we cannot ignore" (*Newsweek*, August 7, 1967, 83).

A fourth possibility is the suggestion that Jesus gave expression to his sexuality in marriage. This view has been most fully developed by William E. Phipps in his two books *Was Jesus Married?* and *The Sexuality of Jesus.* Phipps concludes that "Jesus most probably was married to a Galilean woman in the second decade of life" (*Was Jesus Married?* 70). How does he arrive at such a conclusion? First of all, Phipps begins with an affirmation of Jesus' true humanity which involved sexuality.

Along with all orthodox Christians I believe that Jesus was fully human and, endorsing the sciences of man, I think that sexual desire is intrinsic to human nature. I do not agree with Luther that this desire is so irrepressible among the heterosexually oriented that all must gratify it by coitus. However this means of gratification, in the context of marriage, has been the ordinary way in which most humans throughout history have attempted to deal with the basic psychological as well as physical need. The question that concerns me is whether there are sufficient grounds in the sources pertaining to the life and times of Jesus to substantiate the common assumption that he followed a different pattern of sexual behavior from that of most other humans (13).

Secondly, Phipps argues that in light of the sexual attitudes in Judaism at the time of Jesus, it is highly unlikely that Jesus did not marry. Ancient Judaism highly valued married life and disdained celibacy; it should be assumed that as a first-century Jew, Jesus shared these views.

In the Old Testament licit gratification of sexual passion was encouraged and marriage was a religious duty that every man took seriously. Further, there was virtually no moral contamination associated with marital intercourse and there are no instances of life-long voluntary celibacy in the entire Old Testament history (26). . . .

Celibacy was rejected both in theory and in practice by the Hebrews. Hirschel Revel is not indulging in overstatement when he asserts: "The voluntary renunciation of marriage is a conception utterly foreign to Judaism." It is not found in the Old Testament, the Apocrypha, the Pseudepigrapha, the Qumran scrolls, the Mishnah, or in the Talmud. The traditions that may have influenced Jesus are virtually all contained in these sources. But the Hebrews were much more positive toward sexuality than the mere avoidance of celibacy. They valued sex, in the context of marriage, for procreation, companionship, and recreation. The many-splendored purposes of connubial love were extolled and the extremes of undisciplined license and sexual deprivation were abhorred (33).

As a good Jew, Jesus and his father Joseph would have accepted the responsibility and blessing attendant upon Jesus' marriage.

The Jewish imperative regarding parental duties, accompanied by New Testament information about Jesus' early family relations, gives weighty evidence that Joseph betrothed his children even as he himself had been betrothed. In his time a Jewish father's obligation to a son was clearly defined: "He must circumcise him, redeem him, teach him Torah, teach him a trade, and find a wife for him" [*Talmud, Kiddushin* 29a]. What evidence is there that Joseph fulfilled these five duties? (47).

Phipps argues that Joseph fulfilled these duties because he was a just man who lived by the law. The fulfillment of the first four duties are referred to or can be deduced from the New Testament. The lack of any evidence concerning the fifth can be explained because "the duty of becoming betrothed shortly after puberty was as axiomatic in ancient Judaism as celibacy was in St. Benedict's monastry. Consequently, there is no mention of celibacy in Benedict's *Rule* nor do the Gospels allude to [Jesus'] marriage" (48).

Thirdly, Phipps denies that any of the sayings of Jesus which have traditionally been used to support an ascetic view of sex and a celibate Jesus can be used to disprove the theory that Jesus married.

The alleged evidence in the Gospels for Jesus' celibacy has been weighed and found wanting. The traditional "proof-texts" for his perpetual virginity, which have been ripped from their contexts by ascetically oriented interpreters, not only do not hint that he never married but can more properly be used to show that he endorsed permanent marriage as being of penultimate value. His use of the bridegroom metaphor [Mark 2:19a] proves no more than that he had a life-affirming general outlook and a positive view of weddings. His teaching about sexual desire [Matt 5:27-28] means that the libido should not be adulterated by adulterous schemes. The hyperbolic saying about "hating" one's wife and family [Luke 14:26] means that in cases of irreconcilable conflict domestic allegiance should be subordinated to commitment to God's cause. The eunuch saying [Matthew 19:12], if authentic, pertains to Jesus' sanctioning fidelity to a wayward spouse in hope of eventual mutual reconciliation. His response to the Sadducees [Luke 20:34-36] displays that the resurrected life will surpass but will not negate earthly love between spouses. Thus the five passages from the Gospels that are most frequently relied upon for justifying vows of celibacy and that at first glance may appear to condone or encourage such vows are legitimately open to quite different and even opposing interpretations (98).

Fourthly, Phipps argues that "the Hellenistic sexual asceticism that infiltrated Gentile Christianity in the post-apostolic era has been responsible for the dogma that Jesus was perpetually virginal" (187).

Sexual asceticism can be traced throughout the course of our civilization. It was advocated by a number of Greek philosophers; it waxed in the Roman and medieval eras; and it has continued with diminishing vigor in modern history. Many important philosophers, in their life-styles and teachings, have denigrated the libidinous. They have assumed that devotion to the life of the immaterial intellect should result in antipathy toward satisfying sensual desires.

The influence of Plato has been especially heavy in this regard. He believed that lovers of wisdom should strive to become disincarnate psyches (*The Sexuality of Jesus*, 91). . . .

Through the discipline of crushing tender passions it was thought that the divine immortal soul could best be emancipated from its carnal dungeon. In medieval Catholicism moral dualism was the main, though not the exclusive, theoretical basis for the practice of celibacy. Those theologians in church history who have advocated sexual asceticism have often unwittingly held a doctrine of man closer to Athens than to Jerusalem. The self-mortification they have defended stems more from the dialogues of Plato than from the writings of the Bible (93-94).

14. JESUS: THE CREATION OF THE EARLY CHURCH

The worshippers of the sacred mushroom saw in the fungus a microcosm of nature; it rose from the womb or volva, flourished, and within hours had died again, to be renewed in the continuing cycle of creation. Thus the "Jesus," born of a virgin womb, lifted high on a cross as a sign to men, killed and raised again to eternal life, became a personified enactment of the life cycle of the sacred mushroom, and to the Christian today, persuaded of the historicity of the myth, serves as the supreme example of God's creative and redemptive activity in the world.—John M. Allegro, *The End of a Road* (p. 91)

In the course of modern study of the historical Jesus, several scholars have taken a position which may be called radical skepticism. That is, they have denied the existence of a historical Jesus. Doubting Jesus' historicity, they have viewed him as the product of the faith and imagination of the early church.

Bruno Bauer, for example, argued that the life of Jesus was the creation of the writer of the gospel of Mark. The life of Jesus was produced from elements drawn from Stoic Philosophy and Roman and Alexandrian culture of the second century combined with the influence and personality of the Roman philosopher Seneca.

The Englishman John M. Robertson traced the picture of Jesus back to mythological elements drawn from Judaism and pagan sources. Others have seen astral myths as the ultimate source of the portrait of Jesus.

Albert Kalthoff saw in the figure of Jesus the reflection of and the embodiment of a social movement among the lower classes of the Roman Empire.

The American, William Benjamin Smith, has argued for the idea that the historical Jesus was created out of mythological elements and concepts.

Just after the turn of the century, the most vocal of the scholars denying the historicity of Jesus was the German Arthur Drews. For Drews, the historical Jesus was a creation of the church produced primarily by the historicizing of Old Testament texts.

An historical Jesus, as the Gospels portray him, and as he lives in the minds of the liberal theologians of today, never existed at all; so that he never founded the insignificant and diminutive community of the Messiah at Jerusalem. It will be necessary to concede that the Christ-faith arose quite independently of any historical personality known to us; that indeed Jesus was in this sense a product of the religious "social soul" and was made by Paul, with the required amount of reinterpretation and reconstruction, the chief interest of those communities founded by him. The "historical" Jesus is not earlier but later than Paul; and as such he has always existed merely as an idea, as a pious fiction in the minds of members of the community. The New Testament with its four Gospels is not previous to the Church, but the latter is antecedent to them; and the Gospels are the derivatives, consequently forming a support for the propaganda of the church, and being without any claim to historical significance (*The Christ Myth,* 286). . . .

More or less all the features of the picture of the historical Jesus, at any rate all those of any important religious significance, bear a purely mythical character, and no opening exists for seeking an historical figure behind the Christ myth. It is not the imagined historical Jesus but, if any one, Paul who is that "great personality" that called Christianity into life as a new religion, and by the speculative range of his intellect and the depth of his moral experience gave it the strength for its journey, the strength which bestowed upon it victory over the other competing religions. Without Jesus the rise of Christianity can be quite well understood, without Paul not so (19).

When one studies the Gospels critically, according to Drews, not a single passage can be shown to be historical. "The fact is that there is *nothing, absolutely nothing,* either in the actions or words of Jesus, that has not a mythical character or cannot be traced back to parallel passages in the Old Testament or the Talmud, and is therefore under suspicion of being derived from them" (*The Historicity of Jesus*, 290).

If one asks who the creative personality was who lies behind the historical Jesus other than Paul, Drews would answer: "In the long run the contents of the gospels may be traced to the prophet Isaiah, whose 'predictions,' sayings, penitential appeals, and promises reappear in the Gospels, in the form of a narrative. *Hence Isaiah, not Jesus, would be the powerful personality to whom Christianity would owe its existence.*" "It is more probable that *Jesus and Isaiah are one and the same person* than that the Jesus of liberal theology brought Christianity into existence" (*The Historicity of Jesus*, 296).

Drews saw behind the Christian Jesus not only special mythological elements and the influence of Old Testament references but also a certain idea of the deity.

At the base of all the deeper religions lies the idea of a suffering god, sacrificing himself for humanity, and obtaining spiritual healing for man by his death and his subsequent resurrection. In the pagan religions this idea is conceived naturalistically: the death of the sun, the annual dying of nature, the happy revival of its forces in spring, and the victorious conquering of the power of winter by the new sun—this is the realistic background of the tragic myth of Osiris, Attis, Adonis, Tammuz, Dionysos, Balder, and similar deities. The great advance of Christianity beyond these nature-religions is that it spiritualised this idea by applying it to the man Jesus Christ, blended the many saviour-gods in the idea of the one god-man, and gave it the most plausible form by connecting it with an historical reality (*The Historicity of Jesus*, 305-6).

Behind Drews' arguments against the historicity of Jesus lies his philosophical argument that a purely historical understanding of Jesus does not meet the philosophical needs nor satisfy the religious consciousness of modern man. In a way, he was combating the historical Jesus as reconstructed by liberal theology as much as he was denying the historicity of Jesus. "To bind up religion with history, as modern theologians do, and to represent an *historical religion* as the need of modern man, is no proof of insight, but of a determination to persuade oneself to recognise the Christian religion alone" (*The Historicity of Jesus*, 308).

Religion is a life that emanates from the depths of one's innermost self, an outgrowth of the mind and of freedom. All religious progress consists in making faith more intimate, in transferring the centre of gravity from the objective to the subjective world, by a confident surrender to the God within us. The belief in an historical instrument of salvation is *a purely external appreciation of objective facts*. To seek to base the religious life on it is not to regard the essence of religion, but to make it for ever dependent on a stage of mental development that has long passed in the inner life (x-xi).

In more recent times, many of the ideas of Drews have been restated by the Frenchman P. L. Couchoud who saw the life of the historical Jesus as a mythical fabrication primarily constructed on the basis of Old Testament texts. Like Drews he pointed to the close similarity between Psalms 22 and the depiction of the crucifixion and death of Jesus and argued that the latter were constructed on the basis of the former.

The most recent and extensive attempt to see Jesus as the creation of the church is the work by John M. Allegro, *The Sacred Mushroom and the Cross: A Study of the Nature and Origins of Christianity Within the Fertility Cults of the Ancient Near East*. His ideas have been given a more popular expression in his book *The End of a Road*.

Allegro argues that all Near Eastern religions had their origin in man's questioning about how life originated and how man could ensure his own survival. Man saw himself dependent on the powers and forces of nature and at the same time frustrated by these powers and forces. The same forces that produced his food and provided his sustenance could also parch his crops, destroy his animals, and challenge man himself. Religion was born out of this sense of dependence and frustration.

Man saw that his basic needs centered in the quest for fertility of flock, field, and family. If man were to overcome the needs of life, he must establish communication with the source of fertility and maintain a proper relationship with it. The ultimate powers of fertility were understood by ancient man in terms of human and animal reproduction. The heavenly power was thus conceived as the male whose semen in the form of rain fertilized and fructified the female, the earth. Man's religious rituals were intent on creating, stimulating, and producing this fertilizing sexual union. The deity or forces of nature were not only the source of the life-creating semen but were also the source of knowledge. However much man learned and advanced, he always found some impenetrable mystery which he could not grasp. Man therefore hoped in religion not only to induce the gods to produce fertility and to gain union with the gods but also to grasp and/or experience divine illumination and glimpse the beauty and glory of the divine world. With the gradual evolution of religion, the focus tended to shift away from the cruder desires to control the weather and all forms of fertility and became more concerned with the acquisition of wisdom and knowledge, especially about the future.

In order to understand the essence of religion for ancient man, one must do so through the writings man has left behind. This means, for Allegro, that philology, the science of words is of overriding importance. "The written word is a symbol of thought; behind it lies an attitude of mind, an emotion, a reasoned hypothesis, to which the reader can to some extent penetrate" (*The Sacred Mushroom,* 3). Of special importance is the etymology, the root meaning of words. In language, religious terminology is least susceptible to change. Therefore if the original root meaning of a word can be established, then this meaning can frequently be traced through history in the appearance of this word or the root form.

The first ancient religion for which there exists a written

literature is that of ancient Sumer from the fourth millennium B.C. The Sumerian cuneiform in which these texts are written is seen by Allegro as the bridge, or the common factor, to all the Near Eastern Indo-European and Semitic civilizations. In other words, lying behind the two linguistic families is Sumerian. Thus, on the basis of Sumerian religious terms, one can penetrate to the root-meanings of later religious terminology, related deities, plants, heroes, and so forth and trace the continuity of religious understanding.

In the language and culture of the world's most ancient civilization, Sumerian, it is now possible to find a bridge between the Indo-European and Semitic worlds. The first writing known is found on tablets from the Mesopotamian basin, dating some five thousand years ago, and consisting of crude pictures drawn with a stylus on to soft clay. Later the recognizable pictures became stylized into ideograms made up of nail- or wedge-shape impressions, so-called cuneiform signs, each representing syllables of consonants and vowels. These syllables made up "word-bricks" which resisted phonetic change within the language, and could be joined together to make connected phrases and sentences. To such word-bricks we can now trace Indo-European and Semitic verbal roots, and so begin to decipher for the first time the names of gods, heroes, plants and animals appearing in cultic mythologies. We can also now start penetrating to the root-meanings of many religious and secular terms whose original significance has been obscure (18).

Lying behind the names of the gods in Sumerian, Greek, and Hebrew is the idea of the god as the source of fertility.

If we are to make any enlightened guess at "primitive" man's ideas about god and the universe it would have to be on the reasonable assumption that they would be simple, and directly related to the world of his experience. He may have given the god numerous epithets describing his various functions and manifestations but there is no reason to doubt that the reality behind the names was envisaged as one, all-powerful deity, a life-giver, supreme creator. The etymological examination of the chief god-names that is now possible supports this view, pointing to a common theme of life-giving, fecundity. Thus the principal gods of the Greeks and Hebrews, Zeus and Yahweh (Jehovah), have names derived from Sumerian meaning "juice of fecundity," spermatozoa, "seed of life." The phrase is composed of two syllables, IA (*ya,* dialectally *za*), "juice," literally "strong water," and U, perhaps the most important phoneme in the whole of Near Eastern religion. It is found in the texts represented by a number of different cuneiform signs, but at the root of them all is the idea of "fertility." Thus one U means "copulate" or "mount," and "create"; another "rainstorm," as source of the heavenly sperm; another "vegetation," as the offspring of the god, whilst another U is the name of the storm-god himself. So, far from evincing a multiplicity of gods and conflicting theological notions, our earliest records lead us back to a single idea, even a single letter, "U." Behind Judaism and Christianity, and indeed all the Near Eastern fertility religions and their more sophisticated developments, there lies this single phoneme "U" (20).

Since vegetation was the product of the god's union with earth, plants were assumed to be embodiments of the divine life of the god. Certain plants, however, came to be understood as truer and more complete embodiments than others. Plants endowed with the power to kill or heal, in other words, drug plants, were of special concern, and there grew up in culture a technical knowledge concerning their nature and usage. Likewise there developed a study of man's and individual persons' physiology and psychological make-up in relation to the use of these drug plants often utilizing astrological considerations. From the beginning then religion and drug arts were inseparable. The earliest mystery cults with their secrecy were developed around the collection and transmission of the knowledge of the healing arts and drugs.

Of special importance to ancient man was the mushroom, *Amanita muscaria,* with its characteristic red-and-white spotted cap and powerful hallucinatory poison. The mushroom has always been a mysterious plant. It grows without seed, makes a rapid appearance, grows swiftly, and disappears quickly. According to Allegro, every aspect of the mushroom's existence was fraught with sexual allusions. In its earliest growth, the mushroom button appears like an egg.

As the plant grows it assumes a phallic shape, and finally in its full form it appears as a phallus supporting the female groin. Since mushrooms grow shortly after the rain—that is after the divine fertilization—it was assumed that the mushroom was divinely created and a special embodiment of the divine semen. The mushroom was a "son of god" and a replica of the fertility god himself. When eaten it gave man the experience of union with the heavenly world, a trip to the celestial sphere.

Allegro finds numerous references to the sacred mushroom and the fertility deity throughout the Bible. "Mushroom stories abounded in the Old Testament" (42). We have already seen how he traces the names of the Greek god Zeus and the Hebrew god Yahweh back to a common Sumerian origin. In both testaments, many of the stories and sayings are to be seen as cryptograms and word-plays behind which are references to the fertility god and the mushroom cult. In other words, the biblical traditions are coded to provide the reader with references to fertility and the mushroom cult in what otherwise appear to be ordinary stories. Allegro argues that one must distinguish three levels of understanding which are involved in New Testament texts. There is, first of all, the plain meaning of the Greek text, the story or saying itself. But this is the outer husk with probably little historical reality at this level except for the social and historical background it reflects. Secondly, there is the Semitic level. At this level, when the materials are put back into their Semitic form are word plays, puns, and words with several levels of meaning. Thirdly, there is the level which expresses the basic concepts of the mushroom cult. "Here is the real stuff of the mystery—fertility philosophy." This is the real message being conveyed.

Here, then, was the literary device to spread occult knowledge to the faithful. To tell the story of a rabbi called Jesus, and invest him with the power and names of the magic drug. To have him live before the terrible events that had disrupted their lives, to preach a love between men, extending even to the hated Romans. Thus, reading such a tale, should it fall into Roman hands, even their mortal enemies might be deceived and not probe farther into the activities of the cells of the mystery cults within their territories (xiv).

The Old Testament as well preserved the fertility-mushroom code in its narratives and terminology. For example, the stories of David contain numerous veiled references to the fertility and mushroom cult. David's name means "lover" or "beloved." Allegro's translation of II Sam. 23:1 seeks to demonstrate how the passage teems with sexual references. "The oracle of David, son of Jesse; the oracle of the erect phallus (RSV: the man who was raised on high), the semen-smeared (RSV: anointed) of the God of Jacob, the Na'im (heavenly canopy, RSV: sweet) of the stretched penis (RSV: psalmist) of Israel" (II Sam. 23:1) (141). Even the family name of David, "son of Jesse," reflects an old Sumerian term BAR/USh-SA, "erect penis" (141).

The story of the exodus from Egypt has a mushroom name and epithet as the main ingredients of the story. "The story itself hinges on the play between the name of the fungus as *Mezar,* 'erect, stretched,' and *Masōr,* 'Egypt,' to set the place of the myth; and upon the common Semitic name of the mushroom *Pitrā',* and the root *p-t-r* which gave 'first-born,' 'release,' and 'unleavened bread'" (143-44). In light of such interest in sexual symbolism, Allegro suggests that it is no wonder that cultic prostitution—of both males and females—played such an important function in the cultic life of ancient Israel.

Behind much of the Old Testament, Allegro assumes, there may lie historical reality. There may have been a real David and so forth whose names and titles became the bearer of the secrets of the mushroom cult. But the New Testament is different.

A quite different situation obtains, however, with regard to the New Testament characters. Here, for reasons already stated and which by now should be apparent . . . , we are dealing with a cryptic document. This is a different kind of mythology, based not on pious aggrandizement by later admirers, as has been so often assumed in the past, but a deliberate attempt to mislead the reader. There is every reason why there should *not* have been a real Jesus of Nazareth, at least not one connected with the sect of Christians, nor a real John the Baptist, Peter, John, James, and so on. To have named them, located their homes and families, would have brought disaster upon their associates in a cult which had earned the hatred of the authorities (150).

In the growth of the mushroom, the normal process of fertilization seemed to the ancients to have been bypassed. The god had simply spoken his creative word which was carried to the earth as if by an angelic messenger of the god and the result was the mysterious embodiment of the god. The mushroom was the man child of the god.

Every aspect of the mushroom's existence was fraught with sexual allusions, and in its phallic form the ancients saw a replica of the fertility god himself. It was the "son of God," its drug was a purer form of the God's own spermatozoa than that discoverable in any other form of living matter. It was, in fact, God himself, manifest on earth. To the mystic it was the divinely given means of entering heaven; God had come down in the flesh to show the way to himself, by himself (xv).

Here lies the true background of the story of the virgin birth. "Jesus" was born without earthly father; like the mushroom, he came into existence through the direct creative act of the god.

In the phallic mushroom, the "man-child" born of the "virgin" womb, we have the reality behind the Christ figure of the New Testament story. In a sense he is representative also of the initiates of the cult, "Christians," or "smeared with semen," as the name means. By imitating the mushroom, as well as by eating it and sucking its juice, or "blood," the Christian was taking unto himself the panoply of his god, as the priests in the sanctuary also anointed themselves with the god's spermatozoa found in the juices and resins of special plants and trees. As the priests "served" the god in the temple, the symbolic womb of divine creation, so the

244

Christians and their cultic associates worshipped their god and mystically involved themselves in the creative process. In the language of the mystery cults they sought to be "born again," when, purged afresh of past sin, they could apprehend the god in a drug-induced ecstasy (61).

John the Baptist is also a veiled reference to the mushroom cult. The name John comes from the Sumerian word GAN-NU meaning "red dye," and red was the color of *Amanita muscaria*. The designation Baptist goes back in origin to the Sumerian word TAB-BA-R/LI which means mushroom. His camel's hair clothing points to the two humps of the camel which in turn points to the mushroom volva's two halves. "The name and title of 'John the Baptist' in the New Testament story then, means no more than the 'red-topped mushroom'" (122). The word for camel contains a pun on the Hebrew word, *kirkarah,* and the Greek word for mandrake, *Kirkaia,* both going back to the Sumerian root KUR-KUR, a name for the Holy Plant. The reference to locusts, *gōbāy,* is a play on the word *gab'a,* "mushroom," and both go back to a Sumerian original GUG meaning "pod." The entire story of John's death by beheading must be seen as built around various names from the mushroom. The reference to the platter (*tablā'*) on which his head lay denotes the mushroom TAB-BA-LI. The name Herodias as well as the name Herod serve as vehicles for punning on the names of the mushroom. Herod—which means "heron" which is in Latin *ardeola*—was a term which would reflect the Semitic word *'ardīlā',* "mushroom." Similarily, the name of Rhoda who opened the door to Peter after his release from prison (Acts 12:13).

The opening lines of the Lord's Prayer—"Our father which art in Heaven"—is the Greek version of an Aramaic phrase which was derived by word-play from the Sumerian. "Our father" was originally "Abba, pater," a combination of Aramaic and Greek, but is actually a play on the Sumerian AB-BA-TAB-BA-RI-GI, a mushroom title. "'Our father who art in heaven,' then, is a cryptic way of expressing the name of the Saviour-god, the sacred mushroom'" (162).

245

Throughout the New Testament, Allegro discovers where the writers have gone to the trouble of concealing by ingenious literary devices secret names of the mushroom. A prime example of this is his decipherment of Mark 3:17 which refers to "James the son of Zebedee and John the brother of James, whom he [Jesus] surnamed Boanerges, that is, sons of thunder." Allegro claims that "sons of thunder" was a well-known name for the mushroom fungus "found elsewhere in Semitic texts, and supported by the old Greek name *keraunion*, 'thunder-fungus,' after *keraunos*, 'thunder.' The reference is to the belief that mushrooms were born of thunder, the voice of the god in the storm, since it was noticed that they appeared in the ground after rainstorms" (101-2). Allegro argues that Boanerges cannot under any explanation mean sons of thunder in Aramaic. The title goes back to a Sumerian term—GEShPU-AN-UR—meaning "'mighty man (holding up) the arch of heaven,' a fanciful image of the stem supporting the canopy of the mushroom, seen in cosmographical terms" (101). The conclusion drawn from such an explanation is: "If, for instance, 'Boanerges' is correctly to be explained as a name of the sacred fungus, and the impossible 'translation' appended in the text, 'Sons of Thunder,' is equally relevant to the mushroom, then the validity of the whole New Testament story is immediately undermined" (192-93).

The name Peter is a play on the Semitic word *pitra'* meaning "mushroom" and his surname Bar-jonah goes back to an original BAR-IA-U-NA, a fungus-name cognate with Paeonia, the Holy Plant. The name Barnabas is derived from two words meaning "skin" and "giraffe" or "red-with-white-spots"; thus Barnabas is a veiled reference to the red, white-spotted skin of the *Amanita muscaria*.

The crucifixion is understood in terms of mushroom mythology. "The idea of crucifixion in mushroom mythology was already established before the New Testament myth-makers portrayed their mushroom hero Jesus dying by this method. The fungus itself was probably known as 'The Little Cross'" (106). The cross was a symbol of copulation with the upright phallic symbol holding up the woman's crotch. So the reference to "Christ crucified" is a reference to the "semen-anointed, erected mushroom." And to take up one's cross was a "euphemism for sexual copulation" (105).

Thus the early church was a drug-sex cult whose members in their ritual consumed the body of the Christ—the mushroom—and in their ecstasy experienced union with the divine. The opposition to the early church on the part of the Romans was directed against the drug cult whose secrets its members sought to preserve in the cryptic message of the New Testament. Later Christian generations, the orthodox, lost or suppressed the clue to the true interpretation of the New Testament and thus ascribed historicity to what had originally been merely the means to transmit and protect the secrets of the sex-drug initiates.

If it now transpires that Christianity was only a latter-day manifestation of a religious movement that had been in existence for thousands of years, and in that particular mystery-cult form for centuries before the turn of the era, then the necessity for a founder-figure fades away, and the problems that have so long beset the exegete become far more urgent. The improbable nature of the tale, quite apart from the "miracle" stories, the extraordinarily liberal attitude of the central figure towards the Jewish "quislings" of the time, his friendly disposition toward the most hated enemies of his people, his equivocation about paying taxes to the Roman government, the howling of Jewish citizens for the blood of one of their own people at the hands of the occupying power, features of the Gospel story which have never rung true, now can be understood for what they have always been: parts of a deliberate attempt to mislead the authorities into whose hands it was known the New Testament documents would fall. The New Testament was a "hoax," but nevertheless a deadly serious and extremely dangerous attempt to transmit to the scattered faithful secrets which the Christians dare not permit to fall into unauthorized hands but to whose preservation they were irrevocably committed by sacred oaths (193-94).

The created Jesus of the early sex-drug cult called Christians, who was one of the symbolic carriers of the mushroom mysteries, came however to be looked upon as a historical figure. In the presentations of the Christians, the secrets of the New Testament were lost.

The ruse failed. Christians, hated and despised, were hauled forth and slain in their thousands. The cult well nigh perished. What eventually took its place was a travesty of the real thing, a mockery of the power that could raise men to heaven and give them the glimpse of God for which they gladly died. The story of the rabbi crucified at the instigation of the Jews became a historical peg upon which the new cult's authority was founded. What began as a hoax, became a trap even to those who believed themselves to be the spiritual heirs of the mystery religion and took to themselves the name of "Christian." Above all they forgot, or purged from the cult and their memories, the one supreme secret on which their whole religious and ecstatic experience depended: the names and identity of the source of the drug, the key to heaven—the sacred mushroom (xiv).

BIBLIOGRAPHY

CHAPTER ONE

Anderson, Charles C. *Critical Quests of Jesus*. Grand Rapids: Wm. B. Eerdmans, 1969.

Anderson, Hugh. *Jesus*. Englewood Cliffs, N. J.: Prentice-Hall, 1967.

Braaten, Carl E., and Roy A. Harrisville, eds. *The Historical Jesus and the Kerygmatic Christ: Essays on the New Quest of the Historical Jesus*. Nashville: Abingdon Press, 1964.

Bruce, F. F. *Jesus and Christian Origins Outside the New Testament*. Grand Rapids: Wm. B. Eerdmans, 1974.

Case, S. J. *Jesus Through the Centuries*. Chicago: University of Chicago Press, 1932.

Finegan, Jack. *Hidden Records of the Life of Jesus*. Philadelphia: Pilgrim Press, 1969.

Goguel, Maurice. *Jesus and the Origins of Christianity*. Volume 1: *Prolegomena to the Life of Jesus*. Trans. by Olive Wyon. New York: The Macmillan Company, 1933.

Grant, Robert M. *The Earliest Lives of Jesus*. New York: Harper & Brothers, 1961.

Harnack, Adolf. *What is Christianity?* Trans. by Thomas Bailey Saunders. New York: G. P. Putnam's Sons, 1901.

Keck, Leander. *A Future for the Historical Jesus*. Nashville: Abingdon Press, 1971.

Klausner, Joseph. *Jesus of Nazareth: His Life, Times, and Teaching.* Trans. by Herbert Danby. New York: The Macmillan Company, 1929.

McArthur, Harvey K. *The Quest Through the Centuries: The Search for the Historical Jesus.* Philadelphia: Fortress Press, 1966.

————. *In Search of the Historical Jesus.* New York: Charles Scribner's Sons, 1969.

Renan, Ernest. *Life of Jesus.* Trans. by Charles Edwin Wilbour. New York: Carleton, 1867.

Schweitzer, Albert. *The Quest of the Historical Jesus.* Trans. by W. Montgomery. London: A. & C. Black, 1910.

CHAPTER TWO

Smith, David. *The Days of His Flesh: The Earthly Life of Our Lord and Saviour Jesus Christ.* London: Hodder & Stoughton, 1905.

Stauffer, Ethelbert. *Jesus and His Story.* Trans. by Richard and Clara Winston. New York: Knopf, 1960.

CHAPTER THREE

Schweitzer, Albert. *The Mystery of the Kingdom of God.* Trans. by Walter Lowrie. New York: Dodd, Mead & Company, 1914.

————. *The Quest of the Historical Jesus: A Critical Study of its Progress from Reimarus to Wrede.* Trans. by W. Montgomery. London: A. & C. Black, 1910; New York: The Macmillan Company, 1950, reissued with a new introduction by James M. Robinson, 1968. The second, enlarged German edition was published under the title *Geschichte der Leben-Jesu-Forschung* (Tübingen: J. C. B. Mohr, 1913).

Weiss, Johannes. *Jesus' Proclamation of the Kingdom of God.* Trans. and ed. by Richard H. Hiers and David L. Holland. Philadelphia: Fortress Press, 1971.

Wrede, William, *The Messianic Secret.* Trans. by J. O. G. Greig. Cambridge: J. Clark, 1971.

CHAPTER FOUR

Barton, Bruce. *The Man Nobody Knows.* Indianapolis: The Bobbs-Merrill Company, 1925.

Enslin, Morton. *The Prophet From Nazareth.* New York: McGraw-Hill, 1961.

Bibliography

Matthews, Shailer. *Jesus on Social Institutions*. New York: The Macmillan Company, 1928.

CHAPTER FIVE

Ben-Chorin, Schalom. *Bruder Jesus: Der Nazarener in jüdischer Sicht*. Munich: P. List, 1967.
Buber, Martin. *Two Types of Faith*. Trans. by Norman P. Goldhawk. London: Routledge & Kegan Paul, Ltd., 1951.
Cohn, Haim. *The Trial and Death of Jesus*. New York: Harper, 1971.
Flusser, David. *Jesus*. Trans. by Ronald Walls. New York: Herder & Herder, 1959.
Klausner, Joseph. *Jesus of Nazareth: His Life, Times, and Teaching*. Trans. by Herbert Danby. New York: The Macmillan Company, 1925.
Lapide, Pinchas E. "Jesus in Israeli Literature," *Journal of Theology for Southern Africa,* V (Dec., 1973): 47-56.
Polish, David. *The Eternal Dissent*. New York: Abelard-Schuman, 1961.
Vermes, Geza. *Jesus the Jew: A Historian's Reading of the Gospels*. New York: The Macmillan Company, 1973.

CHAPTER SIX

Bornkamm, Günter. *Jesus of Nazareth*. Trans. by Irene and Fraser McLuskey with James M. Robinson. New York: Harper & Brothers, 1960.
Bultmann, Rudolf. "Is Jesus Risen as Goethe?" in Werner Harenberg, ed., Der Spiegel *on the New Testament*. Trans. by James H. Burtness. New York: The Macmillan Company, 1970, pp. 226-39.
———. *Jesus and the Word*. Trans. by Louise Pettibone Smith and Erminie Huntress Lantero. New York: Charles Scribner's Sons, 1934.
———. *Jesus Christ and Mythology*. New York: Scribner's, 1958.
———. "New Testament and Mythology," in Hans Werner Bartsch, ed., *Kerygma and Myth: A Theological Debate*. Trans. by Reginald H. Fuller. London: S. P.C. K., 1957, pp. 1-44.
———. "A Reply to the Theses of J. Schniewind," *Kerygma and Myth,* pp. 102-23.
———. "The Primitive Christian Kerygma and the Historical

Jesus," in *The Historical Jesus and the Kerygmatic Christ*, pp. 15-42.

————. "The Significance of the Historical Jesus for the Theology of Paul," *Faith and Understanding*, vol. 1. Trans. by Louise Pettibone Smith. New York: Harper, 1969, pp. 220-46.

Fuchs, Ernst. *Studies on the Historical Jesus*. Trans. by Andrew Scobie. London: SCM Press, 1964.

Jaspers, Karl, and Bultmann, Rudolf. *Myth and Christianity: An Inquiry into the Possibility of Religion Without Myth*. New York: Noonday Press, 1958.

Kähler, Martin. *The So-Called Historical Jesus and the Historic, Biblical Christ*. Trans. and ed. by Carl E. Braaten. Philadelphia: Fortress Press, 1964.

Käsemann, Ernst. "The Problem of the Historical Jesus," *Essays on New Testament Themes*. Trans. by W. J. Montague. London: SCM Press, 1964, pp. 15-47.

Robinson, James M. *A New Quest of the Historical Jesus*. London: SCM Press, 1959.

CHAPTER SEVEN

Bowman, John W., *The Intention of Jesus*. Philadelphia: Westminster Press, 1943.

————. "The Life and Teaching of Jesus," in *Peake's Commentary on the Bible*. Ed. by Matthew Black and H. H. Rowley. London: Thomas Nelson and Sons, 1962, pp. 733-47.

————. *Which Jesus?* Philadelphia: Westminster Press, 1970.

Dodd, C. H., *The Apostolic Preaching and its Development*. London: Hodder & Stoughton, 1936.

————. *The Founder of Christianity*. New York: The Macmillan Company, 1970.

Hoskyns, Edwyn, and Davey, Francis Noel. *The Riddle of the New Testament*. London: Faber and Faber, 1931.

Manson, T. W. "The Life of Jesus: Some Tendencies in Present-day Research," in *The Background of the New Testament and its Eschatology*. Ed. by W. D. Davies and D. Daube. London: Cambridge University Press, 1954, pp. 211-21.

————. *The Servant-Messiah: A Study of the Public Ministry of Jesus*. London: Cambridge University Press, 1953.

————. *The Teaching of Jesus: Studies in its Form and Content*. London: Cambridge University Press, 1931.

Taylor, Vincent. *The Formation of the Gospel Tradition*. London: Macmillan and Company, 1933.

Bibliography

CHAPTER EIGHT

Brandon, S.G.F. *Jesus and the Zealots: A Study of the Political Factor in Primitive Christianity.* Manchester: The University Press, 1967.

Carmichael, Joel. *The Death of Jesus.* New York: Macmillan, 1962.

Eisler, Robert. *The Messiah Jesus and John the Baptist (According to Flavius Josephus' recently discovered 'Capture of Jerusalem' and other Jewish and Christian Sources).* English edition by A. H. Krappe. New York: Dial Press, 1931.

Kautsky, Karl. *Foundations of Christianity.* New York: International Publishers, 1925.

Reimarus, H. S. "Concerning the Intention of Jesus and His Teaching," in *Reimarus: Fragments.* Ed. by C. H. Talbert and trans. by Ralph S. Fraser. Philadelphia: Fortress Press, 1970.

Wellhausen, Julius. *Einleitung in die drei ersten Evangelien.* Berlin: Georg Reimer, 1905.

CHAPTER NINE

Cleage, Albert. *The Black Messiah.* New York: Sheed & Ward, 1968.

Cone, James H. *Black Theology and Black Power.* New York: The Seabury Press, 1969.

————. *A Black Theology of Liberation.* Philadelphia: Lippincott, 1970.

Johnson, Joseph A., Jr. "Jesus: The Liberator," *Andover Newton Quarterly* 10 (Sept., 1969–Mar., 1970) 85-96.

Roberts, J. Deotis. *A Black Political Theology.* Philadelphia: Westminster Press, 1974.

————. *Liberation and Reconciliation: A Black Theology.* Philadelphia: Westminster Press, 1971.

Wilmore, Gayraud S. *Black Religion and Black Radicalism.* Garden City, N. Y.: Doubleday, 1972.

CHAPTER TEN

Schonfield, Hugh J. *The Passover Plot.* London: Hutchinson & Co. Ltd., 1965.

CHAPTER ELEVEN

Smith, Morton. *Clement of Alexandria and a Secret Gospel of Mark.* Cambridge: Harvard University Press, 1973.

————. *The Secret Gospel: The Discovery and Interpretation of the Secret Gospel According to Mark.* New York: Harper, 1973.

CHAPTER TWELVE

Davies, A. Powell. *The Meaning of the Dead Sea Scrolls.* New York: Signet Key Books, 1956.

Dupont-Sommer, A. *The Dead Sea Scrolls: A Preliminary Survey.* Trans. by E. Margaret Rowley. Oxford: B. Blackwell, 1952.

Potter, C. F. *The Lost Years of Jesus.* New York: Fawcett Publications, 1958.

Wilson, Edmund. *The Scrolls from the Dead Sea.* New York: Oxford University Press, 1955.

CHAPTER THIRTEEN

Driver, Tom. "Sexuality and Jesus," *Union Seminary Quarterly Review,* 20 (Nov., 1964–May 1965): 235-46.

Eichelbaum, Stanley. "'Superstar' Gospel is Shekels," *Sunday Scene, San Francisco Sunday Examiner and Chronicle,* July 15, 1973, p. 12.

Erskine, John. *The Human Life of Jesus.* New York: William Morrow and Company, 1945.

Montefiore, Hugh. *For God's Sake.* Philadelphia: Fortress Press, 1969.

Phipps, William E. *Recovering Biblical Sensuousness.* Philadelphia: Westminster Press, 1975.

————. *The Sexuality of Jesus: Theological and Literary Perspectives.* New York: Harper, 1973.

————. *Was Jesus Married? The Distortion of Sexuality in the Christian Tradition.* New York: Harper, 1970.

Pittenger, Norman. *Christology Reconsidered.* London: SCM Press, 1960.

CHAPTER FOURTEEN

Allegro, John M. *The End of a Road.* New York: Dial Press, 1971.

————. *The Sacred Mushroom and the Cross: A Study of the Nature and Origin of Christianity Within the Fertility Cults of the Ancient Near East.* London: Hodder & Stoughton, 1970.

Drews, Arthur. *The Christ Myth.* Trans. by C. Delisle Burns. Chicago: Open Court Publishing Company, 1911.

Bibliography

————. *The Witnesses to the Historicity of Jesus.* Trans. by Joseph McCabe. Chicago: Open Court Publishing Company, 1912.

Kalthoff, Albert. *The Rise of Christianity.* Trans. by Joseph McCabe. London: Watts & Co., 1907.

Robertson, John M. *Christianity and Mythology,* 2nd. ed. London: Watts & Co., 1910.

Smith, William Benjamin. *Ecce Deus, Studies of Primitive Christianity.* London: Watts & Co., 1912.